William Howard Doane

Songs of Devotion for Christian Associations

William Howard Doane

Songs of Devotion for Christian Associations

ISBN/EAN: 9783337289799

Printed in Europe, USA, Canada, Australia, Japan

Cover: Foto ©Thomas Meinert / pixelio.de

More available books at **www.hansebooks.com**

SONGS OF DEVOTION

FOR

CHRISTIAN ASSOCIATIONS:

A COLLECTION OF

Psalms, Hymns, and Spiritual Songs,

WITH MUSIC,

FOR

Church Service, Prayer and Conference Meetings,
Religious Conventions, and Family Worship:
Also adapted for use in Schools, Colleges,
and Benevolent Institutions.

W. H. DOANE, Editor,

CINCINNATI, OHIO.

New York and Chicago:
Published by BIGLOW & MAIN,
(Successors to WM. B. BRADBURY,)
425 BROOME STREET, NEW YORK, 726 WABASH AVENUE, CHICAGO.
FOR SALE BY BOOKSELLERS GENERALLY.

RECOMMENDATIONS.

THE General Convention of the YOUNG MEN'S CHRISTIAN ASSOCIATIONS of the United States and British Provinces, convened at Indianapolis last June, passed the following:—

RESOLVED—"That in the Hymn and Tune Book [SONGS OF DEVOTION] prepared at the suggestion of our last Convention, at Portland, by W. H. DOANE, of Cincinnati, Ohio, and published by Messrs. BIGLOW & MAIN, of New York City, we find a work not only admirably adapted for use in our Young Men's Christian Conventions and Associations, but eminently fitted for Devotional Exercises and Social Meetings, and we recommend and urge its adoption for general use.

From Rev. J. H. RAYMOND, President of Vassar College.

" I have examined ' SONGS OF DEVOTION,' and among a multitude of similar works which I have looked through, I know of none in which the proportion of thoroughly good selections seemed to me so large, or where there was so happy a combination of classical correctness and artistic excellence, with popular feeling and spirit. Every page is *singable*, and yet the prevailing taste is pure and high. If my associates agree with me, we shall adopt it for our social worship at ' Vassar' without delay."

" POUGHKEEPSIE, N. Y., July 15th, 1870."

From Rev. R. S. STANTON, President Miami University, Oxford, O.

"My attention has been called to your 'Songs of Devotion' by an esteemed Pastor of Cincinnati. I am highly pleased with it. It is just what every Pastor needs to promote congregational singing. The arrangement, the variety of hymns and tunes, the whole 'getting up,' and the mechanical execution are well adapted to this. I trust it may find great favor among all those who love to sing God's praise in any gathering of His people."

OXFORD, O., July 28, 1870.

From Rev. L. J. EVANS, Lane Seminary.

"I have examined with some care the 'Songs of Devotion,' and have found it to be a very choice collection, and especially well suited for the uses for which it was designed. For general purposes of social devotion it is unexcelled. It will doubtless win favor wherever it is found."

From C. C. WESTON, Esq., Washington, D. C.

"I have given 'Songs of Devotion' a thorough examination. I think it is *just the* Book for *Social Meetings*. We have introduced it in our Church—E Street Baptist."

From Rev. HENRY D. MOORE, Pastor of Vine Street Cong. Ch., Cincinnati, Ohio.

"I feel justified in saying, after examining with some thoroughness the Hymns and Tunes of 'Songs of Devotion,' that I know of no better or more serviceable book of sacred song than it. I heartily comm·nd the book to churches, families and schools for their adoption in the service of praise ; and I devoutly pray the blessing of God to attend its use."

From the Rev. R. JEFFERY, D. D., Pastor 9th Street Baptist Ch., Cincinnati, Ohio.

"The 'Songs of Devotion' need only to be known to become a favorite with all lovers of sacred song. The selection, with excellent discrimination, preserves many of the hymns and tunes that have become dear to all Christian hearts, and presents several original pieces which, instead of being ephemeral, will take a permanent place in the literature of hymns and tunes."

From Rev. A. J. ROWLAND, late President of Mt. Auburn Young Ladies' Institute, Cincinnati, Ohio.

"I have carefully examined 'Songs of Devotion,' and do not hesitate to pronounce it the very best book for social worship that has come under my notice. For service, at the opening of schools, for family prayers, and for the devotional meetings of Christian people, I think it altogether admirable. Its cheapness is also a very great item in its favor, as this brings a large quantity of our very best music within the reach of the poorest church. I wish the book and its author most abundant success."

PREFACE.

THIS collection is presented to the Christian public with the single desire that it may promote in some way the efficiency and usefulness of those who are working for the advancement of Christ's Kingdom. We would call attention to some of its chief features:

1. The hymns have been prepared and selected with unusual care; many original hymns are presented, composed by the best writers; other compilations, as well as the collections of individual authors, have been critically examined; and it is believed that there will be found in this volume only such hymns as will be approved by the entire body of the Protestant Church. The compiler has kept constantly in view the needs, not of a sect, but of a Church universal. The selections are accordingly adapted to the wants of all, and can be used by all.

2. Special attention has been paid to the selection of the music. Those grand old tunes used by the fathers of the Church, and which have been endeared by use and association to the Christian believer, have a prominent place in this collection. Besides these will be found those of modern date, the merits of which are now generally acknowledged, and which will come to be regarded, at no distant day, as among the classical compositions of the Church. Other tunes will be found which are now for the first time published. Most of these are by well-known composers with whose names the public is already familiar, and they are presented in the confident expectation that they will be assigned an honorable and permanent position.

3. The scope of the work is broad and comprehensive. The compiler has sought to adapt both hymns and tunes to all the needs and wants of the Christian. Every department of Christian labor, it is believed, has been completely provided for. The editor has received in his work the thoughtful aid of Christian laymen of large experience, and he has availed himself of their suggestions and advice. The whole field has been carefully gone over, and the publishers feel assured that in its adaptation to Christian wants, "SONGS OF DEVOTION" can safely challenge comparison with any other volume now before the public.

4. To the present work the editor has brought all his experience, and on it he has spent much time and thought.

Thanks are due to the representatives of the late WM. B. BRADBURY, Drs. MASON & HASTINGS, ROBT. LOWRY and others, for permission to use the music found under their respective names. Those bearing the monogram are by the Editor.

W. H. DOANE.

SONGS OF DEVOTION

"Whoso offereth praise, glorifieth me." Ps. 50, Verse 23.

OLD HUNDRED. L. M.

1. Be thou, O God, ex-alt-ed high; And as thy glo-ry fills the sky,

So let it be on earth displayed, Till thou art here, as there, obeyed.

---

1   *Praise to the Great Jehovah.*   L. M.

1 Be thou, O God, exalted high;
And as thy glory fills the sky,
So let it be on earth displayed,
Till thou art here, as there, obeyed.

2 O God, my heart is fixed; 't is bent
Its thankful tribute to present,
And, with my heart, my voice I 'll raise
To thee, my God, in songs of praise.

3 Thy praises, Lord, I will resound,
To all the listening nations round;
Thy mercy highest heaven transcends;
Thy truth beyond the clouds extends.

4 Be thou, O God, exalted high;
And as thy glory fills the sky,
So let it be on earth displayed,
Till thou art here, as there, obeyed.

2   *Doxology.*   L. M.

Praise God, from whom all blessings flow,
Praise him, all creatures here below;
Praise him above, ye heavenly host;
Praise Father, Son, and Holy Ghost.

3   *The Sovereign Jehovah.*   L. M.

1 Before Jehovah's awful throne,
Ye nations bow with sacred joy;
Know that the Lord is God alone;
He can create, and he destroy.

2 His sovereign power without our aid,
Made us of clay, and formed us men;
And when, like wandering sheep, we strayed,
He brought us to his fold again.

3 We are his people; we his care;
Our souls, and all our mortal frame;
What lasting honors shall we rear,
Almighty Father, to thy name?

4 We'll crowd thy gates with thankful songs,
High as the heaven our voices raise;
And earth, with her ten thousand tongues,
Shall fill thy courts with sounding praise.

5 Wide as the world is thy command,
Vast as eternity thy love:
Firm as a rock thy truth shall stand,
When rolling years shall cease to move.

BOYLSTON. S. M.

Moderato.

Dr. L. Mason.

1. A charge to keep I have, A God to glo-ri-fy,

A nev-er-dy-ing soul to save, And fit it for the sky.

4   *Watchfulness.*   S. M.

1 A charge to keep I have,
   A God to glorify,
A never-dying soul to save,
   And fit it for the sky.

2 To serve the present age,
   My calling to fulfill,
Oh, may it all my powers engage
   To do my Master's will.

3 Arm me with jealous care,
   As in thy sight to live,
And oh, thy servant, Lord, prepare
   A strict account to give.

4 Help me to watch and pray,
   And on thyself rely,
Assured if I my trust betray,
   I shall forever die.

5   *Compassion of God.*   S. M.

1 The pity of the Lord,
   To those who fear his name,
Is such as tender parents feel;
   He knows our feeble frame.

2 Our days are as the grass,
   Or like the morning flower;
When blasting winds sweep o'er the
   It withers in an hour.   [field,

3 But thy compassions, Lord,
   To endless years endure;
And children's children ever find
   Thy words of promise sure.

6   *The Redeemer's Tears.*   S. M.

1 Did Christ o'er sinners weep?
   And shall our cheeks be dry?
Let floods of penitential grief
   Burst forth from every eye.

2 The Son of God in tears
   The wond'ring angels see;
Be thou astonished, O my soul;
   He shed those tears for thee.

3 He wept that we might weep;
   Each sin demands a tear:
In heaven alone no sin is found,
   And there's no weeping there.

7   *Prayer for Revival.*   S. M.

1 O Lord, thy work revive
   In Zion's gloomy hour,
And let our dying graces live,
   By thy restoring power.

2 Oh, let thy chosen few
   Awake to earnest prayer;
Their sacred vows again renew,
   And walk in filial fear.

3 Thy spirit then will speak
   Through lips of feeble clay,
Till hearts of adamant shall break,
   Till rebels shall obey.

4 Now lend thy gracious ear;
   Now listen to our cry;
Oh, come and bring salvation near;
   Our souls on thee rely.

Olmutz, Key B♭.   Shirland, Key G.   Dennis, Key G.

DR. HASTINGS.

1. O where shall rest be found, Rest for the wea - ry soul?

'T were vain the ocean depths to sound, Or pierce to either pole.

8   *Life and Death Eternal.*   S. M.

2 The world can never give
   The bliss for which we sigh;
'T is not the whole of life to live,
   Nor all of death to die.

3 Beyond this vale of tears,
   There is a life above;
Unmeasured by the flight of years,
   And all that life is love.

4 There is a death, whose pang
   Outlasts the fleeting breath;
O, what eternal horrors hang
   Around "the second death!"

5 Lord God of truth and grace,
   Teach us that death to shun,
Lest we be banished from thy face,
   And evermore undone.

9   *Death of the Righteous.*   S. M.

1 O for the death of those
   Who slumber in the Lord!
O be like theirs my last repose,
   Like theirs my last reward.

2 Their ransomed spirits soar
   On wings of faith and love,
To meet the Savior they adore,
   And reign with him above.

3 With us their names shall live
   Through long-succeeding years,—
Embalmed with all our hearts can give—
   Our praises and our tears.

10   *The Christian never dies.*   S. M.

1 It is not death to die,
   To leave this weary road,
And, 'mid the brotherhood on high,
   To be at home with God.

2 It is not death to close
   The eye, long dimmed by tears,
And wake, in glorious repose
   To spend eternal years.

3 Jesus, thou Prince of life!
   Thy chosen can not die;
Like thee, they conquer in the strife,
   To reign with thee on high.

11   *Man Condemned before God.*   S. M.

1 Ah! how shall fallen man
   Be just before his God?
If he contend in righteousness,
   We fall beneath his rod.

2 If he our ways should mark
   With strict, inquiring eyes,
Could we for one of thousand faults
   A just excuse devise?

3 All-seeing, powerful God,
   Who can with thee contend?
Or who that tries th' unequal strife
   Shall prosper in the end?

4 Ah! how shall guilty man
   Contend with such a God?
None, none can meet him, and escape
   But through the Savior's blood.

Shawmut, Key D.   Dennis, Key G.   St. Thomas, Key G.

From GARDNER.

1. O speed thee, Christian, on thy way, And to thy ar-mor cling;

With gird-ed loins the call o - bey, That grace and mer-cy bring.

12   *The whole Armor.*   C. M.

2 There is a battle to be fought,
An upward race to run,
A crown of glory to be sought,
A victory to be won.

3 The shield of faith repels the dart
That Satan's hand may throw;
His arrow can not reach thy heart,
If Christ control the bow.

4 The glowing lamp of prayer will light
Thee on thy anxious road;
'T will keep the goal of heaven in sight,
And guide thee to thy God.

5 Oh, faint not, Christian, for thy sighs
Are heard before his throne;
The race must come before the prize,
The cross before the crown.

13   *The Safe Retreat.*   C. M.

1 Dear Father, to thy mercy-seat
My soul for shelter flies:
'T is here I find a safe retreat,
When storms and tempests rise.

2 My great Protector and my Lord,
Thy constant aid impart;
O, let thy kind, thy gracious word
Sustain my trembling heart.

3 O, never let my soul remove
From this divine retreat!
Still let me trust thy power and love,
And dwell beneath thy feet.

14   *Design of Christ's Advent.*   C. M.

1 Hark, the glad sound! the Savior comes,
The Savior promised long;
Let every heart prepare a throne,
And every voice a song.

2 He comes, the prisoner to release,
In Satan's bondage held;
The gates of brass before him burst,
The iron fetters yield.

3 He comes, from thickest films of vice
To clear the mental ray,
And on the eyes long closed in night
To pour celestial day.

4 He comes, the broken heart to bind,
The bleeding soul to cure,
And, with the treasures of his grace,
Enrich the humble poor.

5 Our glad hosannas, Prince of peace,
Thy welcome shall proclaim,
And heaven's eternal arches ring
With thy beloved name.

15   *All-uniting Faith.*   C. M.

1 Let all in whom the spirit glows,
In whom God's word hath place,
The all-uniting faith disclose,—
The all-endearing grace.

2 Then shall the world, admiring,
The gathered flock at rest; [view
And own the Son divinely true,
The saints divinely blest.

Peterboro', G.   Arlington, G.   Woodstock, G.

ENGLISH.

1. Early, my God, without delay, I haste to seek thy face; My thirsty spirit faints a-way, My thirsty spirit faints away, Without thy cheering grace.

16   *"Early will I seek thee."*   C. M.

2 So pilgrims on the scorching sand,
  Beneath a burning sky,
Long for a cooling stream at hand,
  And they must drink or die.

3 I've seen thy glory and thy power
  Through all thy temple shine:
My God! repeat that heavenly hour,
  That vision so divine.

4 Not life itself, with all its joys,
  Can my best passions move,
Or raise so high my cheerful voice,
  As thy forgiving love.

5 Thus, till my last, expiring day,
  I'll bless my God and King:
Thus will I lift my hands to pray,
  And tune my lips to sing.

17   *"Thine, wholly thine."*   C. M.

1 Eternal Father, God of love,
  To thee our hearts we raise;
Thy all-sustaining power we prove,
  And gladly sing thy praise.

2 Thine, wholly thine, O let us be!
  Our sacrifice receive;
Made and preserved and saved by thee,
  To thee ourselves we give.

3 Come, Holy Ghost! the Savior's love
  Shed in our hearts abroad;
So shall we ever live and move
  And be, with Christ, in God.

18   *The Cloud of Witnesses.*   C. M.

1 Give me the wings of faith to rise
  Within the vail, and see
The saints above—how great their joys,
  How bright their glories be!

2 Once they were mourning here below,
  And wet their couch with tears;
They wrestled hard, as we do now,
  With sins, and doubts, and fears.

3 I ask them whence their victory came;
  They, with united breath,
Ascribe their conquest to the Lamb,
  Their triumph to his death.

4 Our glorious Leader claims our praise
  For his own pattern given,
While the long cloud of witnesses
  Show the same path to heaven.

19   *Let me know my Father reigns.*   C. M.

1 My God, my Father, blissful name!
  Oh, may I call thee mine?
May I with sweet assurance claim
  A portion so divine?

2 Whate'er thy providence denies
  I calmly would resign;
For thou art good, and just, and wise:
  Oh, bend my will to thine!

3 Whate'er thy sacred will ordains,
  Oh, give me strength to bear:
And let me know my Father reigns,
  And trust his tender care.

Dundee, Key F.   Marlow, Key G.   Ortonville. Key B♭.

DORRNANCE. 8s & 7s.

I. B. WOODBURY.

1. One there is, a-bove all oth-ers, Well deserves the name of Friend;

His is love be-yond a brother's, Costly, free, and knows no end.

20   *The Sinner's Friend.*   8s & 7s.

1 One there is, above all others,
  Well deserves the name of Friend;
His is love beyond a brother's,
  Costly, free, and knows no end.

2 Which of all our friends, to save us,
  Could or would have shed his blood?
But our Jesus died to have us,
  Reconciled in him to God.

3 O, for grace our hearts to soften!
  Teach us, Lord, at length, to love;
We, alas! forget too often
  What a friend we have above.

21   *Perfections.*   8s & 7s.

1 God is love; his mercy brightens
  All the path in which we rove;
Bliss he wakes, and woe he lightens,
  God is wisdom, God is love.

2 Ev'n the hour that darkest seemeth
  Will his changeless goodness prove;
From the gloom his brightness streameth,
  God is wisdom, God is love.

3 He with earthly cares entwineth
  Hope and comfort from above;
Every-where his glory shineth,
  God is wisdom, God is love.

22   *Before the Cross.*   8s & 7s.

1 Sweet the moments, rich in blessing,
  Which before the cross we spend;
Life and health and peace possessing,
  From the sinner's dying Friend.

2 Truly blessed is this station,
  Low before his cross to lie,
While we see divine compassion,
  Beaming in his gracious eye.

3 Love and grief our hearts dividing,
  With our tears his feet we bathe;
Constant still, in faith abiding,
  Life deriving from his death.

4 Here we feel our sins forgiven,
  While upon the Lamb we gaze;
And our thoughts are all of heaven,
  And our lips o'erflow with praise.

23   *Doxology.*   8s & 7s.

1 Praise the God of our salvation,
  Praise the Father's boundless love;
Praise the Lamb, our expiation;
  Praise the Spirit from above;

2 Praise the mountain of salvation,
  Him by whom our spirits live;
Undivided adoration
  To the one Jehovah give!

Sicily, Key E♭.   Wilmot, Key B♭.   Autumn, Key G.

W. H. DOANE.

Andante.

1. Ev - er near us, ev - er near us, Bending o'er us as we pray;

With his lov - ing presence Je-sus Cheers us on our homeward way.

Chorus.

Ev - er near, ev - er near, Watching o'er us day by day;

Ev - er near, ev - er near, As we tread our homeward way.

24   *Ever near us.*   8s & 7s.

2 Ever near us, ever near us,
  In our bitter loneliness,
Sweetly comes this gentle Jesus,
  Blessing us in tenderness.

3 Ever near us, ever near us,
  When the loves of life depart,
Gently healing comes this Jesus,
  Binding up the wounded heart.

4 Ever near us, ever near us,
  As we cross the swelling tide,
Through the storm our life-boat Jesus
  Bears us to the other side.

25   *Invitation to Jesus.*   8s & 7s.

1 Come to Jesus, all ye weary,
  Burdened with the load of sin;
Come to Jesus, he is ready
  To receive the wanderer in.

Cho. Weary one, weary one,
  Burdened with your load of sin,
  Come to him, come to him,
  He'll receive the wanderer in.

2 Come to Jesus, he'll receive you;
  He will cancel all your guilt;
'T was for this he came to save you,
  'T was for this his blood was spilt.

BALERMA. C. M.

1. For-ev-er here my rest shall be, Close to thy bleeding side;

This all my hope and all my plea, For me the Savior died.

26 *Refuge in Christ.* C. M.

2 My dying Savior, and my God,
    Fountain for guilt and sin!
Sprinkle me ever with thy blood,
    And cleanse, and keep me clean.

3 Wash me, and make me thus thine own;
    Wash me, and mine thou art:
Wash me, but not my feet alone,
    My hauds, my head, my heart.

4 The atonement of thy blood apply,
    Till faith to sight improve;
Till hope in full fruition die,
    And all my soul be love.

27 *Vanity of earthly enjoyments.* C. M.

1 How vain are all things here below,
    How false, and yet how fair!
Each pleasure hath its poison too,
    And every sweet a snare.

2 The brightest things below the sky
    Give but a flatt'ring light;
We should suspect some danger nigh,
    Where we possess delight.

3 Our dearest joys, and nearest friends,
    The partners of our blood,
How they divide our wav'ring minds,
    And leave but half for God.

4 My Savior, let thy beauties be
    My soul's eternal food;
And grace command my heart away
    From all created good.

28 *Providence of God.* C. M.

1 God moves in a mysterious way
    His wonders to perform;
He plants his footsteps in the sea,
    And rides upon the storm.

2 Judge not the Lord by feeble sense,
    But trust him for his grace;
Behind a frowning providence
    He hides a smiling face.

3 His purposes will ripen fast,
    Unfolding every hour;
The bud may have a bitter taste,
    But sweet will be the flower.

29 *Believer's Rest.* C. M.

1 Lord, I believe a rest remains,
    To all thy people known;
A rest where pure enjoyment reigns,
    And thou art loved alone.

2 A rest where all our souls' desire
    Is fixed on things above;
Where fear, and sin, and grief expire,
    Cast out by perfect love.

3 Oh that I now the rest might know,
    Believe, and enter in!
Now, Savior! now the power bestow,
    And let me cease from sin.

4 Remove the hardness of my heart,
    The unbelief remove;
To me the rest of faith impart—
    The Sabbath of thy love.

Downs, Key E♭.   Woodstock, Key G.   Dundee, Key F.

Dr. ARNE.

1. Come, Ho-ly Ghost, our hearts inspire, Let us thine influence prove;

Source of the old pro - phet - ic fire, Fountain of light and love.

30   *Power of the Holy Ghost.*   C. M.

2 Come, Holy Ghost, for moved by thee
  The prophets wrote and spoke;
Unlock the truth, thyself the key,
  Unseal the sacred book.

3 God, through himself, we then shall know,
  If thou within us shine,
And sound, with all thy saints below,
  The depths of love divine.

31   *Running the Christian Race.*   C. M.

1 Awake, my soul, stretch every nerve,
  And press with vigor on :
A heavenly race demands thy zeal,
  And an immortal crown.

2 A cloud of witnesses around
  Hold thee in full survey;
Forget the steps already trod,
  And onward urge thy way.

3 'T is God's all-animating voice
  That calls thee from on high;
'T is his own hand presents the prize
  To thine aspiring eye.

4 Blest Savior, introduced by thee,
  Have I my race begun;
And, crowned with vict'ry, at thy feet,
  I 'll lay my honors down.

32   *Public Humiliation.*   C. M.

1 Lord, look on all assembled here,
  Who in thy presence stand,
To offer up united prayer,
  For this our sinful land.

2 Oh, may we all, with one consent,
  Fall low before thy throne,
With tears the nation's sins lament,
  The church's and our own.

33   *Come, Holy Spirit.*   C. M.

1 Come, Holy Spirit, heavenly Dove,
  With all thy quick'ning powers;
Kindle a flame of sacred love
  In these cold hearts of ours.

2 In vain we tune our formal songs,
  In vain we strive to rise;
Hosannas languish on our tongues,
  And our devotion dies.

3 Father, and shall we ever live
  At this poor dying rate;
Our love so faint, so cold to thee,
  And thine to us so great?

4 Come, Holy Spirit, heavenly Dove,
  With all thy quick'ning powers;
Come, shed abroad a Savior's love,
  And that shall kindle ours.

Naomi, Key D.   Ortonville, Key B♭.   Mear, Key F.

O, REST THEE, BROTHER!

W. H. Doane.

Legato.

1. In darkness art thou walk-ing, Thy sky with clouds o'ercast?

Look back with humble feel-ing, Re-call each blessing past.

Chorus.

O, rest thee, rest thee, Faint and wea-ry heart-ed; O,

rest thee, rest thee, Je-sus still is near.

34

1 In darkness art thou walking,
　　Thy sky with clouds o'ercast?
　Look back with humble feeling,
　　Recall each blessing past.

2 Then like a child confiding,
　　Obey thy Father's will,
　And rest thee in his promise,
　　To keep thee faithful still.

3 Let not thy courage fail thee,
　　O lift thy drooping head;
　Believe in him who taught thee
　　To ask thy daily bread.

4 Has not his tender mercy
　　With grace thy heart supplied?
　Then rest thee in the promise,
　　Thy Father will provide.

5 If tempted, go to Jesus,
　　He knows thy every fear;
　Unburden all thy sorrows,
　　He treasures every tear.

6 The God who made the sunbeam,
　　And feeds the tuneful bird,
　Will surely guard his children;
　　Then rest thee on his word.

Dr. HASTINGS.

Fine.

1. Rock of A - ges, cleft for me, Let me hide my - self in thee;
D. C. Be of sin a dou - ble cure, Save from wrath and make me pure.

D. C.

Let the wa - ter and the blood, From thy wounded side which flowed,

35   *Rock of Ages.*   7s.

2 Could my tears forever flow,
Could my zeal no languor know;
This for sin could not atone;
Thou must save, and thou alone;
In my hand no price I bring,
Simply to thy cross I cling.

3 While I draw this fleeting breath,
When my eyes shall close in death,
When I rise to worlds unknown,
And behold thee on thy throne,
Rock of Ages, cleft for me,
Let me hide myself in thee.

36   *Blessedness of Trust in Christ.*   7s.

1 Savior, happy would I be,
If I could but trust in thee;
Trust thy wisdom me to guide;
Trust thy goodness to provide;
Trust thy saving love and power;
Trust thee every day and hour:

2 Trust thee as the only light
In the darkest hour of night;
Trust in sickness, trust in health;
Trust in poverty and wealth;
Trust in joy, and trust in grief;
Trust thy promise for relief:

3 Trust thy blood to cleanse my soul;
Trust thy grace to make me whole;
Trust thee living, dying, too;
Trust thee all my journey through;
Trust thee till my feet shall be
Planted on the crystal sea!

37   *Only Thee.*   7s.

1 Blessed Savior! thee I love,
All my other joys above;
All my hopes in thee abide,
Thou my hope, and naught beside;
Ever let my glory be,
Only, only, only thee.

2 Once again beside the cross,
All my gain I count but loss;
Earthly pleasures fade away,
Clouds they are that hide my day:
Hence, vain shadows! let me see
Jesus, crucified for me.

3 Blessed Savior! thine am I,
Thine to live, and thine to die;
Height, or depth, or earthly power
Ne'er shall hide my Savior more;
Ever shall my glory be
Only, only, only thee.

Dr. LOWELL MASON.

1. My soul, be on thy guard, Ten thousand foes a - rise;

The hosts of sin are pressing hard To draw thee from the skies.

38 *The Soldier on his Guard.* S. M.

2 Oh, watch, and fight, and pray;
The battle ne'er give o'er;
Renew it boldly every day,
And help divine implore.

3 Ne'er think the victory won,
Nor lay thine armor down;
Thy arduous work will not be done
Till thou obtain thy crown.

4 Fight on, my soul, till death
Shall bring thee to thy God;
He'll take thee at thy parting breath,
To his divine abode.

39 *The Soldier Armed.* S. M.

1 Soldiers of Christ, arise,
And gird your armor on,
Strong in the strength which God supplies,
Through his eternal Son.

2 Strong in the Lord of hosts,
And in his mighty power,
The man who in the Savior trusts
Is more than conqueror.

3 Stand, then, in his great might,
With all his strength endued,
And take, to arm you for the fight,
The panoply of God.

40 *Song of Moses and the Lamb.* S. M.

1 Awake, and sing the song
Of Moses and the Lamb;
Wake every heart, and every tongue,
To praise the Savior's name.

2 Sing of his dying love;
Sing of his rising power;
Sing how he intercedes above
For us, whose sins he bore.

3 Sing, till we feel our heart
Ascending with our tongue;
Sing, till the love of sin depart,
And grace inspire our song.

4 Sing on your heavenly way,
Ye ransomed sinners, sing;
Sing on, rejoicing every day
In Christ, th' eternal King.

5 Soon shall we hear him say,
"Ye blessed children, come!"
Soon will he call us hence away
To our eternal home.

41 *Doxology.* S. M.

To God, the Father, Son,
And Spirit, glory be,
As was, and is, and shall remain,
Through all eternity!

St. Thomas, Key G.   Lisbon, Key B♭.

I. SMITH.

1. Come, sound his praise abroad, And hymns of glo - ry sing;

Je - ho - vah is the sov'reign God, The u - ni - ver - sal King.

42 *Exhortation to praise.* S. M.

2 Come, worship at his throne;
　Come, bow before the Lord:
We are his work, and not our own;
　He formed us by his word.

3 To-day attend his voice,
　Nor dare provoke his rod;
Come, like the people of his choice,
　And own your gracious God.

43 *Redemption by Grace.* S. M.

1 Grace! 't is a charming sound;
　Harmonious to the ear;
Heaven with the echo shall resound,
　And all the earth shall hear.

2 Grace first contrived the way
　To save rebellious man;
And all the steps that grace display,
　Which drew the wondrous plan.

3 Grace led my roving feet
　To tread the heavenly road;
And new supplies each hour I meet,
　While pressing on to God.

4 Grace all the work shall crown,
　Through everlasting days;
It lays in heaven the topmost stone,
　And well deserves the praise.

44 *All one in Christ.* S. M.

1 Let party names no more
　The Christian world o'erspread;
Gentile and Jew, and bond and free,
　Are one in Christ their Lord.

2 Among the saints on earth,
　Let mutual love be found;
Heirs of the same inheritance,
　With mutual blessings crowned.

45 *Call to Praise.* S. M.

1 Stand up, and bless the Lord,
　Ye people of his choice;
Stand up, and bless the Lord your God,
　With heart, and soul, and voice.

2 Oh, for the living flame
　From his own altar brought,
To touch our lips, our souls inspire,
　And wing to heaven our thought!

3 God is our strength and song,
　And his salvation ours:
Then be his love in Christ proclaimed,
　With all our ransomed powers.

4 Stand up, and bless the Lord;
　The Lord your God adore:
Stand up, and bless his glorious name,
　Henceforth, for evermore.

Boylston, Key C.　Shirland, Key G.　Olmutz, Bb.

Fine.

1. Come, thou Fount of every blessing, Tune my heart to sing thy grace; }
Streams of mercy, nev-er ceasing, Call for songs of loudest praise. }
D.C. Praise the mount—O, fix me on it, Mount of God's unchanging love.

Teach me some me - lo-dious sonnet, Sung by flaming tongues above;

46   *The Fount of Blessing.*   8s & 7s.

2 Here I raise my Ebenezer;
  Hither, by thy help I'm come;
And I hope, by thy good pleasure,
  Safely to arrive at home:
Jesus sought me when a stranger,
  Wandering from the fold of God;
He, to save my soul from danger,
  Interposed his precious blood.

3 Oh! to grace how great a debtor
  Daily I'm constrained to be!
Let that grace, Lord, like a fetter,
  Bind my wandering heart to thee.
Prone to wander, Lord, I feel it;
  Prone to leave the God I love;
Here's my heart; Lord, take and seal it;
  Seal it from thy courts above.

47   *"From Grace to Glory."*   8s & 7s.

1 Know, my soul, thy full salvation;
  Rise o'er sin, and fear, and care;
Joy to find in every station
  Something still to do or bear;
Think what Spirit dwells within thee;
  Think what Father's smiles are thine;
Think that Jesus died to win thee:
  Child of heaven, canst thou repine?

2 Haste thee on from grace to glory,
  Armed by faith, and winged by prayer;
Heaven's eternal day before thee—
  God's own hand shall guide thee there.
Soon shall close thine earthly mission,
  Soon shall pass thy pilgrim days;
Hope shall change to glad fruition,
  Faith to sight, and prayer to praise.

48   *The Spirit Invoked.*   8s & 7s.

1 Holy source of consolation,
  Light and life thy grace imparts;
Visit us in thy compassion;
  Guide our minds and fill our hearts.
Heavenly blessings, without measure,
  Thou canst bring us from above;
Lord, we ask that heavenly treasure,
  Wisdom, holiness, and love.

2 Dwell within us, blessed Spirit;
  Where thou art no ill can come;
Bless us now, through Jesus' merit;
  Reign in every heart and home.
Savior, lead us to adore thee,
  While thou dost prolong our days;
Then, with angel hosts before thee,
  May we worship, love, and praise.

Greenville, Key F.   Sicily, Key Eb.   Autumn, Key Ab.

W. H. DOANE.

Andante.

1. Take thy cross without re-pin-ing, Whatso-e'er thy cross may be;
Bear it up the rugged mountain, Je-sus bore a cross for thee.

Chorus.

Take the cross and bear it meekly, Take the cross and bear it meekly,

Take the cross and bear it meekly, Till thy work on earth is done.

---

49   *Take the Cross.*   8s & 7s.

2 Take the cross and learn thy duty,
  Learn of Him who bids thee pray;
He will make it plain before thee,
  Seek his counsel day by day.
    Take the cross, etc.

3 Trials bring the promise nearer,
  Take the cross—thyself deny;
Thro' the might of Him who bore thee,
  Thou shalt conquer by and by.
    Take the cross, etc.

4 Take the cross and bear it meekly,
  Till thy work on earth is done.
Till thy soul shall reach the haven,
  Till thy starry crown is won.
    Take the cross, etc.

50   *Encouragement.*   8s & 7s.

1 Onward, onward. toiling pilgrim,
  Up the rugged steeps of life,
Falter not, though weak and weary,
  In the agony of strife.
    Take the cross, etc.

2 Full of hope, and full of courage,
  Giving not a thought to fear,
Bravely struggle, onward, upward,
  Singing songs of heavenly cheer.
    Take the cross, etc.

3 Yet with soul alive to duty,
  Still press on thy toilsome way,
Good shall come from every trial,
  Strength divine shall win the day.
    Take the cross, etc.

ZEPHYR. L. M.

WM. B. BRADBURY.

1. Come, weary souls, with sin distressed, Come, and accept the promised rest;

The Savior's gracious call o - bey, And cast your gloomy fears away.

51   *Rest for the Weary Penitent.*   L. M.

2 Oppressed with sin, a painful load,
O, come, and spread your woes abroad;
Divine compassion, mighty love,
Will all the painful load remove.

3 Here mercy's boundless ocean flows,
To cleanse your guilt and heal your woes;
Pardon, and life, and endless peace;
How rich the gift! how free the grace!

4 Lord, we accept, with thankful heart,
The hope thy gracious words impart;
We come with trembling, yet rejoice,
And bless the kind, inviting voice.

5 Dear Savior, let thy wondrous love
Confirm our faith, our fears remove;
O, sweetly influence every breast,
And guide us to eternal rest.

52   *Christ's Invitation..*   L. M.

1 Come hither, all ye weary souls;
Ye heavy-laden sinners, come;
I 'll give you rest from all your toils,
And raise you to my heavenly home.

2 They shall find rest that learn of me;
I 'm of a meek and lowly mind;
But passion rages like the sea,
And pride is restless as the wind.

3 Blest is the man whose shoulders take
My yoke, and bear it with delight:
My yoke is easy on his neck,
My grace shall make the burden light.

4 Jesus, we come at thy command,
With faith, and hope, and cheerful zeal;
Resign our spirits to thy hand,
To mold and guide us at thy will.

53   *Christ the Physician of the Soul.*   L. M.

1 Deep are the wounds which sin has made;
Where shall the sinner find a cure?
In vain, alas! is nature's aid;
The work exceeds her utmost power.

2 But can no sovereign balm be found?
And is no kind physician nigh,
To ease the pain, and heal the wound,
Ere life and hope forever fly?

3 There is a great Physician near;
Look up, O fainting soul, and live;
See, in his heavenly smiles appear
Such help as nature can not give.

4 See, in the Savior's dying blood,
Life, health, and bliss abundant flow:
'T is only that dear, sacred flood
Can ease thy pain, and heal thy woe

Federal Street, Key F.   Windham, Key G.   Ward, Key B♭.

ISRAEL HOLDROYD.

1. Show pity, Lord, O Lord forgive, Let a re-pent-ing rebel live;

Are not thy mercies large and free? May not a sinner trust in thee?

54   *Penitence.*   L. M.

2 My crimes are great, but do n't surpass
The power and glory of thy grace;
Great God, thy nature hath no bound,
So let thy pard'ning love be found.

3 O wash my soul from every sin,
And make my guilty conscience clean;
Here on my heart the burden lies,
And past offenses pain my eyes.

4 Yet save a trembling sinner, Lord,
Whose hope, still hov'ring round thy word,
Would light on some sweet promise there,
Some sure support against despair.

55   *Probation in this Life only.*   L. M.

1 Life is the time to serve the Lord,
The time t' insure the great reward;
And while the lamp holds out to burn,
The vilest sinner may return.

2 Life is the hour that God has given
T' escape from hell and fly to heaven;
The day of grace—and mortals may
Secure the blessings of the day.

3 Then what my thoughts design to do,
My hands with all your might pursue,
Since no device, nor work is found,
Nor faith, nor hope, beneath the ground.

56   *The light yoke and easy burden.*   L. M.

1 O that my load of sin were gone;
O that I could at last submit
At Jesus' feet to lay it down—
To lay my soul at Jesus' feet.

2 Rest for my soul I long to find:
Savior of all, if mine thou art,
Give me thy meek and lowly mind,
And stamp thine image on my heart.

3 Fain would I learn of thee, my God,
Thy light and easy burden prove;
The cross all stained with hallowed blood,
The labor of thy dying love.

4 I would, but thou must give the power;
My heart from every sin release;
Bring near, bring near the joyful hour,
And fill me with thy perfect peace.

57   *Seeking.*   L. M.

1 Thus saith the wisdom of the Lord,
"Blessed is the man that hears my word,
Keeps daily watch before my gates,
And at my feet for mercy waits.

2 "The soul that seeks me shall obtain
Immortal wealth and heavenly gain;
Immortal life is his reward;
Life, and the favor of the Lord."

Hebron, Key Bb.   Hamburg, Key Eb.   Rockingham, Key G.

58   HUBERT P. MAIN.

1. Thine, Lord, for-ev - er, Purchased by blood divine, Res-cued and
2. Thine, Lord, for-ev - er, Thro' storm and tempest wild, Trusting con-
3. Thine, Lord, for-ev-er, Cheered by thy precious word, Thro' darkness,

saved by thee, Lord, I am thine.
fi - ding-ly, I am thy child.
doubts, and fears; Thine, thine, O Lord.

4 Thine, Lord, forever,
Tho' death shall lay me low,
E'en in that dreadful hour,
Thine, Lord, I know.

5 Thine, Lord, forever,
When safe before thy throne
I stand, for evermore
Thine, thine, alone.

JESUS WAITS FOR THEE.

59   *Tenderly.*   HUBERT P. MAIN.

1. Come, come to Je - sus! He waits to welcome thee, O Wand'rer,
2. Come, come to Je - sus! He waits to ran-som thee, O Slave, e-

en - ger-ly; Come, come to Je-sus!
ter - nal-ly; Come, come to Je-sus!

2 Come, come to Jesus!
He waits to lighten thee,
O Burdened! graciously;
Come, come to Jesus!

4 Come, come to Jesus!
He waits to give to thee,
O Blind! a vision free;
Come, come to Jesus!

5 Come, come to Jesus!
He waits to shelter thee,
O Weary! blessedly,
Come, come to Jesus!

6 Come, come to Jesus
He waits to carry thee,
O Lamb! so lovingly;
Come, come to Jesus!

T. E. PERKINS.

60

1. Fade, fade each earthly joy, Jesus is mine! Break ev'ry tender tie,

D. S. Je-sus alone can bless,

Fine.

D. S.

Je-sus is mine! Dark is the wilderness, Earth has no resting-place,
Je - sus is mine!

2 Tempt not my soul away,
  Jesus is mine!
Here would I ever stay,
  Jesus is mine!
Perishing things of clay,
Born but for one brief day,
Pass from my heart away,
  Jesus is mine!

3 Farewell, ye dreams of night,
  Jesus is mine!
Lost in this dawning light,
  Jesus is mine!

All that my soul has tried,
Left but a dismal void,
Jesus has satisfied,
  Jesus is mine!

4 Farewell, mortality,
  Jesus is mine!
Welcome, eternity,
  Jesus is mine!
Welcome, O loved and blest,
Welcome, sweet scenes of rest,
Welcome, my Savior's breast,
  Jesus is mine!

COME TO JESUS.

61

1. Come to Je-sus, come to Je-sus, Come to Je-sus, just

now, just now, Come to Je-sus, come to Je-sus, just now.

2 He will save you.
3 O believe him.
4 He is able.
5 He is willing.
6 He'll receive you.

7 Call upon him.
8 He will hear you.
9 Look unto him.
10 He'll forgive you.
11 Flee to Jesus.

12 He will cleanse you.
13 He will clothe you.
14 Jesus loves you.
15 Don't reject him.
16 Only trust him.

Moderato legato.

1. Depth of mer - cy, can there be   Mer - cy still   reserved for me? }
Can my God his wrath forbear, Me,   the chief of sinners, spare? }

Chorus, faster.   *Smoothly.*   *Repeat pp.*

{ God is love, I know, I feel; }
{ Jesus lives and loves me still; } Je - sus lives, He lives and loves me still.

62   *Depth of Mercy.*   7s.
2 I have long withstood his grace;
Long provoked him to his face;
Would not hearken to his calls;
Grieved him by a thousand falls.

3 Now incline me to repent;
Let me now my sins lament;

Now my foul revolt deplore,
Weep, believe, and sin no more.

4 There for me the Savior stands;
Shows his wounds and spreads his hands;
God is love, I know, I feel;
Jesus lives and loves me still.

AMOY. 6s & 4s.

Dr. L. MASON.

1 To - day the Sav-ior calls, Ye wand'rers, come; O, ye benight-ed
2 To - day the Sav-ior calls: O,   lis - ten now; Within these sacred

souls, Why lon - ger roam?
walls To Je - sus bow.

63   *The Savior Calls.*   6s & 4s.
3 To-day the Savior calls:
   For refuge fly;
The storm of justice falls,
   And death is nigh.

4 The Spirit calls to-day:
   Yield to his power;
Oh, grieve him not away,
   'Tis mercy's hour.

S. B. Marsh.

1. Je-sus, lov-er of my soul, Let me to thy bos-om fly, }
While the raging billows roll, While the tempest still is high. }

D. C. Safe in-to the hav-en guide; Oh, receive my soul at last!

Hide me, O my Sav-ior! hide, Till the storm of life is past;

---

64   *Christ the only Refuge.*   7s.

2 Other refuge have I none,—
  Hangs my helpless soul on thee!
Leave, ah! leave me not alone!
  Still support and comfort me;
All my trust on thee is stayed;
  All my help from thee I bring;
Cover my defenseless head
  With the shadow of thy wing.

3 Thou, O Christ, art all I want;
  All and all in thee I find;
Raise the fallen, cheer the faint,
  Heal the sick and lead the blind;
Just and holy is thy name,
  I am all unrighteousness;
Vile, and full of sin I am,
  Thou art full of truth and grace.

65   *Mary at the Savior's Tomb.*   7s.

1 Mary to the Savior's tomb
  Hasted at the early dawn;
Spice she brought, and sweet perfume,
  But the Lord she loved had gone.
For awhile she lingering stood,
  Filled with sorrow and surprise,
Trembling, while a crystal flood
  Issued from her weeping eyes.

2 But her sorrows quickly fled
  When she heard his welcome voice:
Christ had risen from the dead;
  Now he bids her heart rejoice.
What a change his word can make,
  Turning darkness into day!
Ye who weep for Jesus' sake,
  He will wipe your tears away.

66   *Converting Grace.*   7s.

1 Saved by grace, I live to tell
  What the love of Christ has done:
He redeemed my soul from hell;
  Of a rebel made a son.
Oh, I tremble still to think
  How secure I lived in sin,
Sporting on destruction's brink,
  Yet preserved from falling in.

2 Come, my fellow-sinners, try;
  Jesus' heart is full of love;
Oh that you, as well as I,
  May his wondrous mercy prove!
He has sent me to declare
  All is ready, all is free:
Why should any soul despair,
  When he saved a wretch like me?

CHAPIN.

1. God is the refuge of his saints, When storms of sharp distress invade;

Ere we can of-fer our complaints, Behold him present with his aid.

67 *God the Refuge of his People.* L. M.

1 God is the refuge of his saints,
　When storms of sharp distress invade;
Ere we can offer our complaints,
　Behold him present with his aid.

2 Loud may the troubled ocean roar;
　In sacred peace our souls abide;
While every nation, every shore,
　Trembles, and dreads the swelling tide.

3 There is a stream whose gentle flow
　Supplies the city of our God;
Life, love, and joy still gliding thro',
　And watering our divine abode.

4 That sacred stream, thine holy word,
　Supports our faith, our fear controls;
Sweet peace thy promises afford,
　And give new strength to fainting souls.

5 Zion enjoys her Monarch's love,
　Secure against a threatening hour;
Nor can her firm foundation move,
　Built on his truth, and armed with power.

68 *Returning to God.* L. M.

1 Return, my wandering soul, return,
　And seek an injured Father's face;
Those warm desires that in thee burn
　Were kindled by redeeming grace.

Welton, B♭.

2 Return, my wandering soul, return,
　And seek a Father's melting heart.
His pitying eyes thy grief discern,
　His heavenly balm shall heal thy smart.

3 Return, my wandering soul, return;
　Thy dying Savior bids thee live;
Go, view his bleeding side, and learn
　How freely Jesus can forgive.

4 Return, my wandering soul, return,
　And wipe away the falling tear;
'T is God who says, "No longer mourn;"
　'T is mercy's voice invites thee near.

69 *Jesus every-where present.* L. M.

1 Jesus, where'er thy people meet,
　There they behold thy mercy seat;
Where'er they seek thee, thou art found,
　And every place is hallowed ground.

2 For thou, within no walls confined,
　Dost dwell with those of humble mind;
Such ever bring thee where they come,
　And, going, take thee to their home.

3 Great Shepherd of thy chosen few,
　Thy former mercies here renew;
Here, to our waiting hearts, proclaim
　The sweetness of thy saving name.

Duryea, B♭.

T. HASTINGS.

1. From every stormy wind that blows, From every swelling tide of woes,

There is a calm, a sure retreat, 'Tis found beneath the mercy seat.

70 *The Mercy Seat.* L. M.

1 From every stormy wind that blows,
From every swelling tide of woes,
There is a calm, a sure retreat;
'Tis found beneath the mercy seat.

2 There is a place where Jesus sheds
The oil of gladness on our heads—
A place of all on earth most sweet;
It is the blood-bought mercy seat.

3 There is a scene where spirits blend,
Where friend holds fellowship with friend;
Tho' sundered far, by faith they meet
Around one common mercy seat.

4 There, there, on eagle wings we soar,
And sin and sense molest no more;
And heaven comes down our souls to greet,
And glory crowns the mercy seat.

71 *Zion Encouraged.* L. M.

1 Zion, awake; thy strength renew;
Put on thy robes of beauteous hue;
Church of our God, arise and shine,
Bright with the beams of truth divine.

2 Soon shall thy radiance stream afar,
Wide as the heathen nations are:
Gentiles and kings thy light shall view;
All shall admire and love thee too.

Woodworth, E♭.

72 *They that go down to the Sea.* L. M.

1 While o'er the deep thy servants sail,
Send thou, O Lord, the prosperous gale;
And on their hearts, where'er they go,
Oh, let thy heavenly breezes blow.

2 When tempests rock the groaning bark,
Oh hide them safe in Jesus' ark!
When in the tempting port they ride,
Oh keep them safe at Jesus' side.

3 If life's wide ocean smile or roar,
Still guide them to the heavenly shore;
And grant their dust in Christ may sleep,
Abroad, at home, or in the deep.

73 *Heavenly Aspirations.* L. M.

1 Up to the fields where angels lie,
And living waters gently roll,
Fain would my thoughts ascend on high,
But sin hangs heavy on my soul.

2 Oh, might I once mount up and see
The glories of th' eternal skies,
How vain a thing this world would be!
How empty all its fleeting joys!

3 Great All in All, eternal King,
Let me but view thy lovely face,
And all my powers shall bow and sing
Thine endless grandeur and thy grace.

Hebron, B♭.

Dr. L. Mason.

1. My faith looks up to thee, Thou Lamb of Calvary, Savior divine;

Now hear me while I pray; }
Take all my guilt a-way; } O, let me, from this day, Be wholly thine.

---

74   *My Faith looks up.*   6s & 4s.

1 My faith looks up to thee,
  Thou Lamb of Calvary;
    Savior divine,
  Now hear me while I pray;
  Take all my guilt away;
  Oh, let me, from this day,
    Be wholly thine.

2 May thy rich grace impart
  Strength to my fainting heart;
    My zeal inspire;
  As thou hast died for me,
  Oh, may my love to thee
  Pure, warm, and changeless be,
    A living fire.

3 While life's dark maze I tread,
  And griefs around me spread,
    Be thou my guide;
  Bid darkness turn to day,
  Wipe sorrow's tears away,
  Nor let me ever stray
    From thee aside.

4 When ends life's transient dream,
  When death's cold, sullen stream
    Shall o'er me roll,
  Blest Savior, then, in love,
  Fear and distress remove,
  Oh, bear me safe above,
    A ransomed soul.

75   *Savior, I look to thee.*   6s & 4s.

1 Savior, I look to thee,
  Be not thou far from me,
    'Mid storms that lower:
  On me thy care bestow,
  Thy loving kindness show,
  Thine arms around me throw,
    This trying hour.

2 Savior, I look to thee,
  Feeble as infancy,
    Gird up my heart:
  Author of life and light,
  Thou hast an arm of might,
  Thine is the sovereign right,
    Thy strength impart.

3 Savior, I look to thee,
  Let me thy fullness see,
    Save me from fear;
  While at thy cross I kneel,
  All my backslidings heal,
  And a free pardon seal,
    My soul to cheer.

4 Savior, I look to thee,
  Thine shall the glory be,
    Hearer of prayer:
  Thou art my only aid,
  On thee my soul is stayed,
  Naught can my heart invade
    While thou art near.

With Spirit.

1. Christ for the world we sing, The world to Christ we bring, With loving zeal;

The poor and them that mourn, }
The faint and overborne, } Sin-sick and sorrow-worn, Whom Christ doth heal.

---

76 *Christ for all the World.* 6s & 4s.

1 Christ for the world we sing;
  The world to Christ we bring,
    With loving zeal—
  The poor, and them that mourn,
  The faint and overborne,
  Sin-sick and sorrow-worn,
    Whom Christ doth heal.

2 Christ for the world we sing;
  The world to Christ we bring,
    With fervent prayer—
  The wayward and the lost,
  By restless passions tossed,
  Redeemed at countless cost,
    From dark despair.

3 Christ for the world we sing;
  The world to Christ we bring,
    With one accord—
  With us the work to share,
  With us reproach to dare,
  With us the cross to bear,
    For Christ our Lord.

4 Christ for the world we sing;
  The world to Christ we bring,
    With joyful song—
  The new-born souls, whose days,
  Reclaimed from error's ways,
  Inspired with hope and praise,
    To Christ belong.

77 *Come, thou Almighty King.* 6s & 4s.

1 Come, thou Almighty King,
  Help us thy name to sing,
    Help us to praise;
  Father all glorious,
  O'er all victorious,
  Come and reign over us,
    Ancient of days.

2 Jesus, our Lord, arise,
  Scatter our enemies,
    And make them fall.
  Let thine almighty aid
  Our sure defense be made;
  Our souls on thee be stayed;
    Lord, hear our call.

3 Come, holy Comforter,
  Thy sacred witness bear
    In this glad hour.
  Thou, who almighty art,
  Now rule in every heart,
  And ne'er from us depart,
    Spirit of power.

4 To the great One in Three,
  The highest praises be,
    Hence evermore;
  His sovereign majesty
  May we in glory see,
  And to eternity
    Love and adore.

1. Lord, at thy mer-cy seat, Hum-bly I fall; }
Plead-ing thy prom-ise sweet, Lord, hear my call. }

2. Tears of re-pent-ant grief Si-lent-ly fall; }
Help thou my un-be-lief, Hear thou my call. }

Now let thy work be-gin, Oh, make me pure with-in,
Oh, how I pine for thee, 'Tis all my hope, my plea,

Cleanse me from ev-ery sin, Je-sus, my all.
Je-sus has died for me, Je-sus, my all.

78   *Jesus my all.*   6s & 4s.

3 Hark! how the words of love
    Tenderly fall;
Ere to the realms above
    Heard is my call.
Now every doubt has flown,
Broken my heart of stone,
Lord, I am thine alone,
    Jesus, my all.

4 Still at thy mercy seat,
    Humbly I fall;
Pleading thy promise sweet,
    Heard is my call.
Faith wings my soul to'thee,
This all my hope shall be,
Jesus has died for me,
    Jesus, my all.

79   *Weary of Earthly Care.*   6s & 4s.

1 Weary of earthly care,
    Jesus, my Lord,
I want thy love to share,
    Trust in thy Word.
Come, Savior, from above,
Take to thine arms of love,
And from my soul remove
    Each sinful stain.

2 Wash me and make me clean—
    Pure as thou art;
Each root and seed of sin
    Take from my heart;
Make me, in thought and word,
Like unto thee, my Lord;
Then be thy grace adored
    For evermore.

Dr. HASTINGS.

1. Jesus, thy name I love, All other names a-bove, Je-sus, my Lord, Oh thou art

all to me! Nothing to please I see, Nothing apart from thee, Jesus, my Lord!

80   *Jesus, my Soul.*   6s & 4s.

1 Jesus, thy name I love,
  All other names above,
      Jesus, my Lord!
  Oh! thou art all to me!
  Nothing to please I see,
  Nothing apart from thee,
      Jesus, my Lord!

2 Thou blessed Son of God
  Hast bought me with thy blood.
      Jesus, my Lord!
  Oh! how great is thy love,
  All other loves above,
  Love that I daily prove,
      Jesus, my Lord!

3 When unto thee I flee,
  Thou wilt my refuge be,
      Jesus, my Lord!
  What need I now to fear?
  What earthly grief or care,
  Since thou art ever near,
      Jesus, my Lord!

4 Soon thou wilt come again!
  I shall be happy then,
      Jesus, my Lord!
  Then thine own face I'll see,
  Then I shall like thee be,
  Then evermore with thee,
      Jesus, my Lord!

81   *Now I have found a Friend.*   6s & 4s.

1 Now I have found a friend,
  Whose love shall never end;
      Jesus is mine.
  Though earthly joys decrease,
  Though human friendships cease,
  Now I have lasting peace;
      Jesus is mine.

2 Though I grow poor and old,
  He will my faith uphold;
      Jesus is mine.
  He shall my wants supply;
  His precious blood is nigh,
  Naught can my hope destroy
      Jesus is mine.

3 When earth shall pass away,
  In the great judgment day,
      Jesus is mine.
  Oh, what a glorious thing
  Then to behold my King,
  On tuneful harps to sing
      Jesus is mine.

4 Father! thy name I bless;
  Thine was the sovereign grace,
      Praise shall be thine;
  Spirit of holiness!
  Sealing the Father's grace,
  Thou mad'st my soul embrace
      Jesus as mine.

DENNIS. S. M.

H. G. NAGELI.

1. Blest be the tie that binds Our hearts in Christian love;

The fel - low-ship of kindred minds Is like to that a-bove.

82 *Sympathy and Mutual Love.* S. M.

1 Blest be the tie that binds
  Our hearts in Christian love;
The fellowship of kindred minds
  Is like to that above.

2 Before our Father's throne,
  We pour our ardent prayers;
Our fears, our hopes, our aims are one—
  Our comforts and our cares.

3 We share our mutual woes;
  Our mutual burdens bear;
And often for each other flows
  The sympathizing tear.

4 When we asunder part,
  It gives us inward pain;
But we shall still be joined in heart,
  And hope to meet again.

5 This glorious hope revives
  Our courage by the way;
While each in expectation lives,
  And longs to see the day.

83 *Gentleness of God's Commands.* S. M.

1 How gentle God's commands!
  How kind his precepts are!
Come, cast your burdens on the Lord,
  And trust his constant care.

2 Beneath his watchful eye
  His saints securely dwell;
That hand which bears all nature up,
  Shall guard his children well.

3 His goodness stands approved,
  Unchanged from day to day:
I'll drop my burden at his feet,
  And bear a song away.

84 *Christian Love.* S. M.

1 Love is the strongest tie
  That can our hearts unite;
Love makes our service liberty,
  Our every burden light.

2 We run in God's commands,
  When love directs the way;
With willing hearts and active hands,
  Our Maker's will obey.

85 *Purity of Heart.* S. M

1 Blessed are the pure in heart,
  For they shall see our God;
The secret of the Lord is theirs:
  Their soul is Christ's abode.

2 Still to the lowly soul
  He doth himself impart,
And for his cradle and his throne
  Chooseth the pure in heart.

Boylston, Key C.   Tioga, Key Bb.   State Street, Key Bb.

Rev. WM. HUNTER.   Rev. E. W. DUNBAR.

1. And may I still get there? Still reach the heavenly shore?

CHO. There'll be no sor-row there, There'll be no sor-row there;

D. C.

The land for-ev-er bright and fair, Where sorrow reigns no more.

In heaven above, where all is love, There'll be no sorrow there.

86   *The Heavenly Shore.*   S. M.

2 Shall I, unworthy I,
   To fear and doubting given,
Mount up at last, and happy, fly
   On angel's wings to heaven?

3 Hail, love divine and pure,
   Hail, mercy from the skies!
My hopes are bright, and now secure,
   Upborne by faith I rise.

4 I part with earth and sin,
   And shout the danger's past;
My Savior takes me fully in,
   And I am his at last.

87   *No Sorrow There.*   S. M.

1 Oh, sing to me of heaven,
   When I am called to die,
Sing songs of holy ecstasy,
   To waft my soul on high.

2 When the last moment comes,
   Oh, watch my dying face,
To catch the bright seraphic gloam,
   Which o'er my features plays.

3 Then to my raptured soul,
   Let one sweet song be given,
Let music cheer me last on earth,
   And greet me first in heaven.

88   *Heavenly Joy on Earth.*   S. M.

1 Come, we that love the Lord,
   And let our joys be known;
Join in a song with sweet accord,
   And thus surround the throne,

2 The hill of Zion yields
   A thousand sacred sweets,
Before we reach the heavenly fields,
   Or walk the golden streets.

3 Then let our songs abound,
   And every tear be dry;
We're marching thro' Immanuel's ground,
   To fairer worlds on high.

89   *Home in Heaven.*   S. M.

1 My Father's house on high!
   Home of my soul! how near
At times, to faith's foreseeing eye,
   Thy golden gates appear!

2 I hear at morn and even,
   At noon and midnight hour,
The choral harmonies of heaven
   Angelic music pour.

3 Oh, then my spirit faints
   To reach the land I love—
The bright inheritance of saints,
   My glorious home above.

St. Thomas, Key G.   Dover, Key E♭.   Golden Hill, Key E♭.

OLIPHANT. 8s, 7s & 4.

DR. L. MASON.

Allegro. | 1st.

1. In thy name, O Lord, assembling, We, thy people, now draw near;
Teach us to rejoice with trembling, - - - - - -

| 2d.

Speak, and let thy servants hear—Hear with meekness, Hear with meekness,

Hear thy word with god-ly fear, Hear thy word with godly fear.

---

90   *Spiritual Improvement.*   8s, 7s & 4.

1 In thy name, O Lord, assembling,
  We, thy people, now draw near;
Teach us to rejoice with trembling;
  Speak, and let thy servants hear—
    Hear with meekness,
  Hear thy word with godly fear.

2 While our days on earth are lengthened,
  May we give them, Lord, to thee;
Cheered by hope, and daily strengthened,
  We would run, nor weary be,
    Till thy glory,
  Without clouds, in heaven we see.

3 There, in worship, purer, sweeter,
  All thy people shall adore;
Tasting of enjoyment greater
  Than they could conceive before—
    Full enjoyment,
  Holy bliss, for evermore.

91   *God, the Pilgrim's Guide.*   8s, 7s & 4.

1 Guide me, O thou great Jehovah,
  Pilgrim through this barren land;
I am weak, but thou art mighty,
  Hold me with thy powerful hand;
    Bread of heaven,
  Feed me till I want no more.

2 Open now the crystal fountain,
  Whence the healing streams do flow;
Let the fiery, cloudy pillar,
  Lead me all my journey through;
    Strong Deliverer,
  Be thou still my strength and shield.

3 When I tread the verge of Jordan,
  Bid my anxious fears subside;
Bear me through the swelling current,
  Land me safe on Canaan's side;
    Songs of praises
  I will ever give to thee.

Zion, Key D.   Unam, Key G.   Osgood, Key Eb.

WM. B. BRADBURY.

1. Savior, like a Shepherd lead us, Much we need thy tend'rest care;
In thy pleasant pastures feed us, For our use thy folds prepare.

Blessed Je - sus, Blessed Je-sus, Thou hast bought us, thine we are;

Blessed Je-sus, Blessed Je-sus, Thou hast bought us, thine we are.

92 *Savior, like a Shepherd, lead us.* 8s, 7s & 4.

2 We are thine, do thou befriend us,
·Be the Guardian of our way;
Keep thy flock, from sin defend us,
Seek us when we go astray.
Blessed Jesus,
Hear, oh hear us, when we pray.

3 Thou hast promised to receive us,
Poor and sinful though we be;
Thou hast mercy to relieve us,
Grace to cleanse, and power to free.
Blessed Jesus,
We will early turn to thee.

4 Early let us seek thy favor,
Early let us do thy will;
Blessed Lord and only Savior,
With thy love our bosoms fill.
Blessed Jesus,
Thou hast loved us, love us still.

93 *Lead us. Heavenly Father.* 8s. 7s & 4.

1 Lead us, heavenly Father, lead us
O'er the world's tempestuous sea;
Guard us, guide us, keep us, feed us,
For we have no help but thee;
Yet possessing Every blessing,
If our God our Father be.

2 Savior, breathe forgiveness o'er us,
All our weakness thou dost know;
Thou didst tread this earth before us;
Thou didst feel its keenest woe;
Lone and dreary, Faint and weary,
Through the desert thou didst go.

3 Spirit of our God, descending,
Fill our hearts with heavenly joy
Love with every passion blending,
Pleasure that can never cloy;
Thus provided, Pardoned, guided,
Nothing can our peace destroy.

Zion, Key G.   Greenville, Key F.   Oliphant, Key D.

1. A friend there is—your voices join, Ye saints, to praise his name—

Whose truth and kindness are divine, Whose love's a constant flame.

94   *Christ a Friend.*   C. M.

1 A friend there is—your voices join,
  Ye saints, to praise his name—
Whose truth and kindness are divine,
  Whose love's a constant flame.

2 When most we need his helping hand,
  This Friend is always near;
With heaven and earth at his command,
  He waits to answer prayer.

3 When frowns appear to veil his face,
  And clouds surround his throne,
He hides the purpose of his grace,
  To make it better known.

4 And, if our dearest comforts fall
  Before his sovereign will,
He never takes away our all:
  Himself he gives us still.

5 Our sorrows in the scale he weighs,
  And measures out our pains;
The wildest storm his word obeys;
  His word its rage restrains.

95   *Love the test of Discipleship.*   C. M.

1 Our God is love; and all his saints
  His image bear below;
The heart with love to God inspired,
  With love to man will glow.

2 None who are truly born of God
  Can live in enmity;
Then may we love each other, Lord,
  As we are loved by thee.

3 Heirs of the same immortal bliss,
  Our hopes and fears the same,
With bonds of love our hearts unite,
  With mutual love inflame.

4 So may the unbelieving world
  See how true Christians love;
And glorify our Savior's grace,
  And seek that grace to prove.

96   *Saints on Earth and in Heaven.*   C. M

1 In one fraternal bond of love,
  One fellowship of mind,
The saints below and saints above
  Their bliss and glory find.

2 Here, in their house of pilgrimage,
  Thy statutes are their song;
There, thro' one bright, eternal age,
  Thy praises they prolong.

3 Lord, may our union form a part
  Of that thrice happy whole,
Derive its pulse from thee, the heart,
  Its life from thee, the soul.

Siloam, Key D.   Heber, Key C.   Dundee, Key F.

Dr. LOWELL MASON.

1. Dear Refuge of my wea-ry soul, On thee, when sorrows rise,

On thee, when waves of trouble roll, My fainting hope re - lies.

97 *Comfort in God.* C. M.

1 Dear Refuge of my weary soul,
On thee, when sorrows rise,
On thee, when waves of trouble roll,
My fainting hope relies.

2 To thee I tell each rising grief,
For thou alone canst heal;
Thy word can bring a sweet relief
For every pain I feel.

3 But, oh, when gloomy doubts prevail,
I fear to call thee mine;
The springs of comfort seem to fail,
And all my hopes decline.

4 Yet, gracious God, where shall I flee?
Thou art my only trust;
And still my soul would cleave to thee,
Though prostrate in the dust.

98 *Glorying in Christ.* C. M.

1 I'm not ashamed to own my Lord,
Or to defend his cause,
Maintain the honor of his word,
The glory of his cross.

2 Jesus, my God, I know his name;
His name is all my trust;
Nor will he put my soul to shame,
Nor let my hope be lost.

3 Firm as his throne his promise stands,
And he can well secure
What I've committed to his hands
Till the decisive hour.

4 Then will he own my worthless name
Before his Father's face,
And in the New Jerusalem
Appoint my soul a place.

99 *God our Keeper.* C. M.

1 To heaven I lift my waiting eyes;
There all my hopes are laid;
The Lord, who built the earth and skies,
Is my perpetual aid.

2 Their steadfast feet shall never fall
Whom he designs to keep;
His ear attends their humble call,
His eyes can never sleep.

3 Israel, rejoice, and rest secure;
Thy keeper is the Lord;
His wakeful eyes employ his power
For thine eternal guard.

4 He guards thy soul, he keeps thy breath,
Where thickest dangers come;
Go and return, secure from death,
Till God shall call thee home.

Arlington, Key G. I do believe, Key F. Naomi, Key D.

EVEN ME. 8s, 7s & 3.

WM. B. BRADBURY.

1. Lord, I hear of show'rs of blessing, Thou art scatt'ring full and free—
Show'rs, the thirsty land refreshing; Let some drop-pings fall on me—

E - ven me, e - ven me, Let some droppings fall on me.

100 *Longing for Divine Favor.* 8s, 7s & 3.

2 Pass me not, O God, our Father!
Sinful though my heart may be;
Thou might'st leave me, but the rather
Let thy mercy light on me—
Even me.

3 Pass me not, O gracious Savior!
Let me live and cling to thee;
For I am longing for thy favor;
Whilst thou art calling, oh! call me—
Even me.

4 Have I long in sin been sleeping—
Long been slighting, grieving thee?
Has the world my heart been keeping?
Oh! forgive, and rescue me—
Even me.

5 Pass me not, O mighty Spirit!
Thou canst make the blind to see;
Witnesser of Jesus' merit,
Speak some word of power to me—
Even me

CAST YOUR CARE ON JESUS.

R. LOWRY.

1. Cast your care on Je - sus; He will share it, He will bear it—

There is none like Je - sus.

101 2 Cast your sin on Jesus,
He will take it,
Now forsake it—
There is none like Jesus.

3 Cast your heart on Jesus;
Do not grieve him,
Just believe him,
There is none like Jesus.

1. Pass me not, O gen-tle Sav-ior, Hear my hum-ble cry;

While on oth-ers thou art smil-ing, Do not pass me by.

D. S. While on oth-ers thou art call-ing, Do not pass me by.

Chorus. Sav - ior, Sav - ior, Hear my hum - ble cry,

---

102   *Pass me not.*   8s & 5s.

1 Pass me not, O gentle Savior,
  Hear my humble cry;
While on others thou art smiling,
  Do not pass me by.

2 Let me at a throne of mercy
  Find a sweet relief,
Kneeling there in deep contrition,
  Help my unbelief.

3 Trusting only in thy merits,
  Would I seek thy face,
Heal my wounded, broken spirit,
  Save me by thy grace

4 Thou the spring of all my comfort,
  More than life to me.
Whom have I on earth beside thee,
  Whom in heaven but thee.

103   *Doubt not, but Believe*   8s & 5s.

1 Art thou weary? art thou languid?
  Art thou sore distressed?
Come to me, saith One, and, coming,
  On my bosom rest.

CHORUS. Doubting sinner,
  Doubt not, but believe,
He who saved ten thousand others,
  He will thee receive.

2 By what tokens may I know him,
  When I seek my Guide?
In his feet and hands are nail-prints,
  Spear wound in his side.

3 If I ask him to receive me,
  Will he say me nay?
Not till earth and not till heaven
  Shall have passed away.

Animated.   CHAS. ZEUNER.

1. Ye Christian heralds, go proclaim Sal-va-tion in Immanuel's name;

To distant climes the tidings bear, And plant the rose of Sharon there.

104   *Missionaries Encouraged.*   L. M.

1 Ye Christian heralds, go proclaim
Salvation in Immanuel's name;
To distant climes the tidings bear,
And plant the rose of Sharon there.

2 He'll shield you with a wall of fire,
With holy zeal your hearts inspire,
Bid raging winds their fury cease,
And calm the savage breast to peace.

3 And when our labors all are o'er,
Then shall we meet to part no more—
Meet, with the blood-bought throng to fall,
And crown the Savior Lord of all.

105   *The Great Commission.*   L. M.

1 "Go, preach my gospel," saith the Lord,
"Bid the whole earth my grace receive,
He shall be saved that trusts my word,
And he condemned who'll not believe.

2 "I'll make your great commission known,
And ye shall prove my gospel true,
By all the works that I have done,
By all the wonders ye shall do.

3 "Teach all the nations my commands;
I'm with you till the world shall end;
All power is trusted in my hands;
I can destroy and I defend."

106   *The Missionary Charged.*   L. M.

1 Go, messenger of peace and love,
To people plunged in shades of night,
Like angels sent from fields above,
Be thine to shed celestial light.

2 On barren rock and desert isle,
Go, bid the rose of Sharon bloom,
Till arid wastes around thee smile,
And bear to heaven a sweet perfume.

3 Go to the hungry—food impart;
To paths of peace the wanderer guide;
And lead the thirsty, panting heart
Where streams of living water glide.

4 Oh, faint not in the day of toil,
When harvest waits the reaper's hand;
Go, gather in the glorious spoil,
And joyous in his presence stand.

107   *Glory of the Latter Day.*   L. M.

1 Arise, arise; with joy survey
The glory of the latter day:
Already is the dawn begun
Which marks at hand a rising sun.

2 "Behold the way," ye heralds, cry;
Spare not, but lift your voices high;
Convey the sound from pole to pole,
"Glad tidings" to the captive soul.

Uxbridge, Key E♭.   Park Street, Key A.   Duke Street, Key F.

H. K. OLIVER.

1. Je-sus, and shall it ev - er be, A mortal man ashamed of thee?

Ashamed of thee, whom angels praise, Whose glo-ries shine thro' endless days!

108 *Not ashamed of Jesus.* L. M.

2 Ashamed of Jesus!—that dear Friend
On whom my hopes of heaven depend;
No! when I blush, be this my shame,
That I no more revere his Name.

3 Ashamed of Jesus!—yes, I may,
When I've no guilt to wash away;
No tear to wipe, no good to crave,
No fears to quell, no soul to save.

4 Till then—nor is thy boasting vain—
Till then, I boast a Savior slain;
And oh! may this my glory be—
That Christ is not ashamed of me.

109 *Holy Aspirations.* L. M.

1 My God, permit me not to be
A stranger to myself and thee;
Amidst a thousand thoughts I rove,
Forgetful of my highest love.

2 Why should my passions mix with earth,
And thus debase my heavenly birth?
Why should I cleave to things below,
And let my God, my Savior, go?

3 Call me away from flesh and sense;
One sovereign word can draw me thence;
I would obey the voice divine,
And all inferior joys resign.

110 *The Cross.* L. M.

1 Inscribed upon the cross we see,
In glowing letters, "God is love;"
He bears our sins upon the tree;
He brings us mercy from above.

2 The cross! it takes our guilt away;
It holds the fainting spirit up;
It cheers with hope the gloomy day,
And sweetens every bitter cup;—

3 The balm of life, the cure of woe,
The measure and the pledge of love,
The sinner's refuge here below,
The angels' theme in heaven above.

111 *Desiring the presence of Jesus.* L. M.

1 How sweet to leave the world awhile,
And seek the presence of our Lord!
Dear Savior, on thy people smile,
According to thy faithful word.

2 From busy scenes we now retreat,
That we may here converse with thee;
O Lord, behold us at thy feet!
Let this the gate of heaven be.

3 "Chief of ten thousands," now appear,
That we by faith may view thy face;
Oh, speak, that we thy voice may hear,
And let thy presence fill the place.

Hamburg, Key F. Zephyr, Key C. Ward, Key B♭.

1. Come, said Je-sus' sacred voice, Come, and make my paths your choice:

I will guide you to your home; Wea-ry wanderer, hither come!

---

112   *The Voice of Jesus.*   7s.

1 Come, said Jesus' sacred voice,
Come, and make my paths your choice;
I will guide you to your home;
Weary wanderer, hither come!

2 Thou who, homeless and forlorn,
Long hast borne the proud world's scorn,
Long hast roamed the barren waste,
Weary wanderer, hither haste,

3 Hither come! for here is found
Balm that flows for every wound;
Peace that ever shall endure,
Rest, eternal, sacred, sure.

113   *The Throne of Grace.*   7s.

1 They who seek the throne of grace
Find that throne in every place;
If we live a life of prayer,
God is present every-where.

2 In our sickness and our health,
In our want or in our wealth,
If we look to God in prayer,
God is present every-where.

3 Then, my soul, in every strait,
To thy Father come and wait;
He will answer every prayer:
God is present every-where.

114   *Encouragement to Pray.*   7s.

1 Come, my soul, thy suit prepare;
Jesus loves to answer prayer;
He himself invites thee near—
Bids thee ask him, waits to hear.

2 Lord, I come to thee for rest;
Take possession of my breast;
There, thy blood-bought right maintain
And without a rival reign.

3 While I am a pilgrim here,
Let thy love my spirit cheer;
As my guide, my guard, my friend,
Lead me to my journey's end.

4 Show me what I have to do;
Every hour my strength renew;
Let me live a life of faith—
Let me die thy people's death.

115   *Value of Religion.*   7s.

1 'Tis religion that can give
Sweetest pleasure while we live;
'T is religion must supply
Solid comfort when we die.

2 After death its joys shall be
Lasting as eternity;
Be the living God our friend,
Then our bliss shall never end.

Nuremburg, Key G.   Martyn, Key F.   Pleyel's Hymn, Key Ab.

WM. B. BRADBURY.

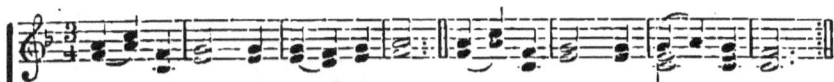

1. Weep-ing soul, no long-er mourn, Je-sus all thy griefs hath borne;
View him bleeding on the tree, Pour-ing out his life for thee;

There thy ev-ery sin he bore, Weep-ing soul, lament no more.

116 *Look to Christ.* 7s.

1 Weeping soul, no longer mourn,
Jesus all thy griefs hath borne;
View him bleeding on the tree,
Pouring out his life for thee;
There thy every sin he bore,
Weeping soul, lament no more.

2 All thy crimes on him were laid;
See, upon his blameless head
Wrath its utmost vengeance pours,
Due to my offense and yours;
Weary sinner, keep thine eyes
On the atoning sacrifice.

3 Cast thy guilty soul on him,
Find him mighty to redeem;
At his feet thy burden lay,
Look thy doubts and fears away;
Now by faith the Son embrace,
Plead his promise, trust his grace.

4 Lord, thy arm must be revealed,
Ere I can by faith be healed;
Since I scarce can look to thee,
Cast a gracious eye on me;
At thy feet myself I lay,
Shine, oh, shine my sins away.

117 *Heart of Stone.* 7s.

1 Heart of stone, relent, relent;
Break, by Jesus' cross subdued;
See his body, mangled, rent,
Covered with the gore of blood;
Sinful soul, what hast thou done?
Crucified th' eternal Son.

2 Yes, thy sins have done the deed,
Driven the nails that fixed him there.
Crowned with thorns his sacred head,
Plunged into his side the spear,
Made his soul a sacrifice,
While for sinful man he dies.

3 Wilt thou let him bleed in vain?
Still to death thy Lord pursue?
Open all his wounds again?
And the shameful cross renew?
"No! with all my sins I'll part;
Savior, take my broken heart."

118 *Doxology.* 7s.

Praise to God on high be given;
Praise him all in earth and heaven;
Praise him at the dawn of light;
Praise him at returning night,
Saints below, and saints above,
Praise, oh, praise the God of love.

T. E. PERKINS.

1. Wea - ry wanderer o'er the main, Seeking for thy home a - gain,

Thro' the gathering mists that rise, Veiling thy na - tal skies

Look be-yond, there's light for thee, Streaming o'er the tur-bid sea,

Soft - ly it smiles tho' distant far, The beautiful po - lar star.

119　　　*Seeking for Home Again.*

2 Stranger, on a rocky strand,
Longing for thy father-land,
Thro' the gathering clouds that rise,
Veiling thy natal skies,
Look beyond, there's hope for thee,
Dawning o'er a tranquil sea,
Softly it smiles though distant far,
The beautiful polar star.

3 Lonely watcher, pale with grief,
Thou shalt find a sweet relief,
Though thy tears unheeded fall,
Jesus will count them all;
Look beyond, there's joy for thee,
Breaking o'er a troubled sea,
Softly it smiles though distant far,
The beautiful polar star.

1. Children of the heavenly King, As we jour-ney let us sing;

Sing our Sav-ior's worthy praise, Glorious in his works and ways.

120 *The Pilgrim's Song.* 7s.

2 We are trav'ling home to God,
In the way our fathers trod;
They are happy now, and we
Soon their happiness shall see.

3 Fear not, brethren, joyful stand
On the borders of our land;
Jesus Christ, our Father's Son,
Bids us undismayed go on.

4 Lord! obediently we'll go,
Gladly leaving all below;
Only thou our leader be,
And we still will follow thee.

121 *Parting and Praise.* 7s.

1 Christians, brethren, ere we part,
Every voice and every heart
Join, and to our Father raise
One last hymn of grateful praise.

2 Tho' we here should meet no more,
Yet there is a brighter shore;
There, released from toil and pain,
There we all may meet again.

3 Now to thee, thou God of heaven,
Be eternal glory given:
Grateful for thy love divine,
May our hearts be ever thine.

122 *Faint not, Christian.* 7s.

1 Faint not, Christian! tho' the road
Leading to thy blest abode
Darksome be, and dangerous too,
Christ, thy Guide, will bring thee through.

2 Faint not, Christian! tho' the world
Has its hostile flag unfurled,
Hold the cross of Jesus fast;
Thou shalt overcome at last.

3 Faint not, Christian! tho' within
There's a heart so prone to sin,
Christ the Lord is over all;
He'll not suffer thee to fall.

4 Faint not, Christian! look on high;
See the harpers in the sky;
Patient wait, and thou wilt join
Chant with them of love divine.

123 *Zion's Children.* 7s.

1 "Give us room that we may dwell,"
Zion's children cry aloud:
See their numbers—how they swell!
How they gather like a cloud!

2 Oh, how bright the morning seems!
Brighter from so dark a night:
Zion is like one that dreams,
Filled with wonder and delight.

Pleyel's Hymn, Key G.   Hendon, Key G.   Fulton, Key Bb.

CORONATION. C. M.

O. HOLDEN.

With Spirit.

1. All hail the power of Je-sus' name! Let an-gels prostrate fall;

Bring forth the roy-al di - a - dem, And crown him Lord of all.

Bring forth the roy-al di - a - dem, And crown him Lord of all.

124 *Crown Him Lord of All.* C. M.

2 Ye chosen seed of Israel's race,
  Ye ransomed from the fall,
Hail him who saves you by his grace,
  And crown him Lord of all.

3 Sinners, whose love can ne'er forget
  The wormwood and the gall;
Go, spread your trophies at his feet,
  And crown him Lord of all.

4 Let every kindred, every tribe,
  On this terrestrial ball,
To him all majesty ascribe,
  And crown him Lord of all.

5 Oh, that with yonder sacred throng
  We at his feet may fall;
We'll join the everlasting song,
  And crown him Lord of all.

125 *This is the Jubilee.* C. M.

1 What heavenly music do I hear,
  Salvation sounding free;
Ye souls in bondage lend an ear,
  This is the Jubilee.

2 The gospel sounds a sweet release,
  To all in misery,
And bids them welcome home to peace;
  This is the Jubilee.

3 Good news, good news to Adam's race,
  Let Christians all agree
To sing redeeming Love and Grace;
  This is the Jubilee.

4 How sweetly do the 'idings roll,
  All round, from sea to sea,
From land to land, from pole to pole;
  This is the Jubilee.

126 *Voice of Praise.* C. M.

1 Lift to God the voice of praise,
  Whose breath our souls inspired;
Loud and more loud the anthems raise,
  With grateful ardor fired.

2 Lift up to God the voice of praise,
  Whose goodness, passing thought,
Loads every moment, as it flies,
  With benefits unsought.

Arlington, Key G.   Dedham, Key A.   Northfield, Key B♭.

GEO. KINGSLEY.

1. And have I, Christ, no love for thee, No passion for thy charms?

No wish my Sav-ior's face to see, And dwell within his arms?

127 *Profession of Love to Christ.* C. M.

1 And have I, Christ, no love for thee,
No passion for thy charms?
No wish my Savior's face to see,
And dwell within his arms?

2 Is there no spark of gratitude,
In this cold heart of mine,
To him whose generous bosom glowed
With friendship all divine?

3 Can I pronounce his charming name,
His acts of kindness tell,
And while I dwell upon the theme,
No sweet emotion feel?

4 Such base ingratitude as this,
What heart but must detest;
Sure Christ deserves the noblest place
In every human breast.

5 A very wretch, Lord, I should prove,
Had I no love for thee;
Rather than not my Savior love,
Oh, may I cease to be.

128 *Redemption by Christ.* C. M.

1 Behold what pity touched the heart
Of God's eternal Son;
Descending from the heavenly court,
He left his Father's throne.

2 His living power, and dying love,
Redeemed unhappy men,
And raised the ruins of our race
To life and God again.

3 To thee, O Lord, our noblest powers
We joyfully resign;
Blest Jesus, take us for thy own,
For we are doubly thine.

129 *Jesus, the Lamb.* C. M.

1 Jesus, with all thy saints above,
My tongue would bear her part;
Would sound aloud thy saving love,
And sing thy bleeding heart.

2 Blest be the Lamb, my dearest Lord,
Who bought me with his blood;
And quenched his Father's flaming sword
In his own vital flood.

3 The Lamb, that freed my captive soul
From Satan's heavy chains;
And sent the lion down to howl,
Where hell and horror reigns.

4 All glory to the dying Lamb
And never-ceasing praise;
While angels live to know his name,
Or saints to feel his grace.

Naomi, Key D.　Siloam, Key D.　Woodstock, Key G.

1. Blow ye the trumpet, blow, The gladly-solemn sound; Let all the nations know,

To earth's re - mot-est bound, The year of ju - bi - lee is come,

The year of ju - bi - lee is come, Return, ye ransomed sinners, home.

130 *The Jubilee Proclaimed.* H. M.

2 Exalt the Lamb of God,
  The sin-atoning Lamb;
Redemption by his blood,
  Through all the lands proclaim;
The year of jubilee is come:
Return, ye ransomed sinners, home.

3 The gospel trumpet hear,
  The news of pardoning grace,
Ye happy souls, draw near;
  Behold your Savior's face:
The year of jubilee is come;
Return, ye ransomed sinners, home.

4 Jesus, our great High Priest,
  Has full atonement made;
Ye weary spirits, rest;
  Ye mourning souls, be glad;
The year of jubilee is come;
Return, ye ransomed sinners, home.

131 *Praise for the Sabbath.* H. M.

1 Awake, ye saints, awake,
  And hail the sacred day;
In loftiest songs of praise
  Your joyful homage pay;
Come, bless the day that God hath blest,
The type of heaven's eternal rest.

2 On this auspicious morn
  The Lord of life arose,
And burst the bars of death,
  And vanquished all our foes;
And now he pleads our cause above,
And reaps the fruit of all his love.

3 All hail, triumphant Lord!
  Heaven with hosannas rings;
And earth, in humbler strains,
  Thy praise responsive sings:
Worthy the Lamb that once was slain,
Thro' endless years to live and reign.

Haddam, Key D.   Lischer, Key G.

1. Sol-diers of Christ, a-rise, And put your ar-mor on,

Strong in the strength which God supplies, Thro' his eternal Son;

Strong in the Lord of Hosts, And in his migh-ty power;

He who in his Re-deemer trusts, Is more than con-quer-or.

132 *The Song of Victory.*   S. M.

2 Stand then in his great might,
   With all his strength endued;
Take ye, to arm you for the fight,
   The panoply of God;
Then when your work is done,
   And all your conflicts past,
Ye shall o'ercome, thro' Christ alone,
   And stand entire at last.

3 Stand then against your foes,
   In close and firm array;
Legions of wily fiends oppose,
   Throughout the evil day:
Leave no unguarded place,
   No weakness of the soul;
Take every virtue, every grace,
   And fortify the whole.

4

133   *Arise, ye Saints.*   S. M.

1 Arise, ye saints, arise!
   The Lord our leader is;
The foe before his banner flies,
   For victory is his.
We hope to see the day
   When all our toils shall cease,
When we shall cast our arms away,
   And dwell in endless peace.

2 This hope supports us here,
   It makes our burdens light;
'T will serve our drooping hearts to cheer,
   Till faith shall end in sight;
Till of the prize possessed,
   We hear of war no more;
And oh, sweet thought! forever rest
   On yonder peaceful shore!

1. Come, with all thy sor - row, Wea - ry, wandering soul;
Come to him who loves thee, He will make - - - thee whole.

Chorus.

There is rest in Je - sus, Sweet, sweet rest,
There is rest in Je - sus, - - - - - - Sweet, sweet rest.

134   *Rest in Jesus.*   6s & 5s.

2 He thy strength in weakness,
    Will thy refuge be;
Cast on him thy burden,
    He will care for thee.

3 Come, in faith believing,
    To his will resigned;
Ask, and he will give thee;
    Seek, and thou shalt find.

4 See the door of Mercy,
    Wouldst thou enter there?
Knock, and he will open;
    Lo! the key is prayer.

135   *Looking unto Jesus.*   6s & 5s.

1 "Onward, upward, homeward!"
    Let my motto be;
Lord, I would press forward,
    Looking unto thee.

CHORUS. Looking unto Jesus,
    Still press on,
Till he bids thee welcome,
    Welcome home.

2 I can run with patience
    All the heavenward race,
If, in cloud or sunshine,
    I may see thy face.

ANGELS HOVERING ROUND.

Arr. by W. H. D.

1. There are angels hov'ring round, There are angels hov'ring round,

There are an - gels, an - gels hov'ring round.

136

2 To carry the tidings home
To the New Jerusalem,
    There are, etc.

3 Let him that heareth come,
Oh, come, while yet there's room:
    There are, etc.

By permission

WM. B. BRADBURY.

1. { Come, brethren, do'nt grow weary, But let us jour-ney on;
The pass-ing scenes all tell us That death will sure-ly come;

The mo-ments will not tar - ry— This life will soon be gone; }
These bod-ies soon will mold - er In the dark and drear-y tomb. }

Chorus.

There is sweet rest in heaven, There is sweet rest in heaven,

Repeat Chorus softly.

There is sweet rest, There is sweet rest, There is sweet rest in heaven.

137

2 Loved ones have gone before us,
  They beckon us away;
O'er aerial plains they're soaring,
  Blest in eternal day;
But we are in the army,
  And dare not leave our post;
We'll fight until we conquer
  The foe's most mighty host.

3 Our Captain's gone before us,
  He kindly calls us home
To yonder world of glory,
  And sweetly bids us come:

The world, the flesh, and Satan
  Will strive to hedge our way,
But we'll o'ercome these powers,
  And hourly watch and pray.

4 And Jesus will be with us,
  E'en to our journey's end,
In every sore affliction
  His present help to lend:
He never will grow weary,
  Though often we request;
He'll give us grace to conquer,
  And take us home to rest.

Arr. by Dr. L. Mason.

1. Ho! every one that thirsts, draw nigh; Thus God invites the fallen race;

Mercy and free salvation buy—Buy wine and milk and gospel grace.

138   *Salvation Free.*   L. M.

1 Ho! every one that thirsts, draw nigh;
Thus God invites the fallen race;
Mercy and free salvation buy—
Buy wine and milk and gospel grace.

2 Come to the living waters, come;
Sinners, obey your Maker's call;
Return, ye weary wand'rers home,
And find my grace is free for all.

3 Nothing ye in exchange shall give;
Leave all you have and are behind;
Frankly the gift of God receive,
Pardon and peace in Jesus find.

4 I bid you all my goodness prove;
My promises for all are free:
Come, taste the manna of my love,
And let your souls delight in me.

139   *Remembering Christ.*   L. M.

1 O thou, my soul, forget no more
The Friend who all thy sorrows bore,
Let every idol be forgot;
But, oh, my soul, forget him not.

2 Renounce thy works and ways, with grief,
And fly to this divine relief;
Nor him forget, who left his throne,
And for thy life gave up his own.

3 Eternal truth and mercy shine,
In him, and he himself is thine:
And canst thou, then, with sin beset,
Such charms, such matchless charms, forget?

4 Oh, no! till life itself depart,
His name shall cheer and warm my heart;
And lisping this, from earth I'll rise,
And join the chorus of the skies.

140   *Longing for Jesus.*   L. M.

1 Far from my thoughts, vain world, begone!
Let my religious hours alone;
Fain would mine eyes my Savior see,
I wait a visit, Lord, from thee.

2 My heart grows warm with holy fire,
And kindles with a pure desire;
Come, my dear Jesus, from above,
And feed my soul with heavenly love.

3 Blest Savior! what delicious fare,
How sweet thine entertainments are!
Never did angels taste above,
Redeeming grace and dying love.

4 Hail, great Immanuel, all divine,
In *thee* thy Father's glories shine:
Thou brightest, sweetest, fairest one,
That eyes have seen or angels known.

Welton, Key B♭.   Dodge, Key A♭.   Uxbridge, Key E♭.

1. Behold! a stranger's at the door! He gently knocks—has knocked before;

Has waited long—is waiting still; You treat no other friend so ill.

141 *The Waiting Savior.* L. M.

2 But will he prove a friend indeed?
He will!—the very friend you need!
The Man of Nazareth!—'t is he,
With garments dyed at Calvary.

3 Oh, lovely attitude!—he stands
With melting heart and laden hands!
Oh, matchless kindness!—and he shows
This matchless kindness to his foes.

4 Admit him, ere his anger burn—
His feet departed ne'er return;
Admit him, or the hour's at hand
When at his door denied you'll stand!

142 *One Thing Needful.* L. M.

1 Why will ye waste on trifling cares
That life which God's compassion spares,
While, in the various range of thought,
The one thing needful is forgot?

2 Shall God invite you from above?
Shall Jesus urge his dying love?
Shall troubled conscience give you pain?
And all these pleas unite in vain?

3 Not so your eyes will always view
Those objects which you now pursue;
Not so will heaven and hell appear,
When death's decisive hour is near.

4 Almighty God, thy grace impart;
Fix deep conviction on each heart;
Nor let us waste on trifling cares
That life which thy compassion spares.

143 *Look unto Jesus.* L. M.

1 See a poor sinner, dearest Lord,
Whose soul, encouraged by thy word,
At mercy's footstool would remain,
And then would look—and look again.

2 Ah! bring a wretched wanderer home,
Now to thy footstool let me come,
And tell thee all my grief and pain,
And wait and look—and look again!

3 Take courage, then, my trembling soul;
One look from Christ will make thee whole,
Trust thou in him, 't is not in vain,
But wait and look—and look again.

4 Look to the Lord, his word, his throne;
Look to his grace, and not your own;
There wait and look, and look again,
You shall not wait, nor look in vain.

5 Ere long that happy day will come,
When I shall reach my blissful home;
And when to glory I attain,
Oh, then I'll look—and look again!

Retreat, Key C.   Hebron, Key B♭.   Hamburg, Key F.

1. More like Je-sus would I be, Let my Sav-ior dwell with me;

Fill my soul with peace and love—Make me gentle as a dove;
D.S. Poor in spir-it would I be, Let my Sav-ior dwell in me.

More like Jesus, while I go, Pil-grim in this world be-low;

144   *More Like Jesus.*   7s.

2 If he hears the raven's cry,
If his ever-watchful eye
Marks the sparrows when they fall,
Surely he will hear my call.
He will teach me how to live,
All my sin-ful thoughts forgive;
Pure in heart I still would be—
Let my Savior dwell in me.

3 More like Jesus when I pray,
More like Jesus day by day,
May I rest me by his side,
Where the tranquil waters glide.
Born of him through grace renewed,
By his love my will subdued,
Rich in faith I still would be—
Let my Savior dwell in me.

145   *Cast thy Burden on the Lord.*   7s.

1 Cast thy burden on the Lord,
Lean thou only on his word;
Ever will he be thy stay,
Though the heavens shall melt away.
Even in the raging storm,
Thou shalt see his cheering form,
Hear his pledge of coming aid,
"It is I, be not afraid."

2 Cast thy burden on the Lord,
Linger near his mercy seat;
He will lead thee by the hand,
Gently to the better land.
He will gird thee by his power,
In thy weary, fainting hour;
Lean, then, loving on his word,
Cast thy burden on the Lord.

Martyn, Key F.   Aletta, Key F.

Rev. Dr. MALAN.

1. Lord, we come before thee now—At thy feet we humbly bow, Oh, do not our

suit disdain! Shall we seek thee, Lord, in vain? Shall we seek thee, Lord, in vain?

146   *Blessing Sought.*   7s.

1 Lord, we come before thee now—
At thy feet we humbly bow:
Oh, do not our suit disdain!
Shall we seek thee, Lord, in vain?

2 Lord, on thee our souls depend;
In compassion, now descend;
Fill our hearts with thy rich grace,
Tune our lips to sing thy praise.

3 In thy own appointed way,
Now we seek thee, here we stay;
Lord, we know not how to go,
Till a blessing thou bestow.

4 Send some message from thy word,
That may peace and joy afford;
Let thy Spirit now impart
Full salvation to each heart.

147   *Christ the Ground of Hope.*   7s.

1 Christ, of all my hopes the ground—
  Christ, the spring of all my joy!
Still in thee let me be found,
  Still for thee my powers employ

2 Fountain of o'erflowing grace!
  Freely from thy fullness give;
Till I close my earthly race,
  Be it "Christ for me to live!"

3 Firmly trusting in thy blood,
  Nothing shall my heart confound;
Safely I shall pass the flood,
  Safely reach Immanuel's ground.

4 Thus, oh, thus an entrance give
  To the land of cloudless sky;
Having known it "Christ to live,"
  Let me know it "gain to die."

148   *The Sweet Communion.*   7s.

1 Lord, 't is sweet to mingle where
Christians meet for social prayer;
Oh, 't is sweet for them to raise
Songs of holy joy and praise!

2 From thy gracious presence flows
Bliss that softens all our woes;
While thy Spirit's holy fire
Warms our hearts with pure desire.

3 Here we supplicate thy throne;
Here, thy pardoning grace is known;
Here, we learn thy righteous ways,
Taste thy love, and sing thy praise.

4 Thus with prayer, and hymns of joy,
We the happy hours employ;
Love, and long to love thee more,
Till from earth to heaven we soar.

Horton, Key Ab.   Pleyel's Hymn, Key Ab.

MERIBAH. C. P. M.

Dr. L. Mason.

1. When thou, my righteous Judge shalt come, To take thy ransomed people home, Shall

I among them stand? { Shall such a worthless worm as I, } Be found at thy right hand?
{ Who sometimes am afraid to die, }

149 *Pleading for Acceptance.* C. P. M.

1 When thou, my righteous Judge, shalt come,
To take thy ransomed people home,
  Shall I among them stand?
Shall such a worthless worm as I,
Who sometimes am afraid to die,
  Be found at thy right hand?

2 I love to meet thy people now,
Before thy feet with them to bow,
  Though vilest of them all:
But—can I bear the piercing thought?—
What if my name should be left out,
  When thou for them shalt call?

3 O Lord, prevent it by thy grace;
Be thou my only hiding-place,
  In this, th' accepted day;
Thy pardoning voice, oh, let me hear,
To still my unbelieving fear,
  Nor let me fall, I pray.

4 Let me among thy saints be found,
Whene'er the archangel's trump shall sound,
  To see thy smiling face;
Then loudest of the crowd I'll sing,
While heaven's resounding mansions ring
  With shouts of sovereign grace.

150 *Complete in Christ.* C. P. M.

1 Come join, ye saints, with heart and voice.
Alone in Jesus to rejoice,
  And worship at his feet;
Come, take his praises on your tongues,
And raise to him your thankful songs,
  "In him ye are complete!"

2 In him, who all our praise excels,
The fullness of the Godhead dwells,
  And all perfections meet:
The head of all celestial powers,
Divinely theirs, divinely ours;
  "In him ye are complete!"

3 Still onward urge your heavenly way,
Dependent on him day by day,
  His presence still entreat;
His precious name forever bless,
Your glory, strength, and righteousness,
  "In him ye are complete!"

4 Nor fear to pass the vale of death;
In his dear arms resign your breath,
  He'll make the passage sweet;
The gloom and fears of death shall flee,
And your departing souls shall see
  "In him ye are complete!"

Ariel, Key E♭.   Winslow, Key D.

1. Oh, could I speak the matchless worth, Oh, could I sound the glories forth

Which in my Savior shine! { I'd soar and touch the heavenly strings, / And vie with Gabriel, while he sings, }

In notes al-most di-vine, In notes al-most di-vine.

151 *The Riches of Christ.* C. P. M.

2 I'd sing the precious blood he spilt,
My ransom from the dreadful guilt
    Of sin and wrath divine:
I'd sing his glorious righteousness,
In which all perfect, heavenly dress
    My soul shall ever shine.

3 I'd sing the characters he bears,
And all the forms of love he wears,
    Exalted on his throne:
In loftiest songs of sweetest praise,
I would to everlasting days
    Make all his glories known.

4 Well, the delightful day will come
When my dear Lord will bring me home,
    And I shall see his face;
Then with my Savior, Brother, Friend,
A blest eternity I'll spend,
    Triumphant in his grace.

152 *Praise for Christ's Mission.* C. P. M.

1 Oh, let your mingling voices rise
In grateful rapture to the skies,
    And hail a Savior's birth;
Let songs of joy the day proclaim,
When Jesus all-triumphant came
    To bless the sons of earth.

2 He came to bid the weary rest;
To heal the sinner's wounded breast;
    To bind the broken heart;
To spread the light of truth around;
And to the world's remotest bound,
    The heavenly gift impart.

3 He came our trembling souls to save,
From sin, from sorrow, and the grave,
    And chase our fears away;
Victorious over death and time,
To lead us to a happier clime,
    Where reigns eternal day.

Meribah, Key E♭.   Cappadocia, Key E♭.

1. Je - sus, I turn to thee, Be thou my guide; Safe in thy loving arms, There let me hide. No other help I know, No other good be - low, Nothing but earthly woe, Nothing be-side.

153   *Jesus a Refuge.*   6s & 4s.

2 Lift up my fainting heart,
   Heavy with sin;
Guilty, and full of wrong,
   Lord, I have been.
Take me, and make me white;
Lord, set my feet aright
Show me the morning light,
   Savior of men.

3 If thou withhold thy love,
   Where shall I flee?
All will be dark and drear,
   All lost to me.
But if thy Spirit brings
Glory on angel's wings,
My soul hosanna sings,
   Ever to thee.

154   *Is Jesus Thine?*   6s & 4s.

1 Say, hast thou found a friend?
   Is Jesus thine?
His love shall never end—
   Is Jesus thine?
Earth's pleasures may decrease,
All human friendship cease,
Wouldst thou have lasting peace?
   Take Jesus thine.

2 He is a friend indeed—
   Is Jesus thine?
He'll be the friend you need—
   Is Jesus thine?
He's knocking—let him in!
There's no other friend like him,
He'll cleanse your soul from sin;
   Take Jesus thine.

Dr. L. MASON.

1. Nearer, my God, to thee, Near-er to thee; E'en though it

be a cross That rais-eth me, Still all my song shall be,

Nearer, my God, to thee, Nearer, my God, to thee, Nearer to thee.

155 *Nearer to God.* 6s & 4s.

2 Though like a wanderer,
Daylight all gone,
Darkness be over me,
My rest a stone,
Yet in my dreams I'd be
Nearer, my God, to thee,
Nearer to thee.

3 There let the way appear,
Steps up to heaven;
All that thou sendest me,
In mercy given,
Angels to beckon me
Nearer, my God, to thee,
Nearer to thee.

4 Then with my waking thoughts,
Bright with thy praise,
Out of my stony griefs,
Bethel I'll raise;
So by my woes to be
Nearer, my God, to thee
Nearer to thee.

5 Or, if on joyful wing,
Cleaving the sky,
Sun, moon, and stars forgot,
Upward I fly,
Still, all my song shall be,
Nearer, my God, to thee,
Nearer to thee.

156 *Fountain of Light Divine.* 6s & 4s.

1 Fountain of life divine!
Thee we adore;
We would be wholly thine
For evermore;
Freely forgive our sin,
Grant heavenly peace within,
Thy light restore.

2 Though to our faith unseen,
While darkness reigns,
On thee alone we lean
While life remains;
By thy free grace restored,
Our souls shall bless the Lord
In joyful strains!

From "SILVER SPRAY."　　　　　　　　　　　　Rev. R. LOWRY.

1. Weeping will not save me— Tho' my face were bathed in tears,

That could not al - lay my fears, Could not wash the sins of years,

Chorus.

Weeping will not save me. { Je - sus wept and died for me; }
{ Je - sus suf-fered on the tree; }

Je - sus waits to make me free, He a - lone can save me.

157

1 Weeping will not save me—
Tho' my face were bathed in tears,
That could not allay my fears,
Could not wash the sins of years
　Weeping will not save me.

2 Working will not save me—
Purest deeds that I can do,
Holiest thought and feelings too,
Can not form my soul anew,
　Working will not save me.

3 Waiting will not save me—
Helpless, guilty, lost, I lie;
In my ear is mercy's cry;
If I wait I can but die—
　Waiting will not save me.

4 Faith in Christ will save me—
Let me trust thy weeping Son;
Trust the work that he has done;
To his arms, Lord, help me run—
　Faith in Christ will save me.

By permission.   WM. B. BRADBURY.

1. There's a light in the win-dow for thee, brother, There's a
2. There's a crown and a robe and a palm, brother, When from

light in the window for thee; A dear one has moved to the
toil and from care you are free; The Savior has gone to pre-

mansions above, There's a light in the window for thee.
pare you a home, With a light in the window for thee.

Chorus.

A mansion in heaven we see, And a light in the window for thee;

A mansion in heaven we see, And a light in the window for thee.

158

3 Oh, watch, and be faithful, and pray, brother,
  All your journey o'er life's troubled sea,
  Though afflictions assail you, and storms beat severe,
  There's a light in the window for thee.

4 Then on, perseveringly on, brother,
  Till from conflict and suffering free,
  Bright angels now beckon you over the stream,
  There's a light in the window for thee.

STOCKWELL. 8s & 7s.

D. E. JONES.

1. He that go-eth forth with weeping, Bearing precious seed in love,

Nev - er tir-ing, nev-er sleep-ing, Findeth mer-cy from a-bove.

159 *Zeal Rewarded.* 8s & 7s.

2 Soft descend the dews of heaven,
  Bright the rays celestial shine ;
Precious fruits will thus be given,
  Through an influence all divine.

3 Sow thy seed, be never weary,
  Let no fears thy soul annoy;
Be the prospect ne'er so dreary,
  Thou shalt reap the fruits of joy.

Lo, the scene of verdure brightening!
  See the rising grain appear;
Look again! the fields are whitening,
  For the harvest time is near.

160 *Pressing Onward.* 8s & 7s.

1 Like the eagle, upward, onward,
  Let my soul in faith be borne :
Calmly gazing, skyward, sunward,
  Let my eye unshrinking turn!

2 Where the cross, God's love revealing,
  Sets the fettered spirit free,
Where it sheds its wondrous healing,
  There, my soul, thy rest shall be!

3 Oh, may I no longer dreaming,
  Idly waste my golden day,
But, each precious hour redeeming,
  Upward, onward press my way!

161 *Life's Work.* 8s & 7s.

1 Following every voice of mercy
  With a trusting, loving heart;
Let us in life's earnest labor
  Still be sure to do our part.

2 Now, to-day, and not to-morrow,
  Let us work with all our might,
Lest the wretched faint and perish
  In the coming stormy night.

162 *Self-denial.* 8s & 7s.

1 Pilgrims in this vale of sorrow,
  Pressing onward toward the prize,
Strength and comfort here we borrow,
  From the Hand that rules the skies.

2 'Mid these scenes of self-denial,
  We are called the race to run;
We must meet full many a trial
  Ere the victor's crown is won.

3 Love shall every conflict lighten,
  Hope shall urge us swifter on,
Faith shall every prospect brighten,
  Till the morn of heaven shall dawn.

4 On the Eternal arm reclining,
  We at length shall win the day;
All the powers of earth combining,
  Shall not snatch our crown away.

Howell, Key G.   Dorrnance, Key E♭.   Wilmot, Key B♭.

1. Cheer thee, brother—art thou weary, Toil-ing in a thirst-y land?
Tho' the soil be rough and sterile, Plant thy seed with bounteous hand.

Chorus.

Work and watch with every hour, Thou shalt labor not in vain;

Sown in weakness, raised in power, Thou shalt reap thy shock of grain.

163   *Cheer Thee, Brother.*   8s & 7s.

1 Cheer thee, brother—art thou weary,
  Toiling in a thirsty land?
Tho' the soil be rough and sterile,
  Plant thy seed with bounteous hand.
  Cho. Work and watch, etc.

2 Do thy warnings seem unheeded?
  Words like drops of rain may fall,
And thy warnings, if repeated,
  May an erring soul recall.

3 Brother, do not be discouraged;
  Shouldst thou gather for the Lord
One bright sheaf to crown the harvest,
  Would it not thy toil reward?

4 Dost thou pray in faith believing,
  When a cloud is o'er thee cast?
God perhaps may stay the answer,
  But 't will surely come at last.

164   *Christian Work.*   8s & 7s.

1 God, who gave us each a talent,
  To employ it gave command;
If we hide it in a napkin,
  He will claim it at our hand.

Chor. Let us then be up and doing,
  Keeping still this truth in view,
Tho' our path be e'er so humble,
  We have all a work to do.

2 With the heralds of the Gospel,
  If we can not bear a part,
We can drop a word of kindness
  That may reach some careless heart.

3 We may touch a chord of feeling
  Guilt and sin have lulled to sleep
To the blessed fold of Jesus
  We may bring some wand'ring sheep.

Arr. by Dr. L. Mason.

1. I love thy king-dom, Lord— The house of thine a-bode—

The Church our blest Redeemer saved With his own precious blood.

165   *Love for Zion.*   S. M.

2 I love thy Church, O God!
Her walls before thee stand,
Dear as the apple of thine eye,
And graven on thy hand.

3 For her my tears shall fall;
For her my prayers ascend;
To her my cares and toils be given,
Till toils and cares shall end.

4 Beyond my highest joy
I prize her heavenly ways;
Her sweet communion, solemn vows,
Her hymns of love and praise.

5 Sure as thy truth shall last,
To Zion shall be given
The brightest glories earth can yield,
And brighter bliss of heaven

166   *Pleasures of Social Worship.*   S. M.

1 How charming is the place
Where my Redeemer, God,
Unveils the beauties of his face,
And sheds his love abroad!

2 Here, on the mercy-seat,
With radiant glory crowned,
Our joyful eyes behold him sit,
And smile on all around.

167   *Encouragement to Faithfulness.*   S. M.

1 Our Captain leads us on;
He beckons from the skies;
He reaches out a starry crown,
And bids us take the prize.

2 "Be faithful unto death,
Partake my victory,
And thou shalt wear his glorious wreath,
And thou shalt reign with me."

3 'Tis thus the righteous Lord
To every soldier saith;
Eternal life is the reward
Of all-victorious faith.

4 Who conquer in his might
The victor's meed receive;
They claim a kingdom in his right,
Which God will freely give.

168   *Danger of Delay.*   S. M.

1 All yesterday is gone;
To-morrow's not our own;
O sinner, come, without delay,
To bow before the throne.

2 Oh, hear his voice to-day,
And harden not your heart;
To-morrow, with a frown, he may
Pronounce the word—"Depart."

Shirland, Key C.   Boylston, Key C.   Laban, Key D.

WOODMAN.

1. Je - sus, who knows full well The heart of ev - ery saint,

In-vites us all our griefs to tell, To pray and nev-er faint.

169   *Invitation.*   S. M.

2 He bows his gracious ear,
  We never plead in vain:
Yet we must wait till He appear,
  And pray, and pray again.

3 Though unbelief suggest,
  Why should we longer wait?
He bids us never give him rest,
  But be importunate.

4 Jesus the Lord will hear
  His chosen when they cry,
Yes, though He may awhile forbear,
  He'll help them from on high.

170   *The Spirit Inviting.*   S. M.

1 The Spirit in our hearts,
  Is whispering, "Sinner, come;"
The bride, the church of Christ, proclaims
  To all his children, "Come!"

2 Let him that heareth say
  To all about him, "Come;"
Let him that thirsts for righteousness,
  To Christ, the fountain, come.

3 Yes, whosoever will,
  Oh, let him freely come,
And freely drink the stream of life;
  'Tis Jesus bids him come.

171   *To-day the Accepted Time.*   S. M.

1 Now is the accepted time,
  Now is the day of grace;
Now, sinners, come without delay,
  And seek the Savior's face.

2 Now is the accepted time,
  The Savior calls to-day;
To-morrow it may be too late—
  Then why should you delay?

3 Now is the accepted time,
  The gospel bids you come;
And every promise in his word
  Declares there yet is room.

172   *A Broken Heart.*   S. M.

1 Unto thine altar, Lord,
  A broken heart I bring;
And wilt thou graciously accept
  Of such a worthless thing?

2 To Christ, the bleeding Lamb,
  My faith directs its eyes;
Thou mayst reject that worthless thing,
  But not his sacrifice.

3 When he gave up his life,
  The law was satisfied;
And now, to its severer claims,
  I answer, "Jesus died."

Dennis, Key F.   Tioga, Key B♭.   Iowa, Key A♭.

5

By permission.   T. E. PERKINS.

1. We've listed in a holy war, Battling for the Lord! E-ternal life, e-ternal joy, Battling for the Lord! We'll work till Jesus comes, We'll work till Jesus comes, We'll work till Jesus comes, And then we'll rest at home.

173

2 Under our Captain, Jesus Christ,
  Battling for the Lord!
We've listed for this mortal life,
  Battling for the Lord!

3 We'll fight against the powers of sin,
  Battling for the Lord!
In favor of our heavenly King,
  Battling for the Lord!

4 And when our warfare here is o'er,
  Battling for the Lord!
This strife we'll leave, and war no more,
  Battling for the Lord!

5 Our friends and kindred there we'll meet,
  On the heavenly shore!
And ground our arms at Jesus' feet,
  On the heavenly shore.

CODA, *for the last verse.*

Home, home, sweet, sweet home! Prepare me, dear Savior, for glory, my home.

From "Song Garden," by per.

Dr. L. MASON.

1. Work, for the night is com - ing, Work thro' the morning hours;

Work while the dew is spark - ling, Work 'mid springing flow'rs:

D. S. Work, for the night is com - ing, When man's work is done.

cres.

Work when the day grows brighter, Work in the glowing sun;

174 *Work.*

2 Work, for the night is coming,
 Work in the sunny noon;
Fill brightest hours with labor,
 Rest comes sure and soon.
Give every flying minute
 Something to keep in store :
Work, for the night is coming,
 When man works no more.

3 Work, for the night is coming,
 Under the sunset skies;
While their bright tints are glowing,
 Work, for the daylight flies.
Work till the last beam fadeth,
 Fadeth to shine no more ;
Work while the night is dark'ning,
 When man's work is o'er.

175 *Clinging to Jesus.*

1 Follow the paths of Jesus,
 Walk where his footsteps lead,
Keep in his beaming presence,
 Every counsel heed;
Watch, while the hours are flying,
 Ready some good to do;
Quick, while his voice is calling,
 Yield obedience true!

2 Cling to the hand of Jesus,
 All through the day and night,
Dark though the way, and dreary,
 He will guide you right.
Live for the good of others,
 Helpless, oppressed, and wrong,
Lift them from depths of sorrow,
 In his strength be strong !

WANDERER INVITED. 8s & 7s.

W. H. DOANE.

1. If thy days are full of sor-row, Full of gloom thy life appears;

If the dawning of to-morrow Brings no resting from thy tears:
D. S. He will not re-fuse to hear thee, Wand'rer, do not tar - ry.

Chorus.

All thy grief to Je - sus car - ry, Je - sus still is near thee;

176   *Wanderer Invited.*   8s & 7s.

2 From thy sinful ways returning,
   Trembling and o'ercome with fear,
Jesus still thy faith discerning,
   Bids thee venture ever near.
All thy sins to Jesus carry,
Jesus still is near thee;
He will not refuse to hear thee,
Wand'rer, do not tarry.

3 When the gloomy waves affright thee,
   When the tempest driveth wild,
Let this cheerful thought delight thee,
   He is near his wandering child.
All thy fears to Jesus carry,
Jesus still is near thee;
He will not refuse to hear thee,
Wand'rer, do not tarry.

177   *Giving the Heart.*   8s & 7s.

1 Take my heart, O Father take it!
   Make and keep it all thine own;
Let thy Spirit melt and break it—
   This proud heart of sin and stone.
Father, make it pure and lowly,
   Fond of peace and far from strife;
Turning from the paths unholy
   Of this vain and sinful life.

2 Ever let thy grace surround it;
   Strengthen it with power divine,
Till thy cords of love have bound it:
   Make it to be wholly thine.
May the blood of Jesus heal it,
   And its sins be all forgiven;
Holy Spirit, take and seal it,
   Guide it in the path to heaven.

By permission.

G. F. ROOT.

1. My days are gliding swiftly by, And I, a pilgrim stranger, Would

S.

End.

not de-tain them as they fly—Those hours of toil and dan-ger.
D. S. just be-fore the shining shore We may al-most dis-cov-er.

Chorus.

D. S. S.

For now we stand on Jordan's strand, Our friends are passing over; And

178 *The Shining Shore.* 8s & 7s.

1 My days are gliding swiftly by,
  And I, a pilgrim stranger,
Would not detain them as they fly,
  Those hours of toil and danger.

2 We'll gird our loins, my brethren dear,
  Our heavenly home discerning;
Our absent Lord has left us word,
  Let every lamp be burning.

3 Should coming days be cold and dark,
  We need not cease our singing;
That perfect rest naught can molest
  Where golden harps are ringing.

4 Let sorrow's rudest tempest blow,
  Each chord on earth to sever,
Our King says come, and there's our home,
  Forever! oh, forever!

179 *The New Year.* 8s & 7s.

1 We meet you here, our brethren dear,
  With ne'er a shade of sorrow;
The old year gone, the new comes on
  With many a glad to-morrow.

CHORUS. But when we stand on Canaan's land,
  And glory shines before us;
To God we'll bring, and ever sing
  Our hallelujah chorus.

2 We meet you here, our friends with cheer,
  A joyous welcome singing;
With prayer and praise our hearts we raise
  With all the joy bells ringing.

3 We meet you here, old dying year,
  Thy solemn voice comes o'er us;
But from thy dust we humbly trust
  A better year before us.

1. Great God of nations, now to thee Our hymn of grat-i-tude we raise;

With humble heart and bending knee, We offer thee our song of praise.

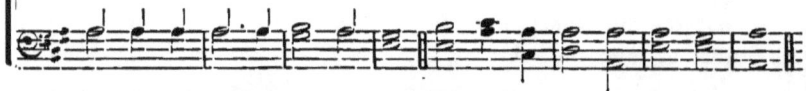

180   *God Acknowledged.*   L. M.

2 Thy name we bless, almighty God,
   For all the kindness thou hast shown
To this fair land the pilgrims trod—
   This land we fondly call our own.

3 Here Freedom spreads her banner wide,
   And casts her soft and hallowed ray;
Here thou our fathers' steps did guide
   In safety through their dangerous way.

4 We praise thee that the gospel's light
   Through all our land its radiance sheds,
Dispels the shades of error's night,
   And heavenly blessings round us spread.

5 Great God, preserve us in thy fear;
   In dangers still our Guardian be;
Oh, spread thy truth's bright precepts here;
   Let all the people worship thee.

181   *The Lord is King.*   L. M.

1 The Lord is King! Lift up thy voice,
O earth, and all ye heavens rejoice!
From world to world the joy shall ring,
"The Lord omnipotent is King!"

2 The Lord is King! who then shall dare
Resist his will, distrust his care?
Holy and true are all his ways;
Let every creature speak his praise.

182   *Arm of the Lord, Awake.*   L. M.

1 Arm of the Lord, awake! awake!
Put on thy strength, the nation shake!
And let the world adoring see
Triumphs of mercy wrought by thee.

2 Let Zion's time of favor come;
Oh! bring the tribes of Israel home;
And let our wondering eyes behold
Gentiles and Jews in Jesus' fold.

3 Almighty God! thy grace proclaim,
In every clime of every name;
Let adverse powers before thee fall,
And crown the Savior Lord of all.

183   *The Goodness of God Celebrated.*   L. M.

1 Bless, oh my soul, the living God;
Call home thy thoughts, that rove abroad;
Let all the powers within me join
In work and worship so divine.

2 Bless, oh my soul, the God of grace;
His favors claim thy highest praise;
Let not the wonders he hath wrought
Be lost in silence, and forgot.

3 Let every land his power confess;
Let all the earth adore his grace;
My heart and tongue with rapture join
In work and worship so divine.

Anvern, Key F.   Park Street, Key A.   Missionary Chant, Key A♭.

GERMAN.

1. Awake, our souls; away, our fears; Let ev'ry trembling thought be gone;

Awake, and run the heavenly race, And put a cheerful courage on.

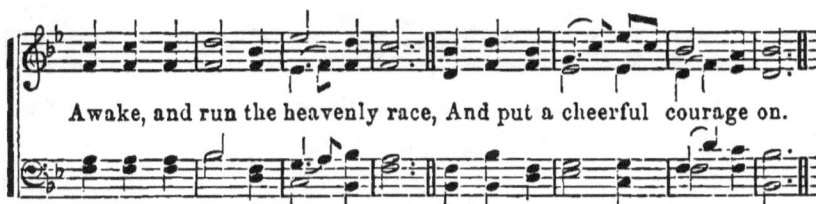

184 *The Heavenly Race.* L. M.

2 True, 't is a strait and thorny road,
  And mortal spirits tire and faint;
But they forget the mighty God,
  Who feeds the strength of every saint.

3 From God, the overflowing spring,
  Our souls shall drink a full supply;
While those who trust their native strength
  Shall melt away, and droop, and die.

4 Swift as an eagle cuts the air,
  We'll mount aloft to thine abode;
On wings of love our souls shall fly,
  Nor tire amid the heavenly road.

185 *The Christian Warfare.* L. M.

1 Stand up, my soul, shake off thy fears,
  And gird the gospel armor on;
March to the gates of endless joy,
  Where Jesus, thy great Captain's, gone.

2 Now let my soul march boldly on,
  Press forward to the heavenly gate;
There peace and joy eternal reign,
  And glittering robes for conquerors wait.

3 There shall I wear a starry crown,
  And triumph in almighty grace,
While all the armies of the skies
  Join in my glorious Leader's praise.

186 *Praise in the Sanctuary.* L. M.

1 Oh, come, loud anthems let us sing,
Loud thanks to our almighty King;
For we our voices high should raise,
When our salvation's Rock we praise.

2 Into his presence let us haste,
To thank him for his favors past;
To him address, in joyful songs,
The praise that to his name belongs.

3 For God the Lord, enthroned in state
Is with unrivaled glory great—
A King superior far to all—
Who by his title God we call.

4 Oh, let us to his courts repair,
And bow with adoration there;
Down on our knees devoutly, all,
Before the Lord, our Maker, fall,

187 *Universal Praise.* L. M.

1 From all who dwell below the skies
Let the Creator's praise arise;
Let the Redeemer's name be sung,
Through every land, by every tongue.

2 Eternal are thy mercies, Lord
Eternal truth attends thy word;
Thy praise shall sound from shore to shore,
Till suns shall rise and set no more.

Rockingham, Key G.   Migdol, Key A.   Hamburg, Key F.

1. Awake, my soul, in joyful lays, And sing thy great Redeemer's praise;

He justly claims a song from me; His loving kindness, oh, how free!

His loving kindness, loving kindness, His loving kindness, oh, how free!

188 *Christ's Loving Kindness.* L. M.

1 Awake, my soul, in joyful lays,
And sing thy great Redeemer's praise;
He justly claims a song from me;
His loving kindness, oh, how free!

2 He saw me ruined by the fall,
Yet loved me, notwithstanding all;
He saved me from my lost estate;
His loving kindness, oh, how great!

3 Though numerous hosts of mighty foes,
Though earth and hell my way oppose,
He safely leads my soul along:
His loving kindness, oh, how strong!

4 I often feel my sinful heart
Prone from my Savior to depart,
But though I oft have him forgot,
His loving kindness changes not.

5 Soon shall I pass the gloomy vale;
Soon all my mortal powers must fail;
Oh, may my last, expiring breath,
His loving kindness sing in death!

6 Then let me mount and soar away,
To the bright world of endless day;
And sing with rapture and surprise,
His loving kindness in the skies.

189 *Praise for Renewing Grace.* L. M.

1 To God, my Savior and my King,
Fain would my soul her tribute bring;
Join me, ye saints, in songs of praise,
For ye have known and felt his grace.

2 With speed he flew to my relief,
Bound up my wounds and soothed my grief,
Poured joy divine into my heart,
And bade each anxious fear depart.

3 These proofs of love, my dearest Lord,
Deep in my breast I will record:
The life which I from thee receive,
To thee, behold, I freely give.

4 My heart and tongue shall tune thy praise,
Through the remainder of my days;
And when I join the powers above,
My soul shall better sing thy love.

From "Wesleyan Sacred Harp."

1. Oh, happy day that fixed my choice On thee, my Savior and my God!
Well may this glowing heart rejoice, And tell its raptures all abroad.

Hap-py day, hap-py day, When Je-sus washed my sins away;
D. S. Hap-py day, hap-py day, When Je-sus washed my sins away.

He taught me how to watch and pray, And live rejoicing every day.

190 *Happy Day.* L. M.

1 Oh happy day that fixed my choice
  On thee, my Savior and my God!
Well may this glowing heart rejoice,
  And tell its raptures all abroad.

2 Oh happy bond, that seals my vows
  To him that merits all my love;
Let cheerful anthems fill his house,
  While to that sacred shrine I move.

3 'Tis done, the great transaction's done;
  I am my Lord's, and he is mine;
He drew me, and I follow'd on,
  Charm'd to confess the voice divine.

4 Now rest, my long-divided heart;
  Fixed on this blissful center, rest;
Nor ever from thy Lord depart:
  With him of every good possess'd.

5 High heaven, that heard the solemn vow,
  That vow renew'd shall daily hear,
Till in life's latest hour I bow,
  And bless in death a bond so dear.

191 *Vows Renewed.* L. M.

1 Now I resolve, with all my heart,
  With all my power to serve the Lord;
Nor from his precepts e'er depart,
  Whose service is a rich reward.

2 Oh, be this service all my joy;
  Around let my example shine;
Till others love the best employ,
  And join in labors so divine.

3 Oh, may I never faint nor tire,
  Nor wandering leave his sacred ways;
Great God, accept my soul's desire,
  And give me strength to live thy praise.

192 *Praise to Jesus.* L. M.

1 With all my powers of heart and tongue,
  I'll praise my Maker in my song;
Angels shall hear the notes I raise,
  Approve the song, and join the praise.

2 I'll sing thy truth and mercy, Lord,
  I'll sing the wonders of thy word;
Not all the works and names below,
  So much thy power and glory show.

| | 1st. | 2d. |

1. Mid scenes of con - fu - sion and crea - ture complaints,
How sweet to my soul is com - mun - ion with ... saints,

To find at the ban-quet of mercy there's room, And feel in the
D. S. Pre-pare me, dear

End.   D. S. S.

pres-ence of Je - sus at home. Home, home, sweet, sweet home.
Sav - ior, for glo - ry, my home.

193   *The Christian Home.*   11s.

2 Sweet bonds that unite all the chil-
    dren of peace!
And thrice precious Jesus, whose love
    can not cease!
Though oft from thy presence in sad-
    ness I roam,
I long to behold thee in glory at
    home

3 Whate'er thou deniest, oh give me
    thy grace,
The Spirit's sure witness, and smiles
    of thy face;
Endue me with patience to wait at
    thy throne,
And find, even now, a sweet foretaste
    of home.

4 I long, dearest Lord, in thy beauties
    to shine;
No more as an exile in sorrow to
    pine;

And in thy dear image arise from
    the tomb,
With glorified millions to praise thee
    at home.

194   *Home, Sweet Home.*   11s.

1 'Mid pleasures and palaces though
    we may roam,
Be it ever so humble, there's no place
    like home;
A charm from the skies seems to hal-
    low us there;
Which, seek thro' the world, is ne'er
    met with elsewhere.

2 An exile from home, splendor dazzles
    in vain,
Oh! give me my lowly thatched cot-
    tage again;
The birds singing gayly, that came at
    my call,
Give me them, with the peace of mind
    dearer than all.

195 *Thy Will be Done.*

1 Thy will be | done! ‖ In devious way
The hurrying stream of ‖ life may | run; ‖
Yet still our grateful hearts shall say, |
    Thy will be | done.

2 Thy will be | done! ‖ if o'er us shine
A gladdening and a | prosperous sun, ‖
This prayer will make it more divine; |
    Thy will be | done.

3 Thy will be | done! ‖ though shrouded o'er
Our path with | gloom, one comfort, | one
Is ours—to breathe, while we adore, |
    Thy will be | done.

TUNE—"HOME," page 74.

196 *My Home in Heaven.* 11s.

1 My home is in heaven, my rest is
    not here,
Then why should I murmur when
    trials are near?
Be hushed, my dark spirit, the worst
    that can come,
But shortens my journey, and hastens
    thee home.
CHO. Home, home, sweet, sweet home,
Prepare me, dear Savior, for glory,
    my home.

2 It is not for thee to be seeking thy
    bliss,
And building thy hopes in a region
    like this;
I look for a city which hands have
    not piled,
I pant for a country by sin un-
    defiled.

3 The thorn and the thistle around
    me may grow,
I would not recline upon roses be-
    low;
I ask not my portion, I seek not my
    rest,
Till I find them forever on Jesus'
    breast.

197 *Sweet Prayer.* 11s.

1 When torn is the bosom by sorrow
    and care,
Be it ever so simple, there's nothing
    like prayer;
It comforts, it softens, subdues, yet
    sustains,
Bids hope rise exulting, and passion
    restrains.
CHO. Prayer, prayer, oh sweet prayer,
Be it ever so simple, there's nothing
    like prayer.

2 When far from the friends that are
    dearest we part,
What fond recollections still cling to
    the heart;
Past scenes and enjoyments live pain-
    fully there;
And restless we languish, till peace
    comes in prayer.

3 When earthly delusions would lead
    us astray,
In folly's gay mazes, or sin's treach-
    erous way,
How strong the enchantment, how
    fatal the snare!
But looking to Jesus, we conquer by
    prayer.

1. How firm a foun-dation, ye saints of the Lord! Is laid for your

D. S. To you, who for

End. D. S. S.

faith in his excellent word! What more can he say, than to you he hath said,

ref - uge to Jesus have fled?

198 *Foundation of Faith.* 11s.

2 "Fear not, I am with thee, oh, be
  not dismayed,
For I am thy God, I will still give thee
  aid :
I 'll strengthen thee, help thee, and
  cause thee to stand,
Upheld by my gracious, omnipotent
  hand.

3 "The soul that on Jesus hath leaned
  for repose,
I will not—I will not desert to his
  foes ;
That soul—though all hell should endeavor to shake,
I 'll never—no never—no never forsake."

199 *Danger of Delay.* 11s.

1 Delay not, delay not; O, sinner,
  draw near ;
The waters of life are now flowing for
  thee ;
No price is demanded ; the Savior is
  here ;
Redemption is purchased, salvation
  is free.

2 Delay not, delay not; why longer
  abuse,
The love and compassion of Jesus,
  thy God ?
A fountain is opened ; how canst thou
  refuse,
To wash and be cleansed in his pardoning blood?

200 *Acquaint Thyself Quickly.* 11s.

1 Acquaint thyself quickly, O sinner,
  with God,
And joy, like the sunshine, shall beam
  on thy road,
And peace, like the dew-drops, shall
  fall on thy head ;
And sleep like an angel shall visit
  thy bed.

2 Acquaint thyself quickly, O sinner,
  with God,
And he shall be with thee when fears
  are abroad ;
Thy safeguard in dangers that threaten
  thy path ;
Thy joy in the valley and shadow of
  death.

1. Oh, turn ye, oh, turn ye, for why will ye die, { When God, in great / Now Je-sus in-

mercy, is coming so nigh? } / vites you, the Spirit says, Come ! } And angels are waiting to welcome you home.

---

201   *Entreaty.*   11s.

2 And now Christ is ready your souls
    to receive,
Oh! how can you question, if you
    will believe?
If sin is your burden, why will you
    not come?
'T is you he bids welcome; he bids
    you come home.

202   *Faint, but Pursuing.*   11s.

1 Tho' faint, yet pursuing, we go on
    our way;
The Lord is our Leader, his word is
    our stay;
Though suffering, and sorrow, and
    trial be near,
The Lord is our refuge, and whom
    can we fear?

2 He raiseth the fallen, he cheereth
    the faint;
The weak, and oppressed—he will
    hear their complaint;
The way may be weary, and thorny
    the road,
But how can we falter? our help is
    in God!

3 Though clouds may surround us,
    our God is our light;
Though storms rage around us, our
    God is our might;
So faint, yet pursuing, still onward
    we come;
The Lord is our leader, and heaven is
    our home!

203   *Expostulation.*   11s.

1 Too long, guilty wanderer, too long
    hast thou been,
In the broad road of ruin, in bondage
    to sin;
Thee the world has allured, and en-
    slaved, and deceived,
While my counsel thou'st spurned,
    and my Spirit hast grieved.

2 Though countless thy sins, and
    though crimson thy guilt,
Yet for crimes such as thine was my
    blood freely spilt:
Come, sinner, and prove me; come,
    mourner, and see
The wounds that I bore when I suf-
    fered for thee.

CROSS AND CROWN. C. M.

WESTERN MELODY.

1. Must Je-sus bear the cross a - lone, And all the world go free?

No, there's a cross for every one, And there's a cross for me.

204 *The Cross and the Crown.* C. M.

2 How happy are the saints above,
　Who once went sorrowing here;
But now they taste unmingled love,
　And joy without a tear.

3 The consecrated cross. I'll bear,
　Till death shall set me free,
And then go home my crown to wear,
　For there's a crown for me!

205 *Christ on the Cross.* C. M.

1 Behold the Savior of mankind,
　Upon the shameful tree;
How great the love that him inclined
　To bleed and die for me!

2 "My God," he cries; all nature shakes,
　And earth's strong pillars bend;
The gate of death in sunder breaks;
　The solid marbles rend.

3 "'T is finished; now, the ransom's paid;
　Receive my soul," he cries;
Behold, he bows his sacred head;
　He bows his head, and dies!

4 But soon he'll break death's tyrant chain,
　And in full glory shine;
O, Lamb of God, was ever pain,
　Was ever love, like thine?

206 *The Savior at the Door.* C. M.

1 Amazing sight! The Savior stands
　And knocks at every door!
Ten thousand blessings in his hands,
　To satisfy the poor.

2 "Behold," he saith, "I bleed and die,
　To bring you to my rest;
Hear, sinners, while I'm passing by,
　And be forever blest.

3 "Say, will you hear my gracious voice
　And have your sins forgiven?
Or will you make that wretched choice,
　And bar yourselves from heaven?"

207 *Christ's Compassion.* C. M.

1 How condescending and how kind
　Was God's eternal Son!
Our misery reached his heavenly mind,
　And pity brought him down.

2 This was compassion, like a God,
　That, when the Savior knew
The price of pardon was his blood,
　His pity ne'er withdrew.

3 Here let our hearts begin to melt,
　While we his death record,
And, with our joy for pardoned guilt,
　Mourn that we pierced the Lord.

Heber, Key C. 　Downs, Key Eb. 　Naomi, Key D.

Dr. HASTINGS.

1. Oh, for a closer walk with God, A calm and heavenly frame; A

light to shine upon the road That leads me to the Lamb! That leads me to the Lamb!

208 *Lamentation.* C. M.

2 Where is the blessedness I knew
When first I saw the Lord?
Where is the soul-refreshing view
Of Jesus and his word?

3 Return, O holy Dove, return,
Sweet messenger of rest:
I hate the sins that made thee mourn,
And drove thee from my breast.

4 The dearest idol I have known,
Whate'er that idol be,
Help me to tear it from thy throne,
And worship only thee.

5 So shall my walk be close with God,
Calm and serene my frame;
So purer light shall mark the road
That leads me to the Lamb.

209 *Prayer for Repentance.* C. M.

1 Oh, for that tenderness of heart
Which bows before the Lord,
That owns how just and good thou art,
And trembles at thy word!

2 Oh, for those humble, contrite tears,
Which from repentance flow,
That sense of guilt, which, trembling fears
The long-suspended blow!

3 O Lord, to me in pity give
For sin the deep distress,
The pledge thou wilt at last receive,
And bid me die in peace.

4 Oh, fill my soul with faith and love,
And strength to do thy will;
Raise my desires and hopes above;
Thyself to me reveal.

210 *Majesty of Jesus.* C. M.

1 Majestic sweetness sits enthroned
Upon the Savior's brow;
His head with radiant glories crown'd,
His lips with grace o'erflow.

2 No mortal can with him compare,
Among the sons of men;
Fairer is he than all the fair
Who fill the heavenly train.

3 To him I owe my life and breath,
And all the joys I have;
He makes me triumph over death,
And saves me from the grave.

4 Since from his bounty I receive
Such proofs of love divine,
Had I a thousand hearts to give,
Lord, they should all be thine.

Brainard, Key C. Balerma. Key Bb. Marlow, Key F.

SOUND THE BATTLE CRY.

From "Bright Jewels," by per.

WM. F. SHERWIN.

Vigorously, in march time.

1. Sound the bat - tle cry, See! the foe is nigh; Raise the standard high

For the Lord; Gird your ar - mor on, Stand firm every one,

Chorus. ff

Rest your cause up - on his ho - ly word. Rouse then, soldiers!

ral - ly round the banner! Ready, steady, pass the word a - long;

Onward, forward, shout aloud Hosanna! Christ is Captain of the mighty throng.

211

2 Strong to meet the foe,
Marching on we go,
While our cause we know
    Must prevail;
Shield and banner bright
Gleaming in the light,
Battling for the right,
    We ne'er can fail.

3 Oh! thou God of all,
Hear us when we call,
Help us one and all
    By thy grace;
When the battle's done,
And the victory won,
May we wear the crown
    Before thy face.

Arr. by W. M. Doane.

1. Sol-diers of the cross, a-rise! Lo! your leader, from the skies,

Waves be-fore you glo-ry's prize, The prize of vic-to-ry.

Seize your ar-mor—gird it on; Now the bat-tle will be won;

See! the strife will soon be done; Then struggle manful-ly.

212 *Soldiers, Arise.* 7s & 5s.

2 Jesus conquered when he fell,
Met and vanquished earth and hell;
Now he leads you on, to swell
The triumphs of his cross.
Though all earth and hell appear,
Who will doubt, or who can fear?
God, our strength and shield is near,
We can not lose our cause.

3 Onward, then, ye hosts of God!
Jesus points the victor's rod—
Follow where your Leader trod;
You soon shall see his face.
Soon, your enemies all slain,
Crowns of glory you shall gain;
Rise to join that glorious train,
Who shout their Savior's praise.
6

213 *Sinners, Rouse Ye.* 7s & 5s.

1 Rouse ye, at the Savior's call,
Sinners, rouse ye, one and all;
Wake! or soon your souls will fall,
Fall in deep despair.
Woe to him who turns away,
Jesus kindly calls to-day;
Come, O sinner, while you may,
Raise your soul in prayer.

2 By the bleeding Savior's love,
By the joys of heaven above,
Let these words your spirits move;
Quick to Jesus fly!
Come and save your souls from death,
Haste! escape Jehovah's wrath!
Fly! for life's a fleeting breath!
Soon, oh soon, you'll die.

From "Songs of Gladness," by per. J. E. GOULD.

1. We dwell this side of Jordan's stream, Yet oft there comes a shining beam
2. The other side! ah, there's the place Where saints in joy past times retrace,
D. S. other side, the other side, When shall we meet our loved ones there?

Across from yonder shore, Across from yonder shore; While visions of a
And think of trials gone, And think of trials gone; The veil withdrawn, they

holy throng, And sound of harp and seraph song, Seem gently wafted o'er,
clearly see That all on earth had need to be, To bring them safely home,

Seem gently wafted o'er. O Zi-on! cit-y fair! O Zi-on! cit-y fair! The
To bring them safely home. O Zion, etc.

214

3 The other side! oh charming side!
Upon its banks, arrayed in white
　For me a loved one waits;
Over the stream he calls to me,
Fear not—I am thy guide to be
　Up to the pearly gates.

4 The other side! the other side!
Who would not brave the swelling tide
　Of earthly toil and care,
To wake one day, when life is past,
Over the stream, at home at last,
　With all the bless'd ones there?

From the "Palm," by per. C. M. Wyman.

Earnestly.

1. The sands of time are sink-ing, The dawn of heaven breaks;

The summer morn I've sighed for, The fair, sweet morn awakes.

Dark, dark hath been the midnight, But day-spring is at hand,

And glo-ry, glo-ry dwelleth, In Im-manuel's land.

215 *Immanuel's Land.* 7s & 6s.

2 I've wrestled on toward heaven,
  'Gainst storm, and wind, and tide,
Now, like a weary trav'ler
  That leaneth on his guide.
Amid the shades of evening,
  While sinks life's ling'ring sand,
I hail the glory dawning,
  From Immanuel's land.

3 Deep waters crossed life's pathway,
  The hedge of thorns was sharp.
Now, these lie all behind me—
  Oh! for a well-tuned harp.
Oh, to join hallelujah
  With yon triumphant band!
Who sing where glory dwelleth,
  In Immanuel's land.

216 *Need of Jesus.* 7s & 6s.

1 I need thee, precious Jesus,
  For I am full of sin,
My soul is dark and guilty,
  My heart is dead within.
I need the cleansing fountain,
  Where I can always flee—
The blood of Christ most precious,
  The sinners only plea.

2 I need thee, precious Jesus,
  For I am very poor,
A stranger and a pilgrim,
  I have no earthly store.
I need the love of Jesus
  To cheer me on my way,
To guide my doubting footsteps,
  To be my strength and stay.

WINDHAM. L. M.

READ.

1. Broad is the road that leads to death, And thousands walk together there,

But wisdom shows a narrow path, With here and there a travel-er.

---

217   *The Broad Road.*   L. M.

2 "Deny thyself and take thy cross,"
  Is the Redeemer's great command;
Nature must count her gold but dross,
  If she would gain this heavenly land.

3 The fearful soul that tires and faints,
  And walks the ways of God no more,
Is but esteemed almost a saint,
  And makes his own destruction sure.

4 Lord, let not all my hopes be vain;
  Create my heart entirely new—
Which hypocrites could ne'er attain,
  Which false apostates never knew.

218   *The Spirit Striving.*   L. M.

1 O, sinner, hear the heavenly voice!
  Oh, hear the Spirit's gracious call!
It bids thee make the better choice,
  And haste to seek in Christ thine all.

2 God's Spirit will not always strive
  With hardened, self-destroying man;
Ye, who persist his love to grieve,
  May never hear his voice again.

3 Sinner, perhaps this very day
  Thy last accepted time may be;
Oh, shouldst thou grieve him now away,
  Then hope may never beam on thee!

219   *Expostulation.*   L. M.

1 O, sinner, why so thoughtless grown?
  Why in such dreadful haste to die?
Daring to leap to worlds unknown!
  Heedless against thy God to fly?

2 Wilt thou despise eternal fate,
  Urged on by sin's delusive dreams?
Madly attempt th' infernal gate,
  And force thy passage to the flames?

3 Stay, sinner, on the gospel plains,
  And hear the Lord of life unfold
The glories of his dying pains—
  Forever telling, yet untold.

220   *The Great Day.*   L. M.

1 The day of wrath, that dreadful day,
  When heaven and earth shall pass away!
What power shall be the sinner's stay?
  How shall he meet that dreadful day?

2 When, shriveling like a parched scroll,
  The flaming heavens together roll,
And louder yet, and yet more dread,
  Resounds the trump that wakes the dead?

3 Oh, on that day, that wrathful day,
  When man to judgment wakes from clay,
Be thou, O Christ, the sinner's stay,
  Though heaven and earth shall pass away.

Ward, Key B♭.   Zephyr, Key C.   Ashwell, Key D.

1. As when the weary traveler gains The height of some commanding hill,

His heart revives, if o'er the plains He sees his home, tho' distant still.

221 *Heaven seen by Faith.* L. M.

2 So, when the Christian pilgrim views,
By faith, his mansion in the skies,
The sight his fainting strength renews,
And wings his speed to reach the prize.

3 The hope of heaven his spirit cheers;
No more he grieves for sorrows past;
Nor any future conflict fears,
So he may safe arrive at last.

4 O Lord, on thee our hopes we stay
To lead us on to thine abode;
Assured, thy love will far o'erpay
The hardest labors of the road.

222 *The Duty of Loving God.* L. M.

1 Yes, I would love thee, blessed God!
Paternal goodness makes thy name;
Thy praises, through thy high abode,
Thy heavenly hosts with joy proclaim.

2 Freely thou gav'st thy dearest Son,
For man to suffer, bleed, and die,
And bid'st me, as a wretch undone,
For all I want on him rely.

3 In him thy reconciled face,
With joy unspeakable I see,
And feel thy powerful, wondrous grace
Draw and unite my soul to thee.

223 *Following the Example of Christ.* L. M.

1 My dear Redeemer and my Lord,
I read my duty in thy word;
But in thy life the law appears,
Drawn out in living characters.

2 Such was thy truth, and such thy zeal,
Such deference to thy Father's will,
Such love and meekness so divine,
I would transcribe and make them mine.

3 Cold mountains, and the midnight air,
Witnessed the fervor of thy prayer,
The desert thy temptations knew,
Thy conflict, and thy victory too.

4 Be thou my pattern; make me bear
More of thy gracious image here;
Then God, the Judge, shall own my name
Among the followers of the Lamb.

224 *Ground of Acceptance.* L. M.

1 How shall the sons of men appear,
Great God, before thine awful bar?
How may the guilty hope to find
Acceptance with th' Eternal mind?

2 Thy blood, dear Jesus, thine alone,
Hath sovereign virtue to atone;
Here will we rest our only plea,
When we approach, great God, to thee.

Federal Street, Key F.   Hebron, Key B♭.   Uxbridge, Key E♭.

HAMBURG. L. M.

GREGORIAN.

1. Kingdoms and thrones to God belong; Crown him, ye nations, in your song;

His wondrous names and powers rehearse; His honors shall enrich your verse.

225   *Majesty of Jehovah.*   L. M.

2 He guides our feet, He guards our ways;
His morning smiles bless all the day;
He spreads the evening veil, and keeps
The silent hours, while Israel sleeps.

3 Israel, a name divinely blest,
May rise secure, securely rest;
Thy holy Guardian's wakeful eyes
Admit no slumber, nor surprise.

226   *Invitation to Sinners.*   L. M.

1 Just as thou art, without one trace
Of love, or joy, or inward grace,
Or meetness for that heavenly place,
Oh, guilty sinner, come, oh come!

2 Thy sins I bore on Calvary's tree;
The stripes thy due, were laid on me,
That peace and pardon might be free,
Oh, wretched sinner, come, oh come!

3 Come, leave thy burden at the cross;
Count all thy gains but empty dross;
My grace repays all earthly loss—
Oh, needy sinner, come, oh come!

4 "The Spirit and thy Bride say, come,"
Rejoicing saints re-echo, Come!
Who faints, who thirsts, who will, may Come;
Thy Savior bids the come, oh come!

227   *The Spirit entreated.*   L. M.

1 Stay, thou insulted Spirit, stay,
Though I have done thee such despite,
Nor cast the sinner quite away,
Nor take thine everlasting flight.

2 Though I have steel'd my stubborn heart,
And shaken off my guilty fears;
And vex'd, and urged thee to depart,
For many long rebellious years.

3 Yet, oh! the chief of sinners spare,
In honor of my great High Priest;
Nor in thy righteous anger, swear
To exclude me from thy people's rest.

228   *Just as I am.*   L. M.

1 Just as I am, without one plea,
But that thy blood was shed for me,
And that thou bid'st me come to thee,
O Lamb of God, I come, I come!

2 Just as I am, though tossed about
With many a conflict, many a doubt,
Fighting within, and fears without,
O, Lamb of God, I come, I come!

3 Just as I am—thy love unknown,
Has broken every barrier down;
Now to be thine, yea, thine alone,
O, Lamb of God, I come, I come!

Federal Street, Key F.   Ward, Key Bb.   Hebron, Key Bb.

BOST.

1. No more, my God, I boast no more Of all the duties I have done

I quit the hopes I held before, To trust the mer - its of thy Son.

229   *Salvation by Grace.*   **L. M.**

1 No more, my God, I boast no more
  Of all the duties I have done;
I quit the hopes I held before,
  To trust the merits of thy Son.

2 Now, for the love I bear his name,
  What was my gain I count my loss;
My former pride I call my shame,
  And nail my glory to his cross.

3 Yes, and I must and will esteem
  All things but loss for Jesus' sake;
Oh, may my soul be found in him,
  And of his righteousness partake.

4 The best obedience of my hands
  Dares not appear before thy throne;
But faith can answer thy demands,
  By pleading what my Lord has done.

230   *Church Union.*   **L. M.**

1 How blest the sacred tie that binds,
In sweet communion kindred minds;
How swift the heavenly course they run,
Whose hearts, whose faith, whose hopes are one!

2 To each the soul of each how dear!
What tender love, what holy fear,
How does the generous flame within,
Refine from earth, and cleanse from sin!

3 Their streaming eyes together flow,
For human guilt and human wo!
Their ardent prayers together rise,
Like mingling flames in sacrifice.

4 Nor shall the glowing flame expire,
When dimly burns frail nature's fire,
Then shall they meet in realms above,
A heaven of joy—a heaven of love.

231   *Seaman's Prayer.*   **L. M.**

1 Beset with snares on every hand,
In life's uncertain path I stand;
Savior divine! diffuse thy light,
To guide my doubtful footsteps right.

2 Engage this roving, treacherous heart,
Great God, to choose the better part;
To scorn the trifles of a day,
For joys that none can take away.

3 Then let the wildest storms arise;
Let tempests mingle earth and skies;
No fatal shipwreck shall I fear,
But all my treasures with me bear.

4 If thou, my Jesus, still art nigh,
Cheerful I live, and cheerful die;
Secure, when mortal comforts flee,
To find ten thousand worlds in thee.

Rockingham, Key G.   Dodge, Key A♭.   Hamburg, Key F.

NEAR THE CROSS.

W. H. DOANE.

1. Je - sus, keep me near the cross, There a precious fountain,

Free to all, a healing stream, Flows from Calvary's mountain,

Chorus.

In the cross, in the cross Be my glo - ry ev - er,

Till my raptured soul shall find Rest be-yond the riv - er.

232   *Near the Cross.*

2 Near the cross, a trembling soul,
  Love and mercy found me;
There the bright and morning star
  Shed its beams around me.

3 Near the cross! O Lamb of God,
  Bring its scenes before me;
Help me walk from day to day,
  With its shadow o'er me.

4 Near the cross I 'll watch and wait,
  Hoping, trusting ever,
Till I reach the golden strand,
  Just beyond the river.

233   *Near to Jesus.*

1 Jesus, am I near to thee?
  Then, no more delaying,
I must in the vineyard be,
  Watching, working, praying.

2 Every heart that 's near to thee,
  Is for sinners seeking;
All their bitter need doth see,
  Is for them entreating.

3 Near to Jesus all the time,
  He will leave me never;
I am his and he is mine,
  I am safe forever

By permission.   W. B. BRADBURY.

1. He leadeth me! Oh! blessed thought, Oh! words with heavenly comfort fraught,

Whate'er I do, where'er I be, Still 't is God's hand that leadeth me!

Refrain.

He lead-eth me! he lead-eth me! By his own hand he leadeth me;

His faith-ful fol-low-er I would be, For by his hand he leadeth me.

234 *He Leadeth Me.* L. M.

1 He leadeth me! Oh! blessed thought,
Oh! words with heav'nly comfort fraught,
Whate'er I do, where'er I be,
Still 't is God's hand that leadeth me!

2 Sometimes 'mid scenes of deepest gloom,
Sometimes where Eden's bowers bloom,
By waters still, o'er troubled sea—
Still 'tis his hand that leadeth me!

3 Lord, I would clasp thy hand in mine,
Nor ever murmur nor repine—
Content, whatever lot I see,
Since 't is my God that leadeth me.

4 And when my task on earth is done,
When, by thy grace, the victory's won,
E'en death's cold wave I will not flee,
Since God through Jordan leadeth me.

235 *Our Guide.* L. M.

1 Come, gracious Spirit, heavenly dove,
With light and comfort from above;
Be thou our Guardian, thou our Guide;
O'er every thought and step beside.
To us the light and truth display,
And make us know and choose thy way;
Plant holy fear in every heart,
That we from God may ne'er depart.

2 Lead us to holiness—the road
Which we must take to dwell with God,
Lead us to Christ—the living way;
Nor let us from his pastures stray.
Lead us to God, our final rest,
To be with him forever blest;
Lead us to heaven, its bliss to share.
Fullness of joy forever there.

THE WATER OF LIFE.

WM. B. BRADBURY.

236

f Chorus.

1. Je - sus the wa - ter of life will give, Freely, freely, freely,
Come to that fountain, oh drink and live, Freely, freely, freely,

Jesus, the water of life will give, Freely to those who love him.
Come to that fountain, oh drink and live, Flowing for those that - - - love him.

Duet. *Chorus.* *Duet.*

The Spirit and the Bride say come, Freely, freely, freely, And

Chorus.

he that is thirsty let him come, And drink of the water of life.

The fountain of life is flowing, Flowing, freely flowing; The fountain of life is flowing, Is flowing for you and for me.

2 Jesus has promised a home in heaven,
Freely, freely, freely,
Treasures unfading will there be given,
Freely, freely, freely,
Treasures unfading will there be given,
Freely to those that love him.

3 Jesus has promised a robe of white,
Freely, freely, freely,
Kingdoms of glory, and crowns of light,
Freely, freely, freely,
Pleasures that never shall pass away,
Freely to those that love him.

4 Jesus has promised eternal day,
Freely, freely, freely,
Pleasure that never shall pass away,
Freely, freely, freely,
Pleasures that never shall pass away,
Freely to those that love him.

5 Jesus has promised a calm repose,
Freely, freely, freely,
Come to the water of life that flows,
Freely, freely, freely,
Come to the water of life that flows,
Freely to all that love him.

REST OF THE WEARY.

By permission.   G. F. Root.

Andantino.   1st.   2d.   End.

1. Rest of the wea-ry, Joy of the sad;
Hope of the drear-y, ... Light of the glad;

Home of the stranger, Strength to the end;
Ref-uge from dan-ger, . . . Sav-ior and Friend.

237   *Savior and Friend.*

2 When my feet stumble,
To thee I'll cry,
Crown of the Humble,
Cross of the High.

When my steps wander,
Over me bend,
Truer and fonder,
Savior and Friend.
Cho. Rest of the weary, etc.

238

Smooth and flowing.

1. Je - sus, most ho - ly one, We lift our souls to thee;
Plead for us, Sav - ior, Lone wand'rers on the sea.

Watch us while shad-ows lie
Far o'er the water spread; Hear the heart's lonely sigh,

Thine too hath bled. Thou that hast looked on death, Aid us when

death is near, Whis-per of heaven to faith—Re-deem-er, Re-

deemer, hear; Hear, oh, hear and save us, Tossed on the deep!

From "Sabbath Carols," by per.

T. E. Perkins.

1. Weary not, my brother, Cheerful be thy song; Is thy burden heavy,

And the journey long? Does the weight oppress thee? Cast it on the Lord;

Chorus.

Run thy race with patience, Trusting in his word. Looking unto Je-sus,

He has died for thee; Oh, glory be to Je-sus, We'll shout salvation free.

2 Seek and thou shalt find him,
　Still in faith believe;
Call and he will hear thee,
　Ask him, and receive;
In the darkest moment—
　In the deepest night,
He will give thee comfort,
　He will give thee light.

3 Trials may befall thee,
　Thorns beset thy way,
Never mind them, brother,
　Only watch and pray;

Through the vale of sorrow
　Once the Savior trod;
Run thy race with patience,
　Pressing on to God.

4 Labor on, my brother,
　Thou shalt reap at last,
Fruits of joy eternal,
　When thy work is past;
Crowds of shining angels
　View thee from the skies;
Run thy race with patience,
　Yonder is the prize.

THE OLD, OLD STORY.

240.

W. H. DOANE.

1. Tell me the old, old sto - ry Of un-seen things a - bove,
2. Tell me the sto - ry slow-ly, That I may take it in—

Of Je - sus and his glo - ry, Of Je - sus and his love.
That wonder - ful re -demption, God's rem - e - dy for sin.

Tell me the story simply, As to a little child, For I am weak and
Tell me the story of - ten, For I for-get so soon, The "early dew" of

Chorus.

weary, And helpless and defiled. Tell me the old, old story, Tell me the old, old
morning Has pass'd away at noon. Tell me, &c.

sto - ry, Tell me the old, old sto - ry Of Je - sus and his love.

3 Tell me the story softly,
  With earnest tones, and grave;
R∶member ! I'm the sinner
  Whom Jesus came to save.
Tell me that story always,
  If you would really be,
In any time of trouble,
  A comforter to me.

4 Tell me the same old story,
  When you have cause to fear
That this world's empty glory
  Is costing me too dear,
Yes, and when that world's glory
  Is drawing on my soul.
Tell me the old, old story:
  "Christ Jesus makes thee whole."

Answer to the Old, Old Story.

241 Not too fast. S:

1. I love to tell the story Of unseen things above, Of Je-sus and his
D. S. It satisfies my

End. D. S. S:

glory, Of Jesus and his love. I love to tell the story, Because I know it's true;
longings As nothing else would do.

Chorus.

Oh! yes, I love to tell the sto - ry, 'T will be my happy theme in

glo - ry To tell the old, old sto - ry Of Je - sus and his love.

2 I love to tell the story;
  More wonderful it seems,
Than all the golden fancies
  Of all our golden dreams.
I love to tell the story,
  It did so much for me!
And that is just the reason
  I tell it now to thee.

3 I love to tell the story;
  'T is pleasant to repeat,
What seems, each time I tell it,
  More wonderfully sweet.

I love to tell the story,
  For some have never heard
The message of salvation,
  From God's own holy word.

4 I love to tell the story;
  For those who know it best,
Seem hungering and thirsting
  To hear it like the rest.
And when, in scenes of glory,
  I sing the New, New Song,
'T will be the Old, Old Story
  That I have loved so long.

CHINA. C. M.

SWAN.

1. Why do we mourn de-part-ing friends, Or shake at death's alarms?

'T is but the voice that Je-sus sends To call them to his arms.

242 *Mourn not the Departed.* C. M.

2 Why should we tremble to convey
  Their bodies to the tomb?
There the dear flesh of Jesus lay,
  And left a long perfume.

3 The graves of all his saints he blest,
  And softened every bed;
Where should the dying members rest,
  But with the dying Head?

4 Thence he arose, ascending high,
  And showed our feet the way;
Up to the Lord our flesh shall fly,
  At the great rising day.

243 *The Death of the Righteous.* C. M.

1 Hear what the voice from heaven proclaims
  For all the pious dead;
"Sweet is the savor of the names,
  And soft their sleeping bed.

2 "They die in Jesus, and are blest;
  How kind their slumbers are!
From suffering and from sin released,
  They 're freed from every snare.

3 " Far from this world of toil and strife
  They 're present with the Lord;
The labors of their mortal life
  End in a large reward."

244 *Death of a Christian.* C. M.

1 Dear as thou wert, and justly dear,
  We will not weep for thee;
One thought shall check the starting tear,
  It is, that thou art free.

2 Triumphant in thy closing eye,
  The hope of glory shone;
Joy breathed in thy expiring sigh,
  To think the race was run.

4 The passing spirit gently fled,
  Sustained by grace divine;
Oh, may such grace on us be shed,
  And make our end like thine.

245 *Death of the Young.* C. M.

1 When blooming youth is snatched away
  By death's resistless hand,
Our hearts the mournful tribute pay,
  Which pity must demand.

2 While pity prompts the rising sigh,
  Oh, may this truth, impressed
With awful power, "I too must die,"
  Sink deep in every breast.

3 Oh, let us fly—to Jesus fly,
  Whose powerful arm can save;
Then shall our hopes ascend on high,
  And triumph o'er the grave.

Mear, Key G.   Woodland. Key G.

TEMPLI CARMINA.

1. O thou who driest the mourner's tear, How dark this world would be,

If, pierced by sins and sorrows here, We could not fly to thee!

246 *Consolation to Bereaved.* C. M.

2 The friends, who in our sunshine live,
  When winter comes, are flown;
And he who has but tears to give,
  Must weep those tears alone.

3 But thou wilt heal that broken heart,
  Which, like the plants that throw
Their fragrance from the wounded part,
  Breathes sweetness out of woe.

4 Oh, who could bear life's stormy doom,
  Did not thy wing of love
Come brightly wafting through the gloom
  Our peace-branch from above?

5 Then sorrow, touched by thee, grows bright,
  With more than rapture's ray;
As darkness shows us worlds of light
  We never saw by day.

247 *A Warning from the Grave.* C. M.

1 Beneath our feet and o'er our head
  Is equal warning given;
Beneath us lie the countless dead,
  And far above is heaven.

2 Death rides on every passing breeze,
  And lurks in every flower;
Each season has its own disease,
  Its peril every hour.

3 Turn, sinner, turn: thy danger know:
  Where'er thy foot can tread,
The earth rings hollow from below,
  And warns thee of her dead.

4 Turn, Christian, turn: thy soul apply
  To truths which hourly tell
That they who underneath thee lie
  Shall live in heaven—or hell.

248 *Life short, and Man frail.* C. M.

1 Teach me the measure of my days,
  Thou Maker of my frame;
I would survey life's narrow space,
  And learn how frail I am.

2 A span is all that we can boast;
  How short the fleeting time!
Man is but vanity and dust,
  In all his flower and prime.

3 What can I wish, or wait for, then,
  From creatures—earth and dust?
They make our expectations vain,
  And disappoint our trust.

4 Now I forbid my carnal hope,
  My fond desire recall;
I give my mortal interest up,
  And make my God my all.

Balerma, Key B♭.   Naomi, Key D.   Mear, Key G.

7

NAOMI. C. M.

Dr. LOWELL MASON.

1. Fa-ther, whate'er of earth-ly bliss Thy sovereign will denies,

Ac - cept-ed   at thy throne of grace, Let this pe - ti - tion rise:

249   *Prayer for needed Grace.*   C. M.

1 Father, whate'er of earthly bliss,
  Thy sovereign will denies,
Accepted at thy throne of grace,
  Let this petition rise: -

2 Give me a calm, a thankful heart,
  From every murmur free;
The blessings of thy grace impart,
  And make me live to thee.

3 Let the sweet hope that thou art mine
  My life and death attend;
Thy presence through my journey shine,
  And crown my journey's end.

250   *Prayer for Faith.*   C. M.

1 Father, I stretch my hands to thee;
  No other help I know;
If thou withdraw thyself from me,
  Ah, whither shall I go?

2 What did thine only Son endure
  Before I drew my breath!
What pain, what labor to secure
  My soul from endless death!

3 Author of faith, to thee I lift
  My weary, longing eyes;
Oh, may I now receive that gift;
  My soul, without it, dies.

251   *Desires for Holiness.*   C. M.

1 Oh, could I find, from day to day,
  A nearness to my God;
Then would my hours glide sweet away,
  While leaning on his word.

2 Lord, I desire with thee to live
  Anew from day to day,
In joys the world can never give,
  Nor ever take away.

3 Blest Jesus, come, and rule my heart,
  And make me wholly thine,
That I may never more depart,
  Nor grieve thy love divine.

252   *Seeking God.*   C. M.

1 Oh that I knew the secret place
  Where I might find my God!
I'd spread my wants before his face,
  And pour my woes abroad.

2 I'd tell him how my sins arise;
  What sorrows I sustain;
How grace decays, and comfort dies,
  And leaves my heart in pain.

3 He knows what arguments I'd take
  To wrestle with my God;
I'd plead for his own mercy's sake,
  And for my Savior's blood.

Miller, Key C.   Downs, Key E♭.   Arlington, Key G.

By permission.

I. B. WOODBURY.

1. By cool Si-lo-am's shad-y rill How sweet the lil-y grows!

How sweet the breath, beneath the hill, Of Sharon's dew-y rose!

253 *The Christian Child.* C. M.

2 Lo! such the child whose early feet
The paths of peace have trod—
Whose secret heart, with influence sweet,
Is upward drawn to God.

3 By cool Siloam's shady rill
The lily must decay;
The rose that blooms beneath the hill
Must shortly fade away.

4 Oh thou who givest life and breath,
We ask thy grace alone,
In childhood, manhood, age, and death,
To keep us still thine own.

254 *Prayer for Seamen.* C. M.

1 We come, O Lord, before thy throne,
And, with united pleas,
We meet and pray for those who roam
Far off upon the seas.

2 Oh, may the Holy Spirit bow
The sailor's heart to thee,
Till tears of deep repentance flow
Like rain-drops in the sea.

3 Then may a Savior's dying love
Pour peace into his breast,
And waft him to the port above
Of everlasting rest.

255 *Prayer for Special Favor.* C. M.

1 Within thy house, O Lord, our God,
In glory now appear;
Make this a place of thine abode,
And shed thy blessings here.

2 When we thy mercy seat surround,
Thy Spirit, Lord, impart;
And let thy gospel's joyful sound
With power reach every heart.

3 Here let the voice of sacred joy
And humble prayer arise,
Till higher strains our tongues employ
In realms beyond the skies.

256 *Purity of Heart.* C. M.

1 Oh, for a heart to praise my God!
A heart from sin set free!
A heart that's sprinkled with the blood
So freely shed for me!

2 Oh, for a heart submissive, meek,
My great Redeemer's throne,
Where only Christ is heard to speak,
Where Jesus reigns alone!

3 Thy temper, gracious Lord, impart;
Come quickly from above;
Oh, write thy name upon my heart;
Thy name, O God, is love.

Brainard, Key C. Heber, Key C. Ortonville, Key B♭.

KEEP ON PRAYING.

By permission.   T. E. PERKINS.

1. Long my spir-it pined in sor-row, Watching, waiting, all in vain;

S.   *End.*

Waiting for a golden morrow, Free from worldly care and pain.
D. S. Cheer up, brother, "keep on praying," Keep on praying to the end.

D. S. S.

When I heard a sweet voice saying, In the accents of a friend,

Chorus.

When our wayward thoughts are straying, When God's mercy seems delaying,

Then in faith we 'll keep on praying, Keep on praying, Keep on praying to the end.

257

2 Ye who sigh for holy pleasures,
  Ye who mourn your load of sin,
Keep on praying, heavenly treasures
  In the end you 're sure to win;
Wrestle with the Lord of glory,
  Lay your troubles at his feet,
Plead with faith in Calvary's story,
  Till your joys are all complete.

3 How the angel band rejoices
  When a kneeling mortal prays;
Hear them cry, in heavenly voices,
  Keep on praying all your days;
Pray until you reach fair Canaan,
  Reach the pearly gates of day,
Then your bliss shall end in glory,
  And shall never pass away.

By permission.   W. B. BRADBURY.

1. Sweet hour of prayer! sweet hour of prayer! That calls me from a world of care,

D.C. And oft escaped the tempter's snare, By thy return, sweet hour of prayer;

And bids me at my Father's throne, Make all my wants and wishes known.

And oft escaped the tempter's snare, By thy return, sweet hour of prayer.

In sea-sons of distress and grief, My soul has often found re - lief,

---

258   *Sweet hour of Prayer.*   L. M.

2 Sweet hour of prayer! sweet hour of prayer!
Thy wings shall my petition bear,
To him whose truth and faithfulness
Engage the waiting soul to bless.
And since he bids me seek his face,
Believe his word, and trust his grace,
I'll cast on him my every care,
And wait for thee, sweet hour of prayer.

3 Sweet hour of prayer! sweet hour of prayer!
May I thy consolation share,
Till from Mount Pisgah's lofty height
I view my home, and take my flight:
This robe of flesh I'll drop, and rise
To seize the everlasting prize;
And shout, while passing thro' the air,
Farewell, farewell, sweet hour of prayer!

259   *Day of Grace.*   L. M.

1 Oh, happy day! blest day of grace!
When Jesus shows his smiling face,
And bids the weary wanderer come
And find in him sweet rest—a home.
The cross uplifted draws us near,
The Spirit whispers words of cheer,
And waits, repenting souls to bless,
In this glad day, this day of grace!

2 Then hasten all who feel your need,
From sin's dread burden to be freed:
To Calvary's victim look and live,
He only can salvation give.
Long have you pleasure sought in vain,
And found but weariness and pain;
Oh come, your sinful steps retrace,
Improve this blessed day of grace.

Solo, Duet, or Trio.   S. WEBBE.

1. Come, ye dis - con - so - late, wher - e'er ye lan - guish,

Come to the mer - cy seat, fer - vent - ly kneel;

1st time, DUET; *2d time,* CHORUS.

Here bring your wounded hearts, here tell your an - guish;

Earth   has   no sor - row that heaven can not heal.

260   *"God is our refuge and strength; a very present help in trouble."*   11s & 10s.

2 Joy to the desolate, light of the straying,
    Hope of the penitent, fadeless and pure;
Here speaks the Comforter, tenderly saying:
    Earth has no sorrow that heaven can not cure.

3 Here see the bread of life; see waters flowing
    Forth from the throne of God, pure from above;
Come to the feast of love; come, ever knowing—
    Earth has no sorrow but heaven can remove.

MAZZINGHI.

1. Peace, troubled soul, whose plaintive moan Hath taught each scene the

notes of woe; Cease thy complaint, suppress thy groan, And let thy

D. S. To lull thy

End.

tears for-get to flow; Be-hold, the precious balm is found,

pain, to heal thy wound.

D. S.

261   *Refuge in Jesus.*   L. M.

1 Peace, troubled soul, whose plaintive moan,
Hath taught each scene the notes of woe;
Cease thy complaint, suppress thy groan,
And let thy tears forget to flow;
Behold, the precious balm is found,
To lull thy pain, to heal thy wound.

2 Come, freely come, by sin oppressed;
On Jesus cast thy weighty load;
In him thy refuge find, thy rest,
Safe in the mercy of thy God;
Thy God's thy Savior—glorious word!
Forever love and praise the Lord.

262   *Jesus a Refuge.*   L. M.

1 Forth from the dark and stormy sky,
Lord, to thine altar's shade we fly;
Forth from the world, its hope and fear,
Father, we seek thy shelter here;
Weary and weak, thy grace we pray,
Turn not, O Lord, thy guests away.

2 Long have we roamed in want and pain,
Long have we sought thy rest in vain;
'Wildered in doubt, in darkness lost,
Long have our souls been tempest-tossed;
Low at thy feet our sins we lay,
Turn not, O Lord, thy guests away.

WEBB. 7s & 6s.

G. J. WEBB.

1. Stand up, stand up for Je - sus, Ye sol-diers of the cross;

Lift high his roy - al ban - ner, It must not suf - fer loss:
D. S. Till ev - ery foe is vanquished, And Christ is Lord indeed.

End.

D. S.

From vic - tory un - to vic - tory His ar - my shall be led,

263 *Stand up for Jesus.* 7s & 6s.

2 Stand up, stand up for Jesus,
  Stand in his strength alone;
The arm of flesh will fail you,
  Ye dare not trust your own.
Put on the Gospel armor,
  And watching unto prayer
Where duty calls, or danger,
  Be never wanting there.

3 Stand up, stand up for Jesus,
  The strife will not be long;
This day the noise of battle,
  The next the victor's song.
To him that overcometh
  A crown of life shall be;
He with the King of glory
  Shall reign eternally.

Moody, Key G.

264 *Anniversary.* 7s & 6s.

1 We meet again in gladness,
  And thankful voices raise;
To God, our heavenly Father,
  We'll tune our grateful praise.
'Twas his kind hand that kept us
  Through all the changing year;
His love it is that brings us
  Again to worship here.

2 We'll thank him for our country,
  The land our fathers trod;
For liberty of conscience,
  And right to worship God.
O Lord, our heavenly Father,
  Accept the praise we bring.
And tune our hearts and voices
  Thy glorious name to sing.

Mendebras, Key F.

265 *"The morning Cometh."* 7s & 6s.

1 The morning light is breaking,
The darkness disappears;
The sons of earth are waking
To penitential tears.
Each breeze that sweeps the ocean
Brings tidings from afar,
Of nations in commotion,
Prepared for Zion's war.

2 Rich dews of grace come o'er us,
In many a gentle shower,
And brighter scenes before us
Are opening every hour.
Each cry, to heaven going,
Abundant answer brings,
And heavenly gales are blowing,
With peace upon their wings.

3 Blest river of salvation,
Pursue thy onward way;
Flow thou to every nation,
Nor in thy richness stay:
Stay not till all the lowly
Triumphant reach their home;
Stay not till all the holy
Proclaim, "The Lord is come!"

266 *Seeking Lost Sheep.* 7s & 6s.

1 How many sheep are straying,
Lost from the Savior's fold,
Upon the lonely mountains?
They shiver with the cold.
Within the tangled thickets,
Where poison vines do creep,
And over rocky ledges,
Wander the poor lost sheep.

2 Oh, who will go to find them,
Who, for the Savior's sake,
Will search, with tireless patience,
Through brier and through brake?
Unheeding thirst and hunger,
Who still, from day to day,
Will seek as for a treasure,
The sheep that go astray?

3 Say, will *you* seek to find them?
From pleasant bowers of ease
Will you go forth, determined
To find the "least of these?"

For still the Savior calls them,
And looks across the world,
And still he holds wide open
The door into his fold.

4 How sweet 't would be at evening,
If you and I could say,
Good Shepherd, we've been seeking
The sheep that went astray;
Heart sore, and faint with hunger,
We heard them making moan,
And lo! we come at nightfall
Bearing them safely home.

267 *Adoration of Jesus.* 7s & 6s.

1 To thee, my God, my Savior,
My soul, exulting, sings;
Rejoicing in thy favor,
Almighty King of kings!
I'll celebrate thy glory,
With all the saints above,
And tell the joyful story
Of thy redeeming love.

2 Soon as the morn with roses
Bedecks the dewy East,
And when the sun reposes
Upon the ocean's breast,
My voice in supplication,
My Savior, thou shalt hear;
Oh, grant me thy salvation,
And to my soul draw near!

3 By thee through life supported,
I pass the dangerous road,
With heavenly hosts escorted
Up to their bright abode:
There cast my crown before thee,
And, all my conflicts o'er,
Unceasingly adore thee;
What would an angel more?

268 *Confidence in Jesus.* 7s & 6s.

1 I lay my sins on Jesus,
The spotless Lamb of God;
He bears them all and frees us
From the accursed load.
I bring my guilt to Jesus,
To wash my crimson stains
White in his blood most precious,
Till not a stain remains.

Farmer, Key B♭.   Tully, Key E♭.

MOODY. 7s & 6s.

W. H. DOANE.

Spirited.

1. Men of the Christian Mis - sion, Go bear the Cross of God!

Be - hold your high com - mis - sion; Go tread the paths he trod.
D. S. Like might-y riv - ers roll - ing, The watch-word pass along.

End.

The great high Cap-tain call-ing, "Stand for the Right, be strong!"

D.S.

269　　*Christian Mission.*　　7s & 6s.

2 Go in the power of Jesus,
　His royal grace proclaim,
Uphold the word so precious,
　The tal'sman of his name!
Go with a *brother's* feeling,
　To sorrowing souls around;
Go pour the oil of healing
　In every mortal wound.

3 In day of Jesus' glory,
　His gracious words may be,
"Each deed of love before me,
　Was even done to me."
Men of the Christian Mission,
　Then bear the Cross of God!
Behold your high commission,
　Go tread the paths he trod.

270　　*Association Hymn.*　　7s & 6s.

1 We're drawing near to Jesus,
　Our banner waves on high,

And this our "watchword" ever,
　We'll work until we die.
We love our Master's service,
　And "seeing eye to eye,"
With grace divine to help us,
　We'll work until we die.

2 Let all "stand up for Jesus,"
　With life, and lip, and eye;
Oh, live the blessed gospel,
　And work until you die.
The "fields are white to harvest,"
　The days are speeding by;
Go forth again, ye workers,
　And work until you die.

3 The "night of death" approaches,
　And angels in the sky
Repeat the chorus ever,
　Go work until you die.
"Come over," now, "and help us,"
　Is our united cry;
And "looking unto Jesus,"
　We'll work until we die.

Webb, Key B♭.　　Mendebras, Key F.

271 *Missionary Progress.* 7s & 6s.

1 Roll on, thou mighty ocean,
  And, as thy billows flow,
Bear messengers of mercy
  To every land below:
Arise, ye gales! and waft them
  Safe to the destined shore;
That man may sit in darkness
  And death's black shade no more.

2 Oh, thou eternal Ruler!
  Who holdest in thine arm
The tempests of the ocean,
  Protect them from all harm!
Thy presence still be with them,
  Wherever they may be;
Though far from us who love them,
  Still let them be with thee.

272 *Spirit of the Gospel.* 7s & 6s.

1 To thee, O blessed Savior,
  Our grateful songs we raise;
Oh, tune our hearts and voices
  Thy holy name to praise:
'Tis by thy sovereign mercy
  We're now allowed to meet,
And join with friends and teachers,
  Thy blessing to entreat.

2 Oh, may thy precious gospel
  Be published all abroad,
Till the benighted heathen
  Shall know and serve the Lord;
Till o'er the wide creation
  The rays of truth shall shine,
And nations now in darkness
  Arise to light divine.

273 *Confidence in God.* 7s & 6s.

1 God is my strong salvation,
  What foe have I to fear?
In darkness and temptation
  My light, my help, is near.
Though hosts encamp around me,
  Firm to the fight I stand·
What terror can confound me,
  With God at my right hand?

2 Place on the Lord reliance,
  My soul, with courage wait;
His truth be thine affiance
  When faint and desolate;

His might thy heart shall strengthen,
  His love thy joy increase;
Mercy thy days shall lengthen,
  The Lord will give thee peace.

274 *Gospel Banner.* 7s & 6s.

1 Now be the gospel banner
  In every land unfurled,
And be the shout, Hosanna!
  Re-echoed through the world:
Till every isle and nation,
  Till every tribe and tongue,
Receive the great salvation,
  And join the happy throng.

2 What though th' embattled legions
  Of earth and hell combine?
His power throughout their regions,
  Shall soon resplendent shine.
Ride on, O Lord, victorious,
  Immanuel, Prince of Peace!
Thy triumph shall be glorious,
  Thy empire still increase!

275 *Missionary's Departure.* 7s & 6s.

1 Go, for the Master calls thee,
  Shed not one bitter tear;
No earthly care enthralls thee,
  Nor hast thou aught to fear.
To him we now commend thee,
  Who rules above the skies;
His blessing will attend thee
  Where'er thy pathway lies.

2 Go, in the midst of dangers
  Declare a Savior's love,
Till distant heathen strangers
  His willing subjects prove;
Till many a crowd assembling,
  Shall hearken to thy voice;
Confess their guilt with trembling,
  And in his name rejoice.

3 Go, for the Master calls thee,
  Far from thy native home,
Whatever there befalls thee,
  Whatever ills may come,
He is thy strong salvation,
  His presence thou shalt share;
He'll aid thy supplication,
  And hearken to thy prayer.

Tully, Key Eb.   Missionary Hymn, Key F.

MISSIONARY HYMN. 7s & 6s.

DR. L. MASON.

1. From Greenland's i - cy mountains, From India's co - ral strand;

Where Afric's sun - ny fountains Roll down their golden sand;

From many an ancient riv - er, From many a palmy plain,—

They call us to de - liv - er Our land from er-ror's chain.

276　　　*Missionary Hymn.*　　　7s & 6s.

2 What though the spicy breezes
　Blow soft o'er Ceylon's isle,
Though every prospect pleases,
　And only man is vile;
In vain, with lavish kindness,
　The gifts of God are strown:
The heathen, in his blindness,
　Bows down to wood and stone.

3 Shall we, whose souls are lighted
　With wisdom from on high,
Shall we to men benighted
　The lamp of life deny?

Salvation! oh, salvation!
　The joyful sound proclaim,
Till earth's remotest nation
　Has learn'd Messiah's name.

4 Waft, waft, ye winds, his story,
　And you, ye waters, roll,
Till, like a sea of glory,
　It spreads from pole to pole;
Till o'er our ransom'd nature
　The Lamb, for sinners slain,
Redeemer, King, Creator,
　In bliss returns to reign.

Moody, Key G.　　Webb, Key B♭.

1. Oh, day of rest and gladness, Oh, day of joy and light,
Oh, balm of care and sad-ness, Most beau-ti - ful and bright;

On thee, the high and low - ly, Bend-ing be - fore the throne,

Sing, Ho - ly, Ho - ly, Ho - ly, To the Great Three in One.

277   *Day of Rest.*   7s & 6s.

2 To-day on weary nations
  The heavenly manna falls;
To holy convocations
  The silver trumpet calls,
Where gospel light is glowing
  With pure and radiant beams,
And living water flowing
  With soul-refreshing streams.

3 New graces ever gaining
  From this our day of rest,
We reach the rest remaining
  To spirits of the blest.
To Holy Ghost be praises,
  To Father and to Son;
The Church her voice upraises
  To three, blest Three in One.

278   *Sabbath.*   7s & 6s.

1 Thine holy day's returning
  Our hearts exult to see,
And with devotion burning,
  Ascend, O God, to thee!

To-day, with purest pleasure,
  Our thoughts from earth withdraw:
We search for heavenly treasure,
  We learn thy holy law.

2 We join to sing thy praises,
  Lord of the Sabbath day;
Each voice in gladness raises
  Its loudest, sweetest lay!
Thy richest mercies sharing,
  Inspire us with thy love,
By grace our souls preparing
  For nobler praise above.

279   *Doxology.*   7s & 6s.

To Father, Son, and Spirit
  Eternal praise be given,
By all that earth inherit,
  And all that dwell in heaven.
Thou triune God! before thee
  Our inmost souls adore:
For thou alone art worthy,
  And shalt be evermore.

Phuvah, Key E.   Missionary Hymn, Key F.

1. Hail to the brightness of Zi-on's glad morning! Joy to the
lands that in dark-ness have lain; Hushed be the ac-cents of
sor-row and mourning, Zi - on in triumph begins her mild reign.

280   *The latter Day.*   11s & 10s.

1 Hail to the brightness of Zion's glad morning!
   Joy to the lands that in darkness have lain;
Hushed be the accents of sorrow and mourning,
   Zion in triumph begins her mild reign.

2 Hail to the brightness of Zion's glad morning,
   Long by the prophets of Israel foretold;
Hail to the millions from bondage returning,
   Gentiles and Jews, the blest vision behold.

3 Lo! in the desert rich flowers are springing,
   Streams ever copious are gliding along;
Loud from the mountain-tops echoes are ringing,
   Wastes rise in verdure, and mingle in song.

4 See, from all lands—from the isles of the ocean
   Praise to Jehovah ascending on high;
Fallen are the engines of war and commotion,
   Shouts of salvation are rending the sky.

Words and Music by Rev. Wm. Hunter.

1. {Joyful-ly, joy-ful-ly onward I move, Bound to the land of bright
{An-gel-ic cho-ris-ters sing as I come, Joy-ful-ly, joy-ful-ly

spi - rits a-bove; } { Soon with my pilgrimage ended below, }
haste to thy home; } { Home to that land of delight will I go; } Pilgrim and

stranger no more shall I roam, Joyfully, joy-ful-ly rest-ing at home.

281   *Joyfully Onward.*   10s.

2 Friends, fondly cherished, have passed on before;
Waiting, they watch me approaching the shore;
Singing, to cheer me through death's chilling gloom,
Joyfully, joyfully haste to thy home.
Sounds of sweet melody fall on my ear;
Harps of the blessed, your voices I hear;
Rings with the harmony heaven's high dome,—
Joyfully, joyfully haste to thy home.

3 Death, with thy weapons of war lay me low,
Strike, king of terrors, I fear not the blow;
Jesus hath broken the bars of the tomb!
Joyfully, joyfully will I go home.
Bright will the morn of eternity dawn,
Death shall be banished, his sceptre be gone:
Joyfully, then, shall I witness his doom,
Joyfully, joyfully, safely at home.

THE ANGEL BOATMAN.

By permission.

T. E. PERKINS.

1. One by one we cross the riv-er, One by one we 're passing o'er;

One by one the crowns are given On the bright, and happy shore.

Youth and childhood oft are passing O'er the dark and rolling tide,

And the bless - ed Ho - ly Spir- it Is the dying Christian's guide;

And the lov- ing, gen- tle Spir- it Bears them o'er the rolling tide.

282

2 One by one we come to Jesus,
　As we heed his gentle voice;
One by one his vineyard enter,
　There to labour and rejoice.
One by one sweet flowers we gather
　In the glorious work of love,
Garlands for the blessed Saviour,
　Gather for the realms above;
And the loving gentle Spirit
　Bears them to our home of love

3 One by one the heavy-laden
　Sink beneath the noontide sun;
And the aged pilgrim welcomes
　Evening shadows as they come.
One by one, with sins forgiven,
　May we stand upon the shore,
Waiting till the blessed Spirit
　Takes our hand and guides us o'er
And the loving, gentle spirit
　Leads us to the shining shore.

Rev. R. Lowry.

Cheerful.

1. Shall we gath-er at the riv-er, Where bright angel feet have trod;

With its crys-tal tide for-ev-er Flowing by the throne of God?

Chorus.

Yes, we'll gather at the river, The beauti-ful, the beautiful riv-er,

Gather with the saints at the river That flows by the throne of God.

283

1 Shall we gather at the river,
  Where bright angel feet have trod;
With its crystal tide forever
  Flowing by the throne of God?

2 On the margin of the river,
  Washing up its silver spray,
We will walk and worship ever,
  All the happy, golden day.

3 On the bosom of the river,
  Where the Savior-king we own,
We shall meet, and sorrow never,
  'Neath the glory of the throne.

4 Ere we reach the shining river,
  Lay we every burden down;
Grace our spirits will deliver,
  And provide a robe and crown.

5 At the smiling of the river,
  Rippling with the Savior's face,
Saints, whom death will never sever,
  Lift their songs of saving grace.

6 Soon we'll reach the shining river,
  Soon our pilgrimage will cease;
Soon our happy hearts will quiver
  With the melody of peace.

8

1. Our heaven-ly Fa-ther calls, And Christ in-vites us near;

With both our friendship shall be sweet, And our communion dear.

284   *Jesus our living Head.*   S. M.

1 Our heavenly Father calls,
   And Christ invites us near;
With both our friendship shall be sweet,
   And our communion dear.

2 God pities all our griefs,
   He pardons every day;
Almighty to protect our souls,
   And wise to guide our way.

3 How large his bounties are!
   What various stores of good,
Diffused from our Redeemer's hand,
   And purchased with his blood!

4 Jesus, our living Head,
   We bless thy faithful care,
Our Advocate before the throne,
   And our Forerunner there.

285   *Christ our Guide.*   S. M.

1 Jesus, my truth, my way,
   My sure, unerring light,
On thee my feeble soul I stay,
   Which thou wilt lead aright.

2 My wisdom, and my guide,
   My counselor, thou art;
Oh, never let me leave thy side,
   Or from thy paths depart.

286   *Consecration to God.*   S. M.

1 Lord, in the strength of grace,
   With a glad heart and free,
Myself, my residue of days,
   I consecrate to thee.

2 Thy ransomed servant, I
   Restore to thee thine own;
And from this moment live or die
   To serve my God alone.

287   *Union with Christ.*   S. M.

1 Dear Savior, we are thine
   By everlasting bonds;
Our names, our hearts, we would resign:
   Our souls are in thy hands.

2 To thee we still would cleave,
   With ever-growing zeal;
If millions tempt us Christ to leave,
   Oh, let them ne'er prevail.

3 Thy Spirit shall unite
   Our souls to thee, our Head;
Shall form us to thy image bright,
   That we thy paths may tread.

4 Since Christ and we are one,
   Why should we doubt or fear?
If he in heaven hath fixed his throne,
   He'll fix his members there.

Shawmut, Key D.   Golden Hill. Key F.

HANDEL.

1. Oh, bless the Lord, my soul; His grace to thee proclaim;

And all that is with-in me, join To bless his ho - ly name.

288 *Praise for Mercies.* S. M.

2 Oh, bless the Lord, my soul;
    His mercies bear in mind;
Forget not all his benefits;
    The Lord to thee is kind.

3 He will not always chide;
    He will with patience wait;
His wrath is ever slow to rise,
    And ready to abate.

4 He clothes thee with his love,
    Upholds thee with his truth,
And like the eagle he renews
    The vigor of thy youth.

5 Then bless his holy name,
    Whose grace hath made thee whole,
Whose loving kindness crowns thy days;
    Oh, bless the Lord, my soul.

289 *The only wise God.* S. M.

1 To God the only wise,
    Our Savior and our King,
Let all the saints below the skies
    Their humble praises bring.

2 'Tis his almighty love,
    His counsel and his care,
Preserves us safe from sin and death,
    And every hurtful snare.

3 He will present our souls,
    Unblemish'd and complete,
Before the glory of his face,
    With joys divinely great.

4 Then all the chosen seed
    Shall meet around the throne;
Shall bless the conduct of his grace,
    And make his wonders known.

290 *Desire for Holiness.* S. M.

1 Prepare me, gracious God,
    To stand before thy face;
Thy Spirit must the work perform,
    For it is all of grace.

2 In Christ's obedience clothe,
    And wash me in his blood:
So shall I lift my head with joy
    Among the sons of God.

3 Do thou my sins subdue,
    Thy sovereign love make known;
The spirit of my mind renew,
    And save me in thy Son.

4 Let me attest thy power,
    Let me thy goodness prove,
Till my full soul can hold no more
    Of everlasting love.

Boylston, Key C.   Olmutz, Key B♭.   Dennis, Key F.

ST. THOMAS. S. M.

A. WILLIAMS.

1. My soul, re - peat his praise, Whose mer - cies are so great;

Whose an - ger is so slow to rise, So read - y to a - bate.

291 *Greatness of God's Mercy.* S. M.

2 His power subdues our sins,
   And his forgiving love,
Far as the east is from the west,
   Doth all our guilt remove.

3 God will not always chide;
   And when his strokes are felt,
His strokes are fewer than our crimes,
   And lighter than our guilt.

4 High as the heavens are raised
   Above the ground we tread,
So far the riches of his grace
   Our highest thoughts exceed.

292 *Christian Fellowship.* S. M.

1 Blest are the sons of peace,
 . Whose hearts and hopes are one;
Whose kind designs to serve and please
   Through all their actions run.

2 Blest is the pious house
   Where zeal and friendship meet;
Their songs of praise, their mingled vows,
   Make their communion sweet.

3 Thus on the heavenly hills
   The saints are blest above,
Where joy like morning dew distills,
   And all the air is love.

293 *Extension of Christ's Kingdom.* S. M.

1 O Lord, our God, arise,
   The cause of Truth maintain,
And wide o'er all the peopled world
   Extend her blessed reign.

2 Thou Prince of life, arise,
   Nor let thy glory cease;
Far spread the conquests of thy grace,
   And bless the earth with peace.

3 O Holy Spirit, rise,
   Expand thy heavenly wing,
And o'er a dark and ruined world
   Let light and order spring.

4 Oh, all ye nations, rise,
   To God the Savior sing;
From shore to shore, from earth to heaven,
   Let echoing anthems ring.

294 *Exhortation to Praise.* S. M.

1 Arise, and bless the Lord,
   Ye people of his choice;
Arise and bless the Lord your God,
   With heart, and soul, and voice.

2 Oh for the living flame
   From his own altar brought,
To touch our lips, our souls inspire,
   And wing to heaven our thought!

Boylston, Key C.   Olmutz, Key B♭.   Labau, Key D.

1. Be-hold the throne of grace! The prom-ise calls me near;

There Je-sus shows a smiling face, And waits to answer prayer.

295 *Blessings sought in Prayer.* S. M.

1 Behold the throne of grace!
  The promise calls me near;
There Jesus shows a smiling face,
  And waits to answer prayer.

2 Thine image, Lord, bestow,
  Thy presence and thy love;
I ask to serve thee here below,
  And reign with thee above.

3 Teach me to live by faith;
  Conform my will to thine,
Let me victorious be in death,
  And then in glory shine.

296 *Ark of Safety.* S. M.

1 Oh cease, my wandering soul,
  On restless wing to roam;
All this wide world, to either pole,
  Has not for thee a home.

2 Behold the ark of God;
  Behold the open door;
Oh, haste to gain that dear abode,
  And rove, my soul, no more.

3 There safe thou shalt abide,
  There sweet shall be thy rest,
And every longing satisfied,
  With full salvation blest.

297 *Salvation through Christ.* S. M.

1 Not what I feel or do
  Can give me peace with God;
Not all my prayers, and sighs, and tears,
  Can bear my awful load.

2 Thy work alone, O Christ,
  Can ease this weight of sin;
Thy blood alone, O Lamb of God,
  Can give me peace within.

3 Thy love to me, O God,
  Not mine, O Lord, to thee,
Can rid me of this dark unrest,
  And set my spirit free.

4 'Tis Christ who saveth me,
  And freely pardon gives;
I love because he loveth me,
  I live because he lives.

298 *Prayer for all Lands.* S. M.

1 O God of sovereign grace,
  We bow before thy throne,
And plead, for all the human race,
  The merits of thy Son.

2 Spread through the earth, O Lord,
  The knowledge of thy ways,
And let all lands with joy record
  The great Redeemer's praise.

Dennis, Key G.   Pond, Key A♭.   Thatcher, Key G.

Dr. L. Mason.

1. The Lord Jehovah reigns; His throne is built on high; The garments he assumes

Are light and majesty; His glories shine with beams so bright, No mortal eye can bear the sight.

299 *Perfections of God's Sovereignty.* H. M.

1 The Lord Jehovah reigns;
 His throne is built on high;
The garments he assumes
 Are light and majesty;
His glories shine with beams so bright,
No mortal eye can bear the sight.

2 The thunders of his hand
 Keep all the world in awe;
His wrath and justice stand
 To guard his holy law;
And where his love resolves to bless,
His truth confirms and seals the grace.

3 Through all his ancient works
 Surprising wisdom shines,
Confounds the powers of hell,
 And breaks their fell designs:
Strong is his arm, and shall fulfill
His great decrees, his sovereign will.

4 And can this mighty King
 Of glory condescend?
And will he write his name
 My Father and my Friend?
I love his name, I love his word;
Join, all my powers, and praise the Lord.

300   *Christ a Priest and King.*   H. M.

1 Join all the glorious names
 Of wisdom, love, and power,
That ever mortals knew,
 Or angels ever bore:
All are too mean to speak his worth,
Too mean to set the Savior forth.

2 Great Prophet of our God,
 Our tongues shall bless thy name;
By thee the joyful news
 Of our salvation came:
The joyful news of sins forgiven,
Of hell subdued, and peace with heaven.

3 Jesus, our great High Priest,
 Has shed his blood and died;
Our guilty conscience needs
 No sacrifice beside:
His precious blood did once atone,
And now it pleads before the throne.

4 Oh, thou almighty Lord,
 Our Conqueror and our King,
Thy scepter and thy sword,
 Thy reigning grace we sing.
Thine is the power; oh, make us sit
In willing bonds beneath thy feet.

Haddam, Key D.   Zebulon, Key F.

Dr. LOWELL MASON.

1. Within these hallowed walls, Our wand'ring feet are brought;)
Where prayer and praise ascend, And heavenly truths are taught.) To

God alone your offerings bring, Let young and old his praises sing.

---

301   *Dedication Hymn.*   H. M.

2 Lord, let this work of love
  Be crowned with full success;
Let thousands, yet unborn,
  Thy sacred name here bless:
To thee, O Lord, all praise to thee
We'll raise throughout eternity.

302   *Corner-stone.*   H. M.

1 Christ is our Corner-stone;
  On him alone we build;
With his true saints alone
  The courts of heaven are filled
On his great love our hopes we place,
Of present grace and joys above.

2 Oh, then, with hymns of praise
  These hallowed courts shall ring!
Our voices we will raise,
  The Three in One to sing:
And thus proclaim in joyful song,
Both loud and long, that glorious name.

3 Here, gracious God, do thou
  For evermore draw nigh;
Accept each faithful vow,
  And mark each suppliant sigh:
In copious shower, on all who pray,
Each holy day thy blessings pour.

Newman, Key B♭.

---

4 Here may we gain from heaven
  The grace which we implore,
And may that grace, once given,
  Be with us evermore,—
Until that day, when all the blest
To endless rest are called away.

303   *Yet there is Room.*   H. M.

1 Ye dying sons of men,
  Immerged in sin and woe,
The gospel's voice attend,
  While Jesus sends to you:
Ye perishing and guilty, come;
In Jesus' arms there yet is room.

2 No longer now delay,
  Nor vain excuses frame;
He bids you come to-day,
  Though poor, and blind, and lame:
All things are ready; sinners, come;
For every trembling soul there's room.

3 Drawn by his dying love,
  Ye wandering sheep, draw near;
He calls you from above,
  The Shepherd's voice now hear:
Let whosoever will now come,
In Jesus' arms there still is room.

Lenox, Key B♭.

Arr. from the German.

1. Welcome, de-light-ful morn, Thou day of sa-cred rest!
I hail thy kind re-turn; Lord, make these moments blest;

From low delights and mor-tal toys I soar to reach im-

mor-tal joys, I soar to reach im-mor-tal joys.

---

304   *Sabbath.*   H. M.

1 Welcome, delightful morn,
  Thou day of sacred rest!
I hail thy kind return;
  Lord, make these moments blest;
From low delights and mortal toys
I soar to reach immortal joys.

2 Now may the King descend,
  And fill his throne of grace;
Thy sceptre, Lord, extend,
  While saints address thy face;
Let sinners feel thy quick'ning word,
And learn to know and fear the Lord.

3 Descend, celestial Dove,
  With all thy quick'ning powers,
Disclose a Savior's love,
  And bless these sacred hours;
Then shall my soul new life obtain,
Nor sabbaths be enjoyed in vain.

305   *Longing for the Sanctuary.*   H. M.

1 Lord of the worlds above,
  How pleasant and how fair
The dwellings of thy love,
  Thine earthly temples, are!
To thine abode my heart aspires,
With warm desires to see my God.

2 Oh, happy souls, who pray
  Where God appoints to hear!
Oh, happy men, who pay
  Their constant service there!
They praise thee still; and happy they
Who love the way to Zion's hill.

3 They go from strength to strength,
  Through this dark vale of tears,
Till each arrives at length,
  Till each in heaven appears;
Oh, glorious seat, when God, our King,
Shall thither bring our willing feet.

Harwich, Key F.   Zebulon, Key F.

1. Let ev-ery crea-ture join To bless Je-ho-vah's name,
And ev-ery power u-nite To swell th' ex-alt-ed theme;

Let nature raise, from every tongue, A general song of grateful praise.

306 *Universal Praise.* H. M.

2 But oh, from human tongues
Should nobler praises flow,
And every thankful heart
With warm devotion glow:
Your voices raise, ye highly blest,
Above the rest declare his praise.

3 Assist me, gracious God,
My heart, my voice, inspire;
Then shall I humbly join
The universal choir;
Thy grace can raise my heart and tongue,
And tune my song to lively praise.

307 *Praise from Heaven and Earth.* H. M.

1 Ye boundless realms of joy
Exalt your Maker's name;
His praise your songs employ
Above the starry frame:
Your voices raise, ye cherubim
And seraphim, to sing his praise.

2 Let all adore the Lord,
And praise his holy name,
By whose almighty word
They all from nothing came:
And all shall last, from changes free,
His firm decree stands ever fast.

308 *United Praise Worship.* H. M.

1 Come, let our voices join
In joyful songs of praise;
To God, the God of love,
Our thankful hearts we'll raise:
To God alone all praise belongs—
Our earliest and our latest songs.

2 Within these hallowed walls
Our wandering feet are brought,
Where prayer and praise ascend,
And heavenly truths are taught:
To God alone your offerings bring;
Let young and old his praises sing.

309 *God's Love to Zion.* H. M.

1 Fixed on the sacred hills,
Its firm foundations rest;
The Lord his temple fills,
With all his glory blest;
He waits where'er his saints adore,
But loves the gates of Zion more.

2 O Zion, sacred place!
Thy name shall spread around;
The city of his grace,
His wonders there abound;
Thy glories will thy God declare,
And earth thy fame resound afar.

Lischer, Key G.   Haddam, Key D.

1. Now the Savior invites you to come, And fly to the arms of his love; In his kingdom of grace there is room, And a mansion of glory a-bove.

Chorus.

Over Jordan a home bright and fair, ... Our Savior has gone to pre - pare; We shall rest by and by from our care, ... In that home ... bright and fair.

310

1 Now the Savior invites you to come,
  And fly to the arms of his love;
In his kingdom of grace there is room,
  And a mansion of glory above.

2 Are you thirsty? remember the call,
  Oh come, and salvation receive;
For the fountain is open to all
  Who will truly repent and believe.

3 Are you weary and sighing for rest?
  To Jesus, your refuge, repair;
He will pillow your head on his breast,
  If you seek him by watching and prayer.

4 To the faithful a promise is given,
  Who meekly his counsel obey,
Of a crown of rejoicing in heaven,
  And a treasure that fades not away.

GO AND TELL JESUS.

By permission.

T. F. SEWARD.

1. Go and tell Je-sus, wea-ry, sin-sick soul; He'll

ease thee of thy burden, make thee whole; Look up to him, he

on-ly can forgive; Believe on him and thou shalt surely live.

Chorus.

Go and tell Je-sus, he on-ly can forgive;
Go and tell Je-sus, oh, turn to him and live! } Go and tell Je-sus,

go and tell Je-sus, Go and tell Je-sus, he on-ly can forgive.

311

2 Go and tell Jesus, when your sins arise
Like mountains of deep guilt before your eyes;
His blood was spilt, his precious life he gave,
That mercy, peace, and pardon you might have.

3 Go and tell Jesus, he'll dispel thy fears,
Will calm thy doubts, and wipe away thy tears;
He'll take thee in his arms, and on his breast
Thou may'st be happy, and forever rest.

J. M. EVANS.

1. "Land ahead!" Its fruits are waving O'er the hills of fadeless green;

And the living waters laving Shores where heavenly forms are seen.

Chorus.

Rocks and storms I'll fear no more, When on that e - ter-nal shore;

Drop the anchor! furl the sail!   I am safe   within the vail!

312   *Land Ahead.*

1 "Land ahead!" its fruits are waving
  O'er the hills of fadeless green;
And the living waters laving
  Shores where heav'nly forms are seen.

2 Onward, bark! the cape I'm rounding;
  See the blessed wave their hands;
Hear the harps of God resounding
  From the bright immortal bands.

3 There, let go the anchor, riding
  On this calm and silv'ry bay;
Sea-ward fast the tide is gliding,
  Shores in sunlight stretch away.

4 Now we're safe from all temptation,
  All the storms of life are past;
Praise the Rock of our salvation,
  We are safe at home at last!

By permission. Rev. J. W. DADMUN.

1. {Out on an o-cean all boundless we ride, We're homeward
   {Tossed on the waves of a rough, restless tide, We're homeward
D. C. Promise of which on us each he bestowed, We're homeward

bound, homeward bound; } {Far from the safe, quiet harbor we rode,}
bound, homeward bound; } {Seeking our Father's celes-tial a-bode,}
bound, homeward bound.

313 *Homeward Bound.*

1 Out on an ocean all boundless we ride,
  We're homeward bound;
Tossed on the waves of a rough, restless tide,
  We're homeward bound;
Far from the safe, quiet harbor we rode,
Seeking our Father's celestial abode,
Promise of which on us each he bestowed,
  We're homeward bound.

2 Wildly the storm sweeps us on as it roars;
  We're homeward bound;
Look! yonder lie the bright heavenly shores;
  We're homeward bound;
Steady! O pilot! stand firm at the wheel,
Steady! we soon shall outweather the gale;
Oh! how we fly 'neath the loud creaking sail;
  We're homeward bound.

3 We'll tell the world, as we journey along,
  We're homeward bound;
Try to persude them to enter our throng,
  We're homeward bound:
Come, trembling sinner, forlorn and oppressed,
Join in our number, oh come and be blest;
Journey with us to the mansions of rest,
  We're homeward bound.

4 Into the harbor of heaven we now glide,
  We're home at last;
Softly we drift on its bright silver tide,
  We're home at last;
Glory to God! all our dangers are o'er;
We stand secure on the glorified shore;
Glory to God! we will shout evermore,
  We're at home at last.

314 *Meet Again.* 7s.

TUNE, HORTON—p. 42.

1 Meet again when life is o'er,
Meet again to part no more;
How it cheers the drooping heart,
When from friends we're call'd to part.

2 Meet again where endless joy
We shall taste without alloy;
Meet where songs shall ne'er grow old,
Sweetly tuned to harps of gold.

3 Meet again! how passing sweet!
Friends long lost again to meet;
Care-worn souls by tempest driven,
Oh, how sweet to meet in heaven.

ERNAN. L. M.

Dr. Mason.

1. Brethren in Christ, and well beloved, To Jesus and his servants dear,

Enter, and show yourselves approved; Enter, and find that God is here.

315 *Christian Fellowship.* L. M.

2 Jesus, attend; thyself reveal;
  Are we not met in thy great name?
Thee in the midst we wait to feel;
  We wait to catch the spreading flame.

3 Truly our fellowship below
  With thee and with the Father is:
In thee eternal life we know,
  And heaven's unutterable bliss.

4 Though but in part we know thee here,
  We wait thy coming from above;
And we shall then behold thee near,
  And be forever lost in love.

316 *Only by Faith.* L. M.

1 Lord, I despair myself to heal;
I see my sin, but can not feel;
I can not, till thy Spirit blow,
And bid th' obedient waters flow.

2 'T is thine a heart of flesh to give;
Thy gifts I only can receive;
Here, then, to thee I all resign;
To draw, redeem, and seal, are thine.

3 With simple faith on thee I call,
My light, my life, my Lord, my all:
I wait the moving of the pool;
I wait the word that speaks me whole.

317 *Exhortation to Prayer.* L. M.

1 What various hindrances we meet
In coming to a mercy-seat;
Yet who that knows the worth of prayer
But wishes to be often there.

2 Prayer makes the darken'd cloud withdraw;
Prayer climbs the ladder Jacob saw;
Gives exercise to faith and love,
Brings every blessing from above.

3 Restraining prayer, we cease to fight;
Prayer keeps the Christian's armor bright;
And Satan trembles when he sees
The weakest saint upon his knees.

318 *Walking by Faith.* L. M.

1 'T is by the faith of joys to come
  We walk through deserts dark as night,
Till we arrive at heaven, our home:
  Faith is our guide, and faith our light.

2 The want of sight she well supplies;
  She makes the pearly gates appear;
Far into distant worlds she pries,
  And brings eternal glories near.

3 With joy we tread the desert through,
  While faith inspires a heavenly ray,
Though lion's roar, and tempests blow,
  And rocks and dangers fill the way.

Hamburg, Key F.   Ward, Key B♭.   Retreat, Key C.

1. Jesus, my Savior, Brother, Friend, On whom I cast my ev - ery care,

On whom for all things I depend,—Inspire, and then accept my prayer.

319 *For the Spirit's Guidance.* L. M.

1 Jesus, my Savior, Brother, Friend,
   On whom I cast my every prayer,
On whom for all things I depend,
   Inspire, and then accept, my prayer.

2 If I have tasted of thy grace,
   The grace that sure salvation brings,
If with me now thy Spirit stays,
   And, hov'ring, hides me in his wings,

3 Still let him with my weakness stay,
   Nor for a moment's space depart;
Evil and danger turn away,
   And keep, till he renews, my heart.

4 If to the right or left I stray,
   His voice behind me may I hear,—
Return, and walk in Christ, thy way:
   Fly back to Christ, for sin is near!

320 *For the Savior's Protection.* L. M.

1 Jesus, I fain would walk in thee,
   From nature's every path retreat;
Thou art my Way—my Leader be,
   And set upon the rock my feet.

2 Uphold me, Savior, or I fall;
   Oh, reach me out thy gracious hand:
Only on thee for help I call,
   Only by faith in thee I stand.

321 *Prayer at Sea.* L. M.

1 Prayer may be sweet in cottage homes,
   Where sire and child devoutly kneel,
While through the open casement nigh
   The vernal blossoms fragrant steal.

2 Prayer may be sweet in stately halls,
   Where heart with kindred heart is blent,
And upward to th' eternal throne
   The hymn of praise melodious sent.

3 But he who fain would know how warm
   The soul's appeal to God may be,
From friends and native land should turn,
   A wanderer on the faithless sea:

4 Should hear its deep, imploring tone
   Rise heavenward o'er the foaming surge,
When billows toss the fragile bark,
   And fearful blasts the conflict urge.

5 Naught, naught appears but sea and sky;
   No refuge where the foot may flee:
How will he cast, O Rock divine,
   The anchor of his soul on thee?

322 *Doxology.* L. M.

To God the Father, God the Son,
And God the Spirit, Three in One,
Be honor, praise, and glory given,
By all on earth, and all in heaven

Zephyr, Key C.　Brainerd, Key C.　Federal Street, Key A♭.

THE SOLID ROCK. L. M.

W. B. BRADBURY.

1. { My hope is built on nothing less Than Je-sus' blood and
   I dare not trust the sweetest frame, But wholly trust on

righteous - ness; }
Je - sus' name. } On Christ the sol - id rock, I stand, All

oth-er ground is sinking sand, All oth-er ground is sinking sand.

323 *The Solid Rock.* L. M.

1 My hope is built on nothing less
Than Jesus' blood and righteousness;
I dare not trust the sweetest frame,
But wholly lean on Jesus' name:
On Christ, the solid rock, I stand;
All other ground is sinking sand.

2 When darkness seems to vail his face,
I rest on his unchanging grace;
In every high and stormy gale
My anchor holds within the vail:
On Christ, the solid rock, I stand;
All other ground is sinking sand.

3 His oath, his covenant, and blood,
Support me in the whelming flood;
When all around my soul gives way,
He then is all my hope and stay:
On Christ, the solid rock, I stand;
All other ground is sinking sand.

324 *The returning Wanderer.* L. M.

1 Weary of wandering from my God,
And now made willing to return,
I hear, and bow beneath the rod;
For thee, not without hope, I mourn:
I have an advocate above,
A Friend before the throne of love.

2 O Jesus, full of truth and grace!
More full of grace than I of sin,
Yet once again I seek thy face,
Open thine arms and take me in;
And freely my backslidings heal,
And love the faithless sinner still.

3 Thou know'st the way to bring me back,
My fallen spirit to restore,
Oh, for thy truth and mercy's sake,
Forgive, and bid me sin no more.
The ruins of my soul repair,
And make my heart a house of prayer.

1. Who can describe the joys that rise, Thro' all the courts of Paradise,

To see a pen-i-tent return, To see an heir of glo-ry born?

325 *Joy in Heaven.* L. M.

1 Who can describe the joys that rise
Through all the courts of Paradise,
To see a penitent return—
To see an heir of glory born?

2 With joy the Father does approve
The fruit of his eternal love;
The Son with joy looks down, and sees
The purchase of his agonies.

3 The Spirit takes delight to view
The holy soul he formed anew;
And saints and angels join to sing
The growing empire of their King.

326 *How to see Jesus.* L. M.

1 Would you see Jesus? come with prayer,
And heart repentant, to his feet;
None who will rightly seek him there
Shall fail his face of love to greet.

2 Would you see Jesus? come with faith,
And search the word his grace hath given,
For help and guidance in the path
That leads to his abode in heaven.

3 Would you see Jesus? day by day
Let thought and converse be on high,
And hastening on the heavenward way,
With Jesus live, with Jesus die.

327 *The Accepted Time.* L. M.

1 While life prolongs its precious light,
Mercy is found, and peace is given;
But soon, ah, soon, approaching night
Shall blot out every hope of heaven.

2 While God invites, how blest the day!
How sweet the gospel's charming sound!
Come, sinners, haste, oh, haste away,
While yet a pardoning God is found.

3 Soon, borne on time's most rapid wing,
Shall death command you to the grave;
Before his bar your spirits bring,
And none be found to hear or save.

4 In that lone land of deep despair,
No Sabbath's heavenly light shall rise;
No God regard your bitter prayer,
No Savior call you to the skies.

5 Now God invites; how blest the day!
How sweet the gospel's charming sound!
Come, sinners, haste, oh, haste away,
While yet a pardoning God is found.

328 *Doxology.* L. M.

Glory to thee, O God, most high!
Father, we praise thy majesty!
The Son, the Spirit, we adore,
One Godhead, blest for evermore!

Forest, Key A♭. Hebron, Key B♭. Ernan, Key B♭.
9

REST. L. M.

WM. B. BRADBURY.

1. Asleep in Jesus! blessed sleep! From which none ever wake to weep;

A calm and un-dis-turbed repose, Un-bro-ken by the last of foes.

329   *Asleep in Jesus.*   L. M.

2 Asleep in Jesus! oh, how sweet
To be for such a slumber meet!
With holy confidence to sing
That death hath lost its venomed sting!

3 Asleep in Jesus! peaceful rest!
Whose waking is supremely blest;
No fear, no woe, shall dim that hour
Which manifests the Savior's power.

4 Asleep in Jesus! oh, for me
May such a blissful refuge be!
Securely shall my ashes lie,
And wait the summons from on high.

330   *The righteous blessed in Death.*   L. M.

1 How blest the righteous when he dies!
When sinks a weary soul to rest!
How mildly beam the closing eyes!
How gently heaves th' expiring breast!

2 So fades a summer cloud away;
So sinks the gale when storms are o'er;
So gently shuts the eye of day;
So dies a wave along the shore.

3 A holy quiet reigns around,
A calm which life nor death destroys;
And naught disturbs that peace profound
Which his unfettered soul enjoys.

4 Life's labor done, as sinks the clay,
Light from its load the spirit flies,
While heaven and earth combine to say,
"How blest the righteous when he dies!"

331   *To the dying Christian.*   L. M.

1 Go, spirit of the sainted dead,
Go to thy longed-for, happy home:
The tears of man are o'er thee shed,
The voice of angels bids thee come.

2 If life be not in length of days,
In silvered locks, and furrowed brow,
But living to the Savior's praise,
How few have lived so long as thou!

3 Though earth may boast one gem the less,
May not e'en heaven the richer be?
And myriads on thy footsteps press,
To share thy blest eternity.

332   *Death Disarmed.*   L. M.

1 Why should we start, and fear to die?
What timorous worms we mortals are!
Death is the gate of endless joy,
And yet we dread to enter there.

2 Jesus can make a dying bed
Feel soft as downy pillows are,
While on his breast I lean my head,
And breathe my life out sweetly there.

Zephyr, Key C.   Repose, Key E♭.   Brainerd. Key C.

1. How sweet the hour of closing day, When all is peaceful and serene,

And when the sun, with cloudless ray, Sheds mellow luster o'er the scene!

333 *The Christian's parting Hour.* L. M.

2 Such is the Christian's parting hour;
So peacefully he sinks to rest;
When faith, endued from heaven with power,
Sustains and cheers his languid breast.

3 Mark but that radiance of his eye,
That smile upon his wasted cheek:
They tell us of his glory nigh
In language that no tongue can speak

4 A beam from heaven is sent to cheer
The pilgrim on his gloomy road;
And angels are attending near,
To bear him to their bright abode.

5 Who would not wish to die like those
Whom God's own Spirit deigns to bless?
To sink into that soft repose,
Then wake to perfect happiness?

334 *Gone Before.* L. M.

1 Dear is the spot where Christians sleep,
And sweet the strains their spirits pour;
Oh, why should we in anguish weep?
They are not lost, but gone before.

2 Secure from every mortal care,
By sin and sorrow vexed no more,
Eternal happiness they share
Who are not lost, but gone before.

335 *She Sleeps, etc.* L. M.

1 She sleeps beneath her native earth,
And near the spot that gave her birth;
Her youthful feet trod flowers that bloom
In beauty o'er her early tomb.

2 She rests beneath her native earth;
With grateful hearts we'll sing her worth;
Her gentle ways shall ever dwell
In hearts that knew and loved her well.

3 And oft we'll lift the tearful eye
To hear her calling from the sky;
Oh, how could we her absence bear,
But that we hope to meet her there!

336 *Asleep in Jesus.* L. M.

1 Sweet is the scene when Christians die,
When sinks a righteous soul to rest;
How mildly beams the closing eye,
How gently heaves the expiring breast!

2 So fades a summer cloud away,
So sinks the gale when storms are o'er,
So gently shuts the eye of day,
So dies a wave along the shore.

3 Triumphant smiles the victor's brow,
Fanned by some guardian angel's wing;
Where is, O grave, thy victory now,
And where, O death, thy venomed sting?

Dodge, Key Ab.   Forest, Key Ab.   Zephyr, Key C.

By permission.   Rev. R. Lowry.

1. One more day's work for Jesus, One less of life for me! But heav'n is

nearer, And Christ is dearer Than yes-ter-day to me; His love and

Chorus.

light Fill all my soul to-night. One more day's work for Jesus, One

more day's work for Jesus, One more day's work for Jesus, One less of life for me.

337   *One more day's work for Jesus.*

2 One more day's work for Jesus!
  How glorious is my King;
    'T is joy, not duty,
    To speak his beauty;
  My soul mounts on the wing
  At the mere thought,
  How Christ my life has bought.

3 One more day's work for Jesus!
  How sweet the work has been,
    To tell the story,
    To show the glory,
  Where Christ's flock enter in!
  How it did shine
  In this poor heart of mine!

4 One more day's work for Jesus!
  Oh, yes, a weary day;
    But heaven shines clearer,
    And rest comes nearer,
  At each step of the way;
  And Christ in all,
  Before his face I fall.

5 Oh, blessed work for Jesus!
  Oh, rest at Jesus' feet!
    There toil seems pleasure,
    My wants are treasure,
  And pain for him is sweet.
    Lord, if I may,
    I 'll serve another day!

By permission.   T. E. PERKINS.

1. Soft - ly on the breath of evening Comes the ten - der

sigh of day; Lone - ly heart, by sor - row lad - en,

Chorus.

'T is the time to pray. Wea - ry pilgrim, cease thy mourning,

Repeat Chorus.

Wea-ry pilgrim, cease thy mourning, Rest beyond for - ev - er.

338   *Pilgrim, watch and pray.*

1 Softly on the breath of evening
  Comes the tender sigh of day ;
Lonely heart, by sorrow laden,
  'T is the time to pray.

2 Pearly dews like tears are falling
  Gently on the sleeping flowers;
Stars like angel eyes are beaming
  From celestial bowers.

3 'T is the hour where hallowed feelings
  Chase our doubts and fears away;
'T is the hour for calm devotion,
  Pilgrim, watch and pray.

4 Tho' temptations dark oppress thee,
  Jesus guides thee on thy way;
He will hear thy lightest whisper,
  Pilgrim, watch and pray.

1. Yes, we trust the day is breaking, Joyful times are near at hand; God, the

mighty God, is speaking, By his word in every land; When he chooses, Darkness

flies at his command, When he chooses, Darkness flies at his command.

339 *Encouraging Prospects.* 8s, 7s & 4.

1 Yes, we trust the day is breaking;
    Joyful times are near at hand;
God, the mighty God, is speaking,
    By his word, in every land:
        When he chooses,
    Darkness flies at his command.

2 While the foe becomes more daring,
    While he enters like a flood,
God, the Savior, is preparing
    Means to spread his truth abroad:
        Every language
    Soon shall tell the love of God.

3 Oh, 't is pleasant, 't is reviving
    To our hearts to hear, each day,
Joyful news, from far arriving,
    How the gospel wins its way:
        Those enlightening
    Who in death and darkness lay.

340   *Installation.*   8s, 7s & 4.

1 Father, by thy heavenly blessing,
    Now confirm this new-born tie;
To thine ear our prayers addressing,
    We beseech thee to be nigh.
        Seal this union;
    Hallow it in courts on high.

2 Now the sacred trust is given;
    Now the solemn charge is made;
Help thy son in strength from heaven,
    Keep these vows upon him laid.
        Thou art ready
    Ever thus to grant thine aid.

3 And when earth's few years have fleeted,
    Grant that in thy home of light,
Past the joys and griefs now meted,
    Pastor, people may unite:
        Ever dwelling
    In the glory of thy sight.

Zion, Key D.   Welcome Song, Key D.

Dr. T. Hastings.

1. For his sake who bought our pardon, Healing, blessing, ever stood,)
And to save us, in the gar-den Freely shed his precious blood:)

Duet.

Let us meek-ly On-ly live in do-ing good:

Let us meek-ly On-ly live in do-ing good:

341 *Doing Good.* 8s, 7s & 4.

2 Giving, feeding, clothing, kneeling,
  Where the outcast's moan is heard;
For the heathen warmly feeling,
  Spreading for God's Holy Word.
      Paid by heaven,
  Till the swelling soul is stirred.

3 Where the widow's weary fingers
  Wipe the death-dews from her child;
Where the sabbath-teacher lingers,
  As if angel faces smiled,
      To their Shepherd,
  Leading lambs by love beguiled.

4 Home, abroad, by mart or altar,
  Land, or sea, 'mid human kind,
May we, toiling, never falter,
  In the strength of Christ resigned.
      Ever trusting,
  Till the tearless land we find.

342 *The Dying Savior.* 8s, 7s & 4.

1 Hark! the voice of love and mercy
  Sounds aloud from Calvary;
See! it rends the rocks asunder,
  Shakes the earth, and vails the sky:
      "It is finished!"
  Hear the dying Savior cry.

2 "It is finished!" Oh, what pleasure
  Do these charming words afford!
Heavenly blessings, without measure,
  Flow to us through Christ the Lord:
      "It is finished!"
  Saints, the dying words record.

3 Tune your harps anew, ye seraphs;
  Join to sing the pleasing theme;
All in earth and heaven uniting,
  Join to praise Immanuel's name:
      Hallelujah!
  Glory to the bleeding Lamb!

Deliverance, Key C.   Oliphant, Key D.

1. Come, ye sinners, poor and needy, Weak and wounded, sick and sore,
D. C. He is a-ble, He is a-ble, He is willing, doubt no more.

Je-sus read-y stands to save you, Full of pit-y, love, and power.

343   *Jesus ready to Save.*   8s, 7s & 4s.

1 Come, ye sinners, poor and needy,
    Weak, and wounded, sick, and sore;
Jesus ready stands to save you,
    Full of pity, love, and power.
        He is able,
        He is willing, doubt no more.

2 Come, ye thirsty, come and welcome;
    God's free bounty glorify;
True belief and true repentance,
    Every grace that brings us nigh,—
        Without money
    Come to Jesus Christ and buy.

3 Come, ye weary, heavy laden,
    Lost and ruined by the fall,
If you tarry till you're better,
    You will never come at all.
        Not the righteous—
    Sinners, Jesus came to call.

4 Let not conscience make you linger,
    Nor of fitness fondly dream;
All the fitness he requireth
    Is to feel your need of him:
        This he gives you—
    'Tis the Spirit's rising beam.

344   *Glad Tidings.*   8s, 7s & 4.

1 Sinners, will you scorn the message
    Sent in mercy from above?
Every sentence, oh, how tender!
    Every line is full of love.
        Listen to it:
    Every line is full of love.

2 Hear the heralds of the gospel
    News from Zion's King proclaim:
"Pardon to each rebel sinner,
    Free forgiveness in his name."
        How important!
    "Free forgiveness in his name."

3 Tempted souls, they bring you succor;
    Fearful hearts, they quell your fears.
And, with news of consolation,
    Chase away the falling tears.
        Tender heralds!
    Chase away the falling tears.

4 Who hath our report believed?
    Who received the joyful word?
Who embraced the news of pardon
    Offered to you by the Lord?
        Can you slight it?
    Offered to you by the Lord?

Greenville, Key F.   Sicily, Key E.

1. Glad we welcome every brother With the love which Christ inspires,

As we gath-er round an-oth-er Of our au-nual council fires.

Duet.

Bless-ed Sav-ior, Blessed Savior, Fill our hearts with warm desires.

345 *Song of Welcome.* 8s, 7s & 4.

2 It has been our joy to meet you
Oft in scenes like this before;
Now with swelling hearts we greet you,
As we press your hands once more.
Heavenly Father,
On our heads thy blessing pour.

3 May our bosoms beat in union;
May our hearts be knit in love;
May the Spirit's blest communion
Teach us wisdom from above.
Thus our meeting
Shall to all a blessing prove.

4 And when all our happy meetings
Shall have ended here below,
May we each exchange our greetings,
Where the living waters flow,
And where Jesus
His own blessing shall bestow.

346 *Sacred Seasons.* 8s, 7s & 4s.

1 Welcome, days of solemn meeting;
Welcome, days of praise and prayer;
Far from worldly scenes retreating,
In your blessings we would share:
Sacred seasons,
In your blessings we would share.

2 Be thou near us, blessed Savior,
Still at morn and eve the same;
Give us faith that can not waver,
Kindle in us heaven's own flame:
Blessed Savior,
Kindle in us heaven's own flame.

3 When the fervent heart is glowing,
Holy Spirit, hear that prayer;
When that song of praise is flowing,
Let that song thine impress bear:
Holy Spirit,
Let that song thine impress bear.

Oliphant, Key D. Savior, like a Shepherd, Key E♭. Zion, Key D.

1. Je-sus! the ver-y thought of thee, With sweetness fills my breast;

But sweeter far, thy face to see, And in thy presence rest.

347   *Christ our only Joy.*   C. M.

2 No voice can sing, no heart can frame,
  Nor can the memory find,
A sweeter sound than Jesus' name,
  The Savior of mankind.

3 Oh, hope of every contrite heart,
  Oh, joy of all the meek,
To those who fall how kind thou art,
  How good to those who seek!

4 But what to those who find? Ah, this
  Nor tongue, nor pen, can show;
The love of Jesus, what it is,
  None but his loved ones know.

5 Jesus, our only joy be thou,
  As thou our prize wilt be;
Jesus, be thou our glory now,
  And through eternity.

348   *Retreat in Prayer.*   C. M.

1 Far from the world, O Lord, I flee,
  From strife and tumult far;
From scenes where Satan wages still
  His most successful war.

2 The calm retreat, the silent shade,
  With prayer and praise agree;
And seem by thy sweet bounty made
  For those who follow thee.

349   *Thirsting after God.*   C. M.

1 As pants the hart for cooling streams,
  When heated in the chase,
So longs my soul, O God, for thee,
  And thy refreshing grace.

2 For thee, my God, the living God,
  My thirsty soul doth pine;
Oh, when shall I behold thy face,
  Thou Majesty divine?

3 Why restless, why cast down, my soul?
  Trust God; who will employ
His aid for thee, and change these sighs
  To thankful hymns of joy.

350   *Rejoicing in God.*

1 Oh, render thanks and bless the Lord;
  Invoke his sacred name;
Acquaint the nations with his deeds,
  His matchless deeds proclaim.

2 Sing to his praise in lofty hymns
  His wondrous works rehearse;
Make them the theme of your discourse,
  And subject of your verse.

3 Rejoice in his almighty name,
  Alone to be adored;
And let their hearts o'erflow with joy
  That humbly seek the Lord.

Balerma, Key B♭.   Siloam, Key D.   Naomi, Key D.

By permission.

W. B. BRADBURY.

1. The Savior! oh, what endless charms Dwell in that blissful sound!

Its influence ev-ery fear disarms, And spreads delight around.

351 *Condescension of Christ.* C. M.

1 The Savior! oh, what endless charms
Dwell in that blissful sound!
Its influence ev'ry fear disarms,
And spreads delight around.

2 Here pardon, life, and joy divine
In rich profusion flow,
For guilty rebels, lost in sin,
And doomed to endless woe.

3 How rich the depths of love divine!
Of bliss, a boundless store!
Dear Savior, let me call thee mine;
I can not wish for more.

4 On thee alone my hope relies;
Beneath thy cross I fall,
My Lord, my life, my sacrifice,
My Savior and my all.

352 *Sanctuary Blessing.* C. M.

1 Dear Shepherd of thy people, here
Thy presence now display;
As thou hast given a place for prayer,
So give us hearts to pray.

2 Within these walls let holy peace
And love and concord dwell;
Here give the troubled conscience ease,
The wounded spirit heal.

3 The feeling heart, the melting eye,
The humble mind bestow;
And shine upon us from on high,
To make our graces grow.

4 May we in faith receive the word,
In faith present our prayers;
And in the presence of our Lord
Unbosom all our cares.

353 *The Savior's Invitation.* C. M.

1 The Savior calls; let every ear
Attend the heavenly sound;
Ye doubting souls, dismiss your fear;
Hope smiles reviving round.

2 For every thirsty, longing heart,
Here streams of bounty flow;
And life, and health, and bliss impart,
To banish mortal woe.

3 Ye sinners, come; 't is mercy's voice;
That gracious voice obey;
'T is Jesus calls to heavenly joys,
And can you yet delay?

4 Dear Savior, draw reluctant hearts;
To thee let sinners fly,
And take the bliss thy love imparts,
And drink, and never die.

Arlington, Key G.   Heber, Key C.   Ortonville, Key B♭.

FOUNTAIN. C. M.

Dr. L. Mason.

1. There is a fountain filled with blood, Drawn from Immanuel's veins;
And sinners, plunged beneath that flood,

Lose all their guilt - y stains, Lose all their guilt - y stains.

354 *Fountain for Sinners.* C. M.

2 The dying thief rejoiced to see
That fountain in his day;
And there may I, though vile as he,
Wash all my sins away.

3 Dear, dying Lamb, thy precious blood
Shall never lose its power.
Till all the ransomed church of God
Be saved, to sin no more.

4 E'er since, by faith, I saw the stream
Thy flowing wounds supply,
Redeeming love has been my theme,
And shall be till I die.

5 Then in a nobler, sweeter song
I'll sing thy power to save,
When this poor lisping, stammering tongue
Lies silent in the grave.

355 *Resolution.* C. M.

1 Come, humble sinner, in whose breast
A thousand thoughts revolve,
Come, with your guilt and fear oppressed,
And make this last resolve:

2 I'll go to Jesus, though my sin
Like mountains round me close;
I know his courts, I'll enter in,
Whatever may oppose.

356 *Rejoicing in the Gospel.* C. M.

1 Blest are the souls that hear and know
The gospel's joyful sound;
Peace shall attend the paths they go,
And light their steps surround.

2 Their joy shall bear their spirits up,
Through their Redeemer's name;
His righteousness exalts their hope,
Nor Satan dares condemn.

3 The Lord, our glory and defense,
Strength and salvation gives;
Israel, thy King forever reigns,
Thy God forever lives.

357 *Invitation.* C. M.

1 Come, humble souls, ye mourners, come,
And wipe away your tears;
Adieu to all your sad complaints,
Your sorrows and your fears.

2 Come, shout aloud the Father's grace,
And sing the Savior's love;
Soon shall you join the glorious theme
In loftier strains above.

3 Transporting hope! still on my soul
With radiant glories shine,
Till thou thyself art lost in joys
Immortal and divine.

Lucius, Key C.   Naomi, Key D.   Downs, Key E♭.

THANE. C. M.

1. There is a name I love to hear, I love to speak its worth;
It sounds like mu-sic in mine ear, The sweetest name on earth.
D. C. No saint on earth its worth can tell, No heart conceive how dear!

Chorus.

Je-sus! the name I love so well, The name I love to hear!

358   *The name I Love.*   C. M.

2 It tells me of a Savior's love,
Who died to set me free;
It tells me of his precious blood,
The sinner's perfect plea.

3 It tells of one whose loving heart
Can feel my deepest woe,
Who in my sorrow bears a part
That none can bear below.

4 It bids my trembling heart rejoice,
It dries each rising tear;
It tells me, in a "still small voice,"
To trust and never fear.

359   *Prayer for Sincerity.*   C. M.

1 Lord, when we bow before thy throne,
And our confessions pour,
Oh, may we feel the sins we own,
And hate what we deplore!

CHO. Let faith each meek petition fill,
And waft it to the skies,
And teach our hearts 't is goodness still
That grants it or denies.

2 Our contrite spirits, pitying, see;
True penitence impart;
And let a healing ray from thee
Beam hope on every heart.

360   *Access to Christ.*   C. M.

1 I heard the voice of Jesus say,
"Come unto me and rest;
Lay down, thou weary one, lay down
Thy head upon my breast!"
I came to Jesus as I was,
Weary, and worn, and sad;
I found in him a resting-place,
And he hath made me glad.

2 I heard the voice of Jesus say,
"Behold, I freely give
The living water, thirsty one,
Stoop down, and drink, and live!"
I came to Jesus, and I drank
Of that life-giving stream;
My thirst was quenched, my soul revived,
And now I live in him.

3 I heard the voice of Jesus say,
"I am this dark world's light;
Look unto me, thy morn shall rise
And all thy day be bright!"
I looked to Jesus, and I found
In him my Star, my Sun;
And in that light of life I'll walk,
Till all my journey's done.

Balerma, Key Bb.   Heber, Key C.   Farwell, Key Eb.

HANDEL.

1. Come, let us lift our joyful eyes Up to the courts a-bove, And

smile to see our Father there, Upon a throne of love, Upon a throne of love.

---

361   *Access to God by a Mediator.*   C. M.

2 Come, let us bow before his feet,
     And venture near the Lord;
No fiery cherub guards his seat,
     Nor double-flaming sword.

3 The peaceful gates of heavenly bliss
     Are opened by the Son;
High let us raise our notes of praise,
     And reach th' almighty throne.

4 To thee ten thousand thanks we bring.
     Great Advocate on high,
And glory to th' eternal King,
     Who lays his anger by.

362   *The Lord my Portion.*   C. M.

1 Eternal Source of joys divine,
     To thee my soul aspires;
Oh! could I say: The Lord is mine!
     'T is all my soul desires.

2 My hope, my trust, my life, my Lord,
     Assure me of thy love;
Oh, speak the kind, transporting word,
     And bid my fears remove!

3 Then shall my thankful powers rejoice,
     And triumph in my God,
Till heavenly rapture tune my voice,
     To spread thy praise abroad.

363   *For laying a Corner-stone.*   C. M.

1 Builder of mighty worlds on worlds,
     How poor the house must be,
That with our human, sinful hands,
     We may erect for thee.

2 O Christ, thou art our Corner-stone,
     On thee our hopes are built;
Thou art our Lord, our light, our life,
     Our sacrifice for guilt.

3 In thy blest name we gather here,
     And consecrate the ground:
The walls that on this rock shall rise
     Thy praises shall resound.

4 May many a soul, from death redeemed,
     In heavenly regions fair,
With joy exclaim, " I learned the path
     To God and glory there."

364   *Perseverance.*   C. M.

1 Firm as the earth thy gospel stands,
     My Lord, my hope, my trust;
If I am found in Jesus' hands,
     My soul can ne'er be lost.

2 His honor is engaged to save
     The meanest of his sheep;
All whom his heavenly Father gave,
     His hands securely keep.

Downs, Key E♭.   Farwell, Key E♭.   Believe, Key G.

By permission.

WM. B. BRADBURY.

1. Ye va-liant sol-diers of the cross, Ye hap-py, pray-ing band,
Tho' in this world ye suffer loss, You'll reach fair Canaan's land;

Chorus.

Let us nev-er mind the scoffs nor the frowns of the world,

For we all have the cross to bear, It will only make the crown the

bright-er to shine, When we have the crown to wear.

365 *Forsaking earthly Pleasures.* C. M.

1 Ye valiant soldiers of the cross,
Ye happy, praying band,
Though in this world you suffer loss,
You'll reach fair Canaan's land.
Let us never mind, etc.

2 All earthly pleasures we'll forsake,
When heaven appears in view,
In Jesus' strength we'll undertake
To fight our passage through.

3 Oh, what a glorious shout there'll be,
When we arrive at home!
Our friends and Jesus we shall see,
And God shall say "Well done!"

366 *Christian Soldier.* C. M.

1 Am I a soldier of the cross,
A follower of the Lamb;
And shall I fear to own his cause,
Or blush to speak his name?
Let us never mind, etc.

2 Must I be carried to the skies
On flowery beds of ease,
While others fought to win the prize,
And sailed through bloody seas?

3 Are there no foes for me to face?
Must I not stem the flood?
Is this vile world a friend to grace,
To help me on to God?

Lanesboro, Key C.   Arlington, Key G.   Dedham, Key A.

I WILL SING FOR JESUS.

By permission.   PHILIP PHILLIPS.

1. I will sing for Je - sus, With his blood he bought me; And

all a - long my pilgrim way His lov - ing hand has brought me.

Chorus.

Oh, help me sing for Je - sus! Help me tell the sto - ry Of

him who did re - deem us, The Lord of life and glo - ry.

367   *Singing for Jesus.*

1 I will sing for Jesus.
  With his blood he bought me;
And all along my pilgrim way,
  His loving hand has brought me.

2 Can there overtake me
  Any dark disaster,
While I sing for Jesus,
  My blessed, blessed Master?

3 I will sing for Jesus,
  His name alone prevailing,
Shall be my sweetest music
  When heart and flesh are failing.

4 Still I'll sing for Jesus.
  Oh, how will I adore him!
Among the cloud of witnesses
  Who cast their crowns before him.

By permission.

S. J. VAIL.

Solo.

1. Where do you journey, my brother, Oh where do you journey, I pray?

Where do you journey, my sis - ter? For stormy and dark is the way.

Duet.

We 're journeying onward to Canaan, Thro' suff'ring and trial and care,

Ritard.

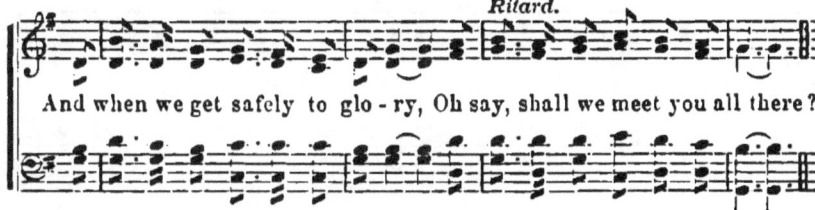

And when we get safely to glo - ry, Oh, say, shall we meet you all there?

Chorus.

Oh say, shall we meet you all there? Oh say, shall we meet you all there?

Ritard.

And when we get safely to glo - ry, Oh say, shall we meet you all there?

368   *Traveling to Heaven.*

2 What is your mission, my brother?
  What is your mission below?
What is your mission, my sister,
  As journeying onward you go?
Our mission is practicing mercy,
  Sweet charity, patience, and love,
And following the footsteps of Jesus,
  That lead to the mansions above.

3 Oh, yes, you will meet us, my brother,
  God helping our weakness and sin;
Bearing the cross, we, my sister,
  The crown will endeavor to win.
We 'll walk through the vale and the shadow,
  Thro' suff'ring, and trial, and care;
And when you get safely to glory,
  You 'll meet, yes, you 'll meet us all there!

10

JESUS PAID IT ALL.

W. B. BRADBURY.

1. Naught of mer-it or of price Re-mains to jus-tice due;

Je - sus died, and paid it all— Yes, all the debt I owe.

Chorus.

Je - sus paid it all, All the debt I owe,

Je - sus paid it, paid it all,

Je - sus died and paid it all—Yes, all the debt I owe.

369   *Jesus paid it All.*

2 When he, from his lofty throne,
  Stoop'd down to do and die,
Every thing was fully done;
  " 'T is finished!" was his cry.

3 Weary not, oh toiling one,
  Whate'er thy conflict be,
Work for him with cheerful heart,
  Who suffered all for thee.

4 Clinging to the Savior's cross,
  Look up by simple faith,
Praise him for the pardoning love
  That saves from endless death.

5 Bring a willing sacrifice,
  Thy soul, to Jesus' feet;
Stand in him, in him alone,
  All glorious and complete.

W. H. DOANE.

Slow and gliding.

1. On a fear-ful brink I stood, By sin con-demned to die;

Threat'ning clouds above me rolled; I knew not where to fly.

Chorus.

Saved by grace a-lone, This my song shall be:

Je-sus now the debt has paid, And Je-sus died for me.

370   *Sinner Pardoned.*

2 While my guilt before me rose,
  In all its dark array,
Justice claimed, with stern demand,
  The debt I could not pay.

3 Trembling, at the cross I knelt,
  And heard my Savior's voice:
" All is cancel'd, look and live,
  In me, thy God, rejoice."

4 Boundless mercy, vast and deep,
  A mighty ocean wide,
Lost in wonder, filled with praise,
  I plunge beneath the tide.

5 Hope celestial plumes her wings,
  And lifts my thoughts above;
Now the eye of faith is clear,
  And all my life is love.

1. My country, 't is of thee, Sweet land of liberty, Of thee I sing; Land where my

fathers died, Land of the pilgrim's pride, From every mountain side Let freedom ring.

371   *National Hymn.*   6s & 4s.

1 My country, 't is of thee,
  Sweet land of liberty,
    Of thee I sing;
  Land where my fathers died,
  Land of the pilgrim's pride,
  From ev'ry mountain side
    Let freedom ring.

2 My native country! thee,
  Land of the noble free,
    Thy name I love;
  I love thy rocks and rills,
  Thy woods and templ'd hills,
  My heart with rapture thrills
    Like that above.

3 Let music swell the breeze,
  And ring from all the trees
    Sweet freedom's song!
  Let mortal tongues awake;
  Let all that breathe partake;
  Let rocks their silence break:
    The sound prolong.

4 Our father's God! to thee,
  Author of liberty,
    To thee we sing:
  Long may our land be bright
  With freedom's holy light;
  Protect us by thy might,
    Great God, our King!

372   *On to the Battle-field.*   6s & 4s.

1 On to the battle-field,
  There sword and spear to wield,
    Right onward press;
  Field where our fathers fought,
  Where martyr spirits wrought,
  It shall by blood be bought,
    Lord Jesus, bless.

2 Lift up the banner high,
  Ring out the battle cry,
    Jesus, our Lord!
  To him we stand or fall,
  Him we our Captain call,
  Round him we rally all,
    In glad accord.

3 Strong in his strength we fight,
  Only for truth and right,
    Careless of fame;
  By all his pains and throes,
  By all his griefs and woes,
  Down with our Leader's foes,
    Up with his name.

4 Fling out our banner's folds,
  Stay up the hand that holds,
    Ours is the day!
  Shout till the echoes ring,
  Till rocks and rivers sing
  Praises to Christ, our King,
    Praises for aye.

373 *Soldiers of Christ.* 6s & 4s.

1 Soldiers of Christ are we,
Marching to victory—
Marching to heaven!
In his bright armor dressed,
His cross our chosen crest,
And for our food and rest
His word is given.

2 Though foes our paths surround,
Though toils and cares abound,
Onward we tread!
We hear our Lord's command,
We grasp each shining brand,
And, like a banner grand,
Hope waves o'erhead.

3 Thou blessed Prince of Peace!
Give thou our strength increase,
Our courage raise.
And when our course is run,
Warfare and labor done,
To thee our hearts, in one,
Shall give thee praise.

4 Soldiers of Christ are we:
Light, Love, and Liberty,
Our battle call!
Till truth shall win the day,
Till right shall gain the sway,
Till sin is driven away,
We fight or fall.

374 *"God save the State."* 6s & 4s.

1 God bless our native land!
Firm may she ever stand,
Through storm and night;
When the wild tempests rave,
Ruler of winds and wave,
Do thou our country save
By thy great might.

2 For her our prayer shall rise
To God, above the skies;
On him we wait:
Thou who art ever nigh,
Guarding with watchful eye,
To thee aloud we cry,
God save the State!

375 *Worthy is the Lamb.* 6s & 4s.

1 Come, all ye saints of God;
Wide through the earth abroad
Spread Jesus' fame;
Tell what his love has done;
Trust in his name alone;
Shout to his lofty throne,
"Worthy the Lamb."

2 Hence, gloomy doubts and fears!
Dry up your mournful tears;
Swell the glad theme;
Praise ye our gracious King;
Strike each melodious string;
Join heart and voice to sing, ·
"Worthy the Lamb!"

3 Hark! how the choirs above
Filled with the Savior's love,
Dwell on his name!
There, too, may we be found,
With light and glory crowned,
While all the heavens resound,
"Worthy the Lamb!"

376 *Worthy the Lamb.* 6s & 4s.

1 Glory to God on high!
Let heaven and earth reply;
Praise ye his name;
His love and grace adore,
Who all our sorrows bore,
And sing for evermore,
"Worthy the Lamb!"

2 Ye who surround the throne,
Join cheerfully in one,
Praising his name:
Ye who have felt his blood
Sealing your peace with God,
Sound his dear name abroad,—
"Worthy the Lamb!"

3 Soon must we change our place;
Yet will we never cease
Praising his name:
To him our songs we'll bring,
Hail him our gracious King,
And through all ages sing,
"Worthy the Lamb!"

Dr. LOWELL MASON.

1. I'm but a traveler here, Heav'n is my home;
Earth is a desert drear, Heav'n is my home; } Danger and sorrow stand

Round me on ev'ry hand, Heav'n is my fatherland, Heav'n is my home.

377   *Heaven is my Home.*   6s & 4s.

2 What tho' the tempest rage,
  Heav'n is my home;
Short is my pilgrimage,
  Heav'n is my home;
Time's cold and wintry blast
Soon will be over past,
I shall reach home at last,
  Heav'n is my home.

3 There at my Savior's side,
  Heav'n is my home,
I shall be glorified,
  Heav'n is my home;
There are the good and blest,
Those I loved most and best,
There, too, I soon shall rest,
  Heav'n is my home.

ENTREATY.   6s & 4s.

Dr. T. HASTINGS.

1. Child of sin and sorrow, Filled with dismay;
Wait not for to-morrow, Yield thee to-day. } Heaven bids thee come While yet there's room,
D.C. Child of sin and sorrow, Hear, and obey.

378   *Entreaty.*   6s & 4s.

2 Child of sin and sorrow!
  Why wilt thou die?
Come while thou canst borrow
  Help from on high:
  Grieve not that love
  Which from above,
Child of sin and sorrow,
  Would bring thee nigh.

3 Child of sin and sorrow!
  Thy moments glide,
Like the flitting arrow,
  Or rushing tide;
  Ere time is o'er,
  Heaven's grace implore;
Child of sin and sorrow,
  In Christ confide.

1. More love to thee, O Christ! More love to thee. Hear thou the

prayer I make, On bended knee; This is my earnest plea,

More love, O Christ, to thee, More love to thee, More love to thee.

379 *More Love to thee, O Christ.* 6s & 4s.

1 More love to thee, O Christ,
    More love to thee!
  Hear thou the prayer I make,
    On bended knee;
  This is my earnest plea:
  More love, O Christ, to thee,
    More love to thee!

2 Once earthly joy I craved,
    Sought peace and rest,
  Now thee alone I seek,
    Give what is best:
  This all my prayer shall be,
  More love, O Christ, to thee,
    More love to thee!

3 Let sorrow do its work,
    Send grief and pain,
  Sweet are thy messengers,
    Sweet their refrain,
  When they can sing with me,—
  More love, O Christ, to thee,
    More love to thee!

4 Then shall my latest breath
    Whisper thy praise;
  This be the parting cry
    My heart shall raise,
  This still its prayer shall be:
  More love, O Christ, to thee,
    More love to thee!

Bethany, Key G.   Maclean, Key A♭.

1. I'm a pilgrim, and I'm a stranger, I can tarry, I can tarry but a night;

Do not detain me, for I am going To where the fountains are ever flowing.

380 *A Pilgrim and Stranger.*

2 There the glory is ever shining;
I am longing, I am longing for the sight;
Here in this country so dark and dreary,
I have been wand'ring, forlorn and weary;
I'm a pilgrim, and I'm a stranger,
I can tarry, I can tarry but a night.

3 There's the city to which I journey;
My Redeemer, my Redeemer is its light;
There is no sorrow, nor any sighing,
There is no sin there, nor any dying.
I'm a pilgrim, and I'm a stranger,
I can tarry, I can tarry but a night.

GENTLE SHEPHERD.

GERMAN.

1. Gentle Shepherd, grant thy blessing On us now, While before thy throne we bow.

381 *Prayer to the Shepherd.*

1 Gentle Shepherd, grant thy blessing
    On us now,
While before thy throne we bow.

2 Gentle Shepherd, we thy children
    Seek thy face:
Give us now thy heavenly grace.

3 Gentle Shepherd, bless the children
    Of this fold:
Cleanse the hearts of young and old.

4 Gentle Shepherd, when life's ended,
    Take us home,
Never from thy side to roam.

By permission.   Rev. W. McDonald.

1. In the Christian's home in glory, There remains a land of rest;

There my Savior's gone be-fore me, To ful-fill my soul's request.

Chorus.

{ There is   rest   for the wea-ry, There is rest for the wea-ry,
{ On   the oth-er   side of Jor-dan, In   the sweet fields of E - den,

There is   rest   for the wea-ry, There is rest for   you. }
Where the tree of life is blooming, There is rest for   you. }

382   *Rest for the Weary.*

2 He is fitting up my mansion,
    Which eternally shall stand;
For my stay shall not be transient,
    In that holy, happy land.

3 Pain nor sickness ne'er shall enter,
    Grief nor woe my lot shall share;
But in that celestial center
    I a crown of life shall wear.

4 Death itself shall then be vanquished,
    And his sting shall be withdrawn;
Shout for gladness, oh ye ransomed,
    Hail with joy the rising morn.

5 Sing, oh sing, ye heirs of glory!
    Shout your triumph as you go!
Zion's gate will open for you,
    You shall find an entrance through.

1. This is not my place of resting—Mine's a cit-y yet to come;

On-ward to it I am hast-ing—On to my e-ter-nal home.
D. S. Nev-er-more be sad or wea-ry, Nev-er-more to sin a-gain.

Chorus.

Nev-er-more, nev-er-more, Nev-er-more to sin a-gain;

383   *Nevermore.*   8s & 7s.

1 This is not my place of resting—
  Mine's a city yet to come;
Onward to it I am hasting—
  On to my eternal home.

2 In it all is light and glory;
  O'er it shines a nightless day;
Every trace of sin's sad story,
  All the curse, hath passed away.

3 There the Lamb, our Shepherd, leads us
  By the streams of life along;
On the freshest pastures feeds us,
  Turns our sighing into song.

4 Soon we pass this desert dreary,
  Soon we bid farewell to pain;
Never more are sad and weary,
  Never, never sin again.

384   *Rest for the Burdened.*   8s & 7s.

1 Hear the Savior's precious promise,
  Heavy-laden, grief oppressed:
"Come, and in my bosom tarry,
  Come, and I will give you rest."

2 I am weary, Savior, sinning,
  Grieving love and care divine:
I would feel thy Spirit winning,
  Molding all my will to thine.

3 I am weary clasping treasures,
  But to see their brightness wane;
Weary pruning earthly pleasures,
  But to garner fruits of pain.

4 I am weary, Savior, weary;
  Tempest-tossed, I seek thy breast;
Tenderly thy weak one carry
  To thy everlasting rest.

By permission.
A. J. ABBEY.

1. By faith I view my Sa-vior bleeding, On the tree, On the tree!

To ev - ery na-tion he is crying, "Look to me! Look to me!"
D. S. Hark! hark! what precious words I hear, "Mercy's free, Mercy's free."

Chorus.

He bids the guilty now draw near, Repent, believe, dismiss their fear;

385   *Mercy's Free.*   .

1 By faith I view my Savior bleeding
    On the tree;
To every nation he is crying,
    "Look to me!"
    He bids the guilty now draw near,
    Repent, believe, dismiss their fear;
    Hark! hark! what precious words I hear,
    "Mercy's free!"

2 Did Christ, when I was sin pursuing,
    Pity me?
And did he snatch my soul from ruin?
    Can it be?
    Oh, yes, he did salvation bring;
    He is my Prophet, Priest, and King;
    And now my happy soul can sing,
    "Mercy's free!"

3 Jesus my weary soul refreshes,
    Mercy's free!
And every moment Christ is precious
    Unto me.
    None can describe the bliss I prove,
    While through this wilderness I rove;
    All may enjoy the Savior's love,
    Mercy's free!

4 Long as I live, I'll still be crying,
    "Mercy's free!"
And this shall be my theme when dying,
    "Mercy's free!"
    And when the vale of death I've passed,
    When safe beyond the stormy blast,
    I'll sing while endless ages last,
    "Mercy's free!"

L. MASON.

1. My son, know thou the Lord; Thy fa-thers' God o-bey;

Seek his pro-tect-ing care by night, His guardian hand by day.

386　　*Parental Entreaty.*　　S. M.

1 My son, know thou the Lord;
　Thy fathers' God obey;
Seek his protecting care by night,
　His guardian hand by day.

2 Call, while he may be found;
　Oh, seek him while he's near;
Serve him with all thy heart and mind,
　And worship him with fear.

3 If thou wilt seek his face,
　His ear will hear thy cry;
Then shalt thou find his mercy sure,
　His grace forever nigh.

4 But if thou leave thy God,
　Nor choose the path to heaven,
Then shalt thou perish in thy sins,
　And never be forgiven.

387　　*Death of an aged Minister.*　　S. M.

1 "Servant of God, well done;
　Rest from thy loved employ:
The battle fought, the victory won,
　Enter thy Master's joy."

2 Tranquil amid alarms,
　It found him on the field,
A veteran slumbering on his arms,
　Beneath his red-cross shield.

3 The pains of death are past;
　Labor and sorrow cease;
And, life's long warfare closed at last,
　His soul is found in peace.

4 Soldier of Christ, well done;
　Praise be thy new employ;
And, while eternal ages run,
　Rest in thy Savior's joy.

388　　*Temperance.*　　S. M.

1 Mourn for the tarnished gem—
　For reason's light divine,
Quenched from the soul's bright diadem,
　Where God hath bid it shine.

2 Mourn for the ruined soul—
　Eternal life and light
Lost by the fiery, maddening bowl,
　And turned to hopeless night.

3 Mourn for the lost; but call,
　Call to the strong, the free;
Rouse them to shun that dreadful fall,
　And to the refuge flee.

4 Mourn for the lost; but pray,
　Pray to our God above,
To break the fell destroyer's sway,
　And show his saving love.

Olmutz, Key Bb.　Boylston, Key C.　Fond, Key D.

1. In Je - sus' name we come; Thy Spir - it, Lord, im-part:

A fore-taste of our heavenly home Be-stow on ev - ery heart.

389 *A Prayer.* S. M.

2 With gratitude and praise,
  With fearless, hopeful love,
Our faith looks up, and trusting, says:
  We will no longer rove.

3 As at thine altar, here,
  We take our solemn vows,
Give us the penitential tear
  Which blesses as it flows.

4 Give us the needful strength
  Life's journey to pursue;
Patience to suffer, till, at length,
  Thine heavenly rest we view.

5 So may we labor, fight,
  Endure, believe, and pray,
Until the darkness of our night
  Vanish in endless day.

390 *Devout Gratitude.* S. M.

1 While I thy mercies trace,
  Thy love enwraps my soul;
Naught can exceed thy sovereign grace
  In Christ, so free and full!

2 To thee I owe my life,
  Its breath each moment given,
My home, my friends, freedom from strife,
  All joys this side of heaven!

3 Thou givest me thy word
  My steps to guide aright;
A place among thy people, Lord,
  And strength for thee to fight!

4 Thy Spirit's witness, too,
  Accredits me as thine;
And when I stray doth gently woo
  This wandering heart of mine!

5 To all these mercies add
  A grateful heart, O Lord!
To sing thy praises, loud and glad,
  And all thy gifts record.

391 *For closing Prayer Meetings.* S. M.

1 Lord, at this closing hour,
  Establish every heart
Upon thy word of truth and power,
  To keep us when we part.

2 Peace to our brethren give;
  Fill all our hearts with love;
In faith and patience may we live,
  And seek our rest above.

3 Through changes, bright or drear,
  We would thy will pursue,
And toil to spread thy kingdom here,
  Till we its glory view.

Dennis, Key G.   State Street, Key Bb.   Tioga, Key Bb.

MORNINGTON.

1. How beauteous are their feet Who stand on Zi - on's hill;

Who bring salva - tion on their tongues, And words of peace reveal!

392   *The Gospel Ministry.*   S. M.

1 How beauteous are their feet
  Who stand on Zion's hill;
Who bring salvation on their tongues,
  And words of peace reveal!

2 How charming is their voice!
  How sweet their tidings are!—
"Zion, behold thy Savior King;
  He reigns and triumphs here!"

3 How happy are our ears,
  That hear this joyful sound!
Which kings and prophets waited for,
  And sought, but never found!

4 How blessed are our eyes,
  That see this heavenly light!
Prophets and kings desired it long,
  But died without the sight.

5 The watchmen join their voice,
  And tuneful notes employ;
Jerusalem breaks forth in songs,
  And deserts learn the joy.

6 The Lord makes bare his arm
  Through all the earth abroad;
Let every nation now behold
  Their Savior and their God.

393   *Season for Prayer.*   S. M.

1 Come at the morning hour,
  Come, let us kneel and pray;
Prayer is the Christian pilgrim's staff
  To walk with God all day.

2 At noon, beneath the Rock
  Of Ages, rest and pray;
Sweet is that shelter from the sun
  In the weary heat of day.

3 At evening, in thy home,
  Around its altar, pray;
And finding there the house of God,
  With heaven then close the day.

394   *Heavenly Rest.*   S. M.

1 As strangers here below,
  With various woes oppressed,
We must through tribulation go
  To our eternal rest.

2 Thus Christ, our glorious Head,
  Ascended to his throne;
Why should his servants fear to tread
  The way their Lord hath gone?

3 The path to glory lies
  Through conflict and distress;
But joyful we at length shall rise,
  The kingdom to possess.

Pond, Key D.   Rowland, Key E♭.   St. Thomas, Key G.

Gently.

1. With grateful hearts, we raise An al - tar, Lord, to thee;

Deign to ac-cept our fee - ble praise, Thy face grant us to see.

395 *Dedication Hymn.* H. M.

2 Our Father and our Friend,
We, sinners saved by grace,
Entreat that thou wilt condescend
To glorify this place.

3 Dear Savior, fill each heart
With faith, and hope, and love;
Thy blessing graciously impart,
Thy presence ne'er remove.

4 Blest Spirit, hover o'er
This consecrated ground;
Upon our souls thine influence pour,
Thy peace diffuse around.

5 Our life and all our powers
We dedicate anew;
Lord, make the swiftly-passing hours
Witness that we are true.

6 And when life's work is done,
Its conflicts o'er at last,
Give us to meet where every one
The joys of heaven shall taste.

396 *Sow beside all Waters.* S. M.

1 Sow in the morn thy seed;
At eve hold not thy hand;
To doubt and fear give thou no heed;
Broadcast it o'er the land.

2 Thou canst not toil in vain;
Cold, heat, and moist, and dry,
Shall foster and mature the grain
For garners in the sky.

3 Thence, when the glorious end,
The day of God, shall come,
The angel reapers shall descend,
And heaven cry, "Harvest home!"

397 *The Bible the Guide.* S. M.

1 With humble heart and tongue,
My God, to thee I pray:
Oh, bring me now, while I am young,
To thee, the living way.

2 My heart, to folly prone,
Renew by power divine;
Unite it to thyself alone,
And make me wholly thine.

3 Oh, let thy word of grace
My warmest thoughts employ;
Be this, through all my following days,
My treasure and my joy.

4 To what thy laws impart
Be my whole soul inclined;
Oh, let them dwell within my heart,
And sanctify my mind.

Laban, Key D.   Thatcher, Key E♭.   State Street, Key B♭.

HUNTINGTON. S. M.

T. E. PERKINS.

1. When, overwhelmed with grief, My heart within me dies,

Helpless, and far from all re-lief, To heaven I lift mine eyes.

398 *Comfort in God.* S. M.

1 When, overwhelmed with grief,
  My heart within me dies,
Helpless, and far from all relief,
  To heaven I lift mine eyes.

2 Oh, lead me to the Rock
  That's high above my head,
And make the covert of thy wings
  My shelter and my shade.

3 Within thy presence, Lord,
  Forever I'll abide;
Thou art the tower of my defense,
  The refuge where I hide.

399 *Sanctifying Influence.* S. M.

1 Come, Holy Spirit, come;
  Let thy bright beams arise;
Dispel the sorrow from our minds,
  The darkness from our eyes.

2 Convince us all of sin;
  Then lead to Jesus' blood,
And to our wondering view reveal
  The mercies of our God.

3 Revive our drooping faith,
  Our doubts and fears remove,
And kindle in our breasts the flame
  Of never-dying love.

4 'T is thine to cleanse the heart,
  To sanctify the soul,
To pour fresh life in every part,
  And new create the whole.

5 Dwell, Spirit, in our hearts;
  Our minds from bondage free;
Then shall we know, and praise, and love
  The Father, Son, and thee.

400 *Ingratitude Deplored.* S. M.

1 Is this the kind return?
  Are these the thanks we owe?
Thus to abuse eternal love,
  Whence all our blessings flow?

2 To what a stubborn frame
  Has sin reduced our mind!
What strange, rebellious wretches we,
  And God as strangely kind!

3 Turn, turn us, mighty God,
  And mold our souls afresh;
Break, sovereign grace, these hearts of stone,
  And give us hearts of flesh.

4 Let past ingratitude
  Provoke our weeping eyes;
And hourly, as new mercies fall,
  Let hourly thanks arise.

Olmutz, Key B♭.   Crowell, Key C.   Tioga, Key B♭.

1. The day is past and gone, The eve-ning shades ap-pear;

Oh, may we all re-mem-ber well, The night of death draws near.

401 *Evening Hymn.* S. M.

1 The day is past and gone,
The evening shades appear;
Oh, may we all remember well
The night of death draws near.

2 We lay our garments by,
Upon our beds to rest;
So death will soon disrobe us all
Of what we here possess.

3 Lord, keep us safe this night,
Secure from all our fears;
May angels guard us while we sleep,
Till morning light appears.

4 And when we early rise,
And view th' unwearied sun,
May we set out to win the prize,
And after glory run.

5 And when our days are past,
And we from time remove,
Oh, may we in thy bosom rest,
The bosom of thy love.

402 *Evening Devotion.* S. M.

1 Another day is past,
The hours forever fled,
And time is bearing us away,
To mingle with the dead.

2 Our minds in perfect peace
Our Father's care shall keep;
We yield to gentle slumber now,
For thou canst never sleep.

3 How blessed, Lord, are they
On thee securely stayed!
Nor shall they be in life alarmed,
Nor be in death dismayed.

403 *Flight of Time.* S. M.

1 To-morrow, Lord, is thine,
Lodged in thy sovereign hand;
And if its sun arise and shine,
It shines by thy command.

2 The present moment flies,
And bears our life away;
Oh, make thy servants truly wise,
That they may live to-day.

3 Since on this fleeting hour
Eternity is hung,
Awake, by thine almighty power,
The aged and the young.

4 To Jesus may we fly,
Swift as the morning light,
Lest life's young, golden beams should die
In sudden, endless night.

Dover, Key G. Boylston, Key C. Mornington, Key E♭.
11

1. And are we yet a-live, And see each oth-er's face?

Glo-ry and praise to Je-sus give, For his re-deem-ing grace.

404   *Meeting after Absence.*   S. M.

1 And are we yet alive,
   And see each other's face?
Glory and praise to Jesus give
   For his redeeming grace.

2 Preserved by power divine
   To full salvation here,
Again in Jesus' praise we join,
   And in his sight appear.

3 What troubles have we seen!
   What conflicts have we past!
Fightings without, and fears within,
   Since we assembled last!

4 But out of all the Lord
   Hath brought us by his love;
And still he doth his help afford,
   And hides our life above.

5 Then let us make our boast
   Of his redeeming power,
Which saves us to the uttermost,
   Till we can sin no more.

6 Let us take up the cross,
   Till we the crown obtain;
And gladly reckon all things loss,
   So we may Jesus gain.

405   *Laborers in the Vineyard.*   S. M.

1 And let our bodies part,
   To diff'rent climes repair;
Still ever, ever join'd in heart
   The friends of Jesus are.

2 Oh, let us still proceed
   In Jesus' work below;
And, foll'wing our triumphant Head,
   To further conquests go.

3 The vineyard of the Lord
   Before his laborers lies;
And lo! we see the vast reward
   Which waits us in the skies.

4 Oh, let our heart and mind
   Continually ascend,
That haven of repose to find,
   Where all our labors end;

5 Where all our toils are o'er,
   Our suff'ring and our pain:
Who meet on that eternal shore
   Shall never part again.

406   *Doxology.*   S. M.

1 Ye angels 'round the throne,
   And saints that dwell below,
Adore the Father, love the Son,
   And bless the Spirit too.

Boylston, Key C.   Olmutz, Key B♭.   Dennis, Key G.

D. READ.

1. Welcome, sweet day of rest, That saw the Lord a-rise; Wel-come to this re-viv-ing breast, And these rejoicing eyes!

407 *The Sabbath Welcomed.* S. M.

2 The King himself comes near,
And feasts his saints to-day;
Here we may sit, and see him here,
And love, and praise, and pray.

3 One day in such a place,
Where thou, my God, art seen,
Is sweeter than ten thousand days
Of pleasurable sin.

4 My willing soul would stay
In such a frame as this,
And sit and sing herself away
To everlasting bliss.

408 *The perfect Word.* S. M.

1 O Lord, thy perfect word
Directs our steps aright,
Nor can all other books afford
Such profit and delight!

2 Celestial beams it sheds
To cheer this vale below;
To distant lands its glory spreads,
And streams of mercy flow.

3 True wisdom it imparts,
Commands our hope and fear;
Oh, may we hide it in our hearts,
And feel its influence there.

409 *Increase from God.* S. M.

1 Lord, if at thy command,
The word of life we sow,
Watered by thy Almighty hand,
The seed shall surely grow.

2 Now, then, the ceaseless shower
Of gospel blessing send,
And let the soul-converting power
Thy laborers attend.

410 *Jesus Enthroned.* S. M.

1 Enthroned is Jesus now,
Upon his heavenly seat;
The kingly crown is on his brow,
The saints are at his feet.

2 In shining white they stand,
A great and countless throng;
A palmy scepter in each hand,
On every lip a song.

3 They sing the Lamb of God,
Once slain on earth for them;
The Lamb through whose atoning blood
Each wears his diadem.

4 Thy grace, O Holy Ghost,
Thy blessed help supply,
That we may join that radiant host,
Triumphant in the sky.

Dover, Key E♭. Silver Street, Key C. Laban, Key D.

Spirited.

1. In the har-vest field there is work to do, For the
2. Crowd the gar-ner well with the sheaves all bright, Let the

grain is ripe, and the reapers few, And the Master's voice bids the
song be glad, and the heart be light, Fill the precious hours, ere the

work-ers true, Heed the call that he gives to-day.
shades of night Take the place of the gold-en day.

Chorus.

Labor on,   Labor on,   Keep the bright reward in view; 'T is the

Labor on,   Labor on,

Savior's command, He will strength renew, Labor on till the close of day.

411

3 In the gleaner's path may be rich reward,
Though the time seems long, and the labor hard;
For the Master's joy, with his chosen shared,
   Drives the gloom from the darkest day.

4 Lo! the Harvest Home in the realms above
Shall be gained by each who has toiled and strove,
When the Master's voice, in sweet words of love,
   Calls away to eternal day.

PLANTING SHARON'S ROSE.

JAS. M. NORTH.

1. Lord, thou callest for the workers, Glad we come at thy command;

Give us each the worker's out-fit, Loving heart and ready hand.
In the virgin soul of childhood, Planting Sharon's fadeless Rose.

End.

Great the honor, sweet the du-ty, That thy love on us be-stows,

D. S.

412   *Planting Sharon's Rose.*   8s & 7s.

1 Lord, thou callest for the workers,
  Glad we come at thy command;
Give us each the worker's outfit,
  Loving heart and ready hand.
Great the honor, sweet the duty
  That thy love on us bestows,
In the virgin soul of childhood,
  Planting Sharon's fadeless Rose!

2 Bless our labors, God of heaven;
  Aid thy laborers, Lord of earth;
Oh, 't is hard to set our garden
  With the plant of priceless worth!
Patient all the day we labor,
  Still at night the tempter sows
Tares of sin, where we had planted
  Sharon's fair and fadeless Rose!

3 Ours is toil that knows no season;
  Day and night to us are one;
Winter with us blooms as summer,
  Ours is an eternal sun.
So when heat of summer scorches,
  And when storm of winter blows,
Still we toil within our garden,
  Planting Sharon's fadeless Rose.

4 Wake, oh North-wind! come, oh South-wind!
  O'er our garden softly blow;
Bid the Rose's sacred perfume
  From our tender plants to flow.
Come, Beloved, to thy garden;
  All its sweets to thee it owes;
Shed thy holy fragrance o'er us,
  Sharon's fair and fadeless Rose!

Rev. R. Lowry.

1. { 'Mid Christian hosannas, O'er conquering banners, There breaks on our
   { With pit - i - ful moaning, With sorrowful groaning, The guilty im-

shou-ting a des - o - late cry; }
[*Omit.* . . . . . } plore us for help ere they die.

Chorus. f

Oh, work while 't is day, For the light flees away, And the hand of the

cres.

toil - er will soon work no more; But the faithful will rise To the

cres.

Lord in the skies, With the plaudit, "Well done," when the toiling is o'er.

413

2 Oh, up and be doing,
  Our duty pursuing,
Nor drown with rejoicing the wailing
        of woe:
  Our hearts will be lighter,
  Our path will be brighter,
The nearer our Master's own foot-
        prints we go.

3 With watching and praying,
  No longer delaying,
We 'll follow with gladness the voice
        of our Lord:
  The field is before us,
  The crown is just o'er us,
And working for Jesus brings pre-
        cious reward.

1. In the name of Je - sus, March to meet the foe; Nothing can with-
Chorus. Saints and angels watch us From their bright abode; Yes we will go

End.

stand you, God is God, you know. Do not pale and trem - ble—
on - ward, Help us, mighty God.

D. C. Chorus.

Let the foeman shout; In the name of Je - sus, Fling your colors out.

414   *" Christian Battle Hymn."*

1 In the name of Jesus
  March to meet the foe ;
Nothing can withstand you,
  God is God, you know.
Do not pale and tremble,
  Let the foeman shout ;
In the name of Jesus
  Fling your colors out.

2 This is war in earnest,
  Not a childish play :
Swords and martial music
  On a festal day.
Oh, thou Christian soldier,
  To the cause be true !
In the day of battle
  There is work to do.

3 Let your bugles always
  Give a certain sound ;
Spread your tent, at evening,
  On the foeman's ground.
Let the cross uplifted
  For a banner be ;
That you fight for Jesus
  Let the nations see.

4 Onward! Christians, onward!
  Do not stop nor stay ;
Through the ranks of Satan
  Make a shining way.
Bear the cross of Jesus
  Over hill and plain :
This indeed is glory,
  Worthy of the name.

415

2 Come, let us work for Jesus,
  By faith and earnest prayer.
The wandering ones from Jesus
  Should claim our constant care;
Come, let us work for Jesus,
  For hearts are bleeding sore,
While 'neath the wings of Jesus
  There's healing evermore.

3 Come, let us work for Jesus,
  We've many jewels rare
To gather yet for Jesus,
  To crown our labors there;
Then let us work for Jesus
  Before the sun goes down:
We've hearts to win for Jesus
  Ere we can wear a crown.

By permission.   GEO. F. ROOT.

Not too fast.

1. Oh, we are volunteers in the army of the Lord, Forming into line at our
2. The glory of our flag is the emblem of the dove, Gleaming are our swords from the

Captain's word; We are under marching orders to take the battle field, And we'll
forge of love: We go forth, but not to battle for earthly honors vain, 'Tis a

Chorus.

ne'er give o'er the fight till the foe shall yield. Come and join the army, the
bright immortal crown that we seek to gain. Come, etc.

ar-my of the Lord, Je-sus is our Captain, we rally at his word;

Sharp will be the conflict with the powers of sin, But with such a leader we are sure to win.

416

3 Our foes are in the field, pressing hard on every side,
  Envy, anger, hatred, with self and pride;
  They are cruel, fierce and strong, ever ready to attack;
  We must watch, and fight, and pray, if we'd drive them back.

4 Oh, glorious is the struggle in which we draw the sword,
  Glorious in the kingdom of Christ our Lord;
  It shall spread from sea to sea, it shall reach from shore to shore,
  And his people shall be blessed for evermore.

WHAT SHALL THE HARVEST BE?

W. H. DOANE.

Marching time.

1. Some are sowing their seed in the daylight fair; They are sowing seed in the noonday's glare; They are sowing seed in the soft twilight; They are sowing their seed in the solemn night. What shall the harvest be?

Chorus.

What shall the harvest be? What shall the harvest be? What shall the harvest be?

417

The Harvest.

2 Some are sowing their seed of word and deed,
Which the cold know not, nor the careless heed;
Oh! the gentle word, and the kindest deed,
That have blest the sad heart in its sorest need.
Sweet shall the harvest be, etc.

3 Some are sowing the seed of noble deed,
With a sleepless watch and an earnest heed;
With a ceaseless hand in the earth they sow,
And the fields are all whitening where'er they go.
Rich will the harvest be, etc.

4 Whether sown in the darkness, or sown in the light;
Whether sown in weakness, or sown in might;
Whether sown in meekness, or sown in wrath,
In the broadest highway or the shadowy path:
Sure will the harvest be, etc.

Arr. from E. H. NEVIN.

1. Live on the field of battle, Be earnest in the fight, Stand forth with manly courage,

And struggle for the right. Live! live! live! live! On the field of battle.

418 *The Christian Hero.*

2 Watch on the field of battle!
The foe is every-where;
His fiery darts fly thickly,
Like lightning thro' the air,
Watch! watch! watch! watch!
On the field of battle!

3 Pray on the field of battle!
God works with those who pray,

His mighty arm can nerve us,
And make us win the day.
Pray! pray! pray! pray!
On the field of battle.

4 Die on the field of battle!
'Tis noble thus to die;
God smiles on valiant soldiers,
Their record is on high.
Die! die! die! die!
On the field of battle!

SAY BROTHERS.

1. Say, brothers, will you meet us, Say, brothers, will you meet us,

Say, brothers, will you meet us, On Canaan's hap-py shore?

419 *Say Brothers.*

2 Say, sisters, will you meet us
On Canaan's happy shore?

3 That will be a happy meeting
On Canaan's happy shore.

4 Jesus lives and reigns forever
On Canaan's happy shore.

5 Glory! glory! hallelujah!
Forever, evermore!

1. Hark! 't is the watchman's cry, Wake, brethren, wake! Jesus our Lord is nigh, Wake, brethren, wake! Sleep is for sons of night, Children are ye of light, Yours is the glory bright, Wake, brethren, wake! Hark! 't is the watchman's cry,

Chorus.

Wake, brethren, wake! Wake, brethren, wake! Jesus our Lord is nigh, Wake, brethren, wake!

420

2 Call to each working band,
  Watch, brethren, watch!
Clear is our Lord's command,
  Watch, brethren, watch!
Be ye as men that wait
All at the Master's gate,
E'en though he tarry late,
  Watch, brethren, watch!

3 Heed we the Steward's call,
  Work, brethren, work!
There's work enough for all:
  Work, brethren, work!

This vineyard of the Lord
Fresh labor will afford;
Yours is a sure reward,
  Work, brethren, work!

4 Hear we the Shepherd's voice,
  Pray, brethren, pray!
Would ye his heart rejoice?
  Pray, brethren, pray!
Sin calls for constant fear;
Long as we struggle here,
We need the Strong One near—
  Pray, brethren, pray.

Allegro.

1. Soldiers for Je-sus, remember our du-ty, He is our leader, and
2. Nev-er give up when the conflict is raging, Sin is our foe, and the

strong to defend; Gird on our ar-mor, and face every danger,
world is the field; Stand by the cross, with our banner up-lift-ed,

Chorus.

Pray without ceasing, and fight to the end. {Nev-er give up,
Glo-ry our watchword, the Bi-ble our shield. {Nev-er give up,

| 1st. | 2d. |

never give up, But onward, march onward, and never give up;
never give up, But onward, march onward, and . . . . never give up.

421

3 Never give up when the night is the darkest,
Why should we tremble? there's nothing to fear;
Grace will support us. the Savior still whispers,
Lo! I am with you, then be of good cheer.

4 Cling to the hope that is sure as an anchor;
Trials, though often they mingle our cup,
Leave to the faithful a blessing behind them,
Bear them with patience, but never give up.

5 Never give up till the foe we have conquered;
Firm at our post till our duty is done,
Stand we like heroes, and face every danger;
Never give up till the battle is won.

1. { As, pant-ing in the sul - try beam, The
So to thy pres - ence, Lord, I flee; So

hart de - sires the cool - ing stream, }
longs my soul, O God, for thee; } A - thirst to taste thy

liv - ing grace, And see thy glo - ry face to face.

422   *Seeking God.*   L. M

2 But rising griefs distress my soul,
And tears on tears successive roll;
For many an evil voice is near,
To chide my woe and mock my fear;
And silent memory weeps alone
O'er hours of peace and gladness flown.

3 For I have walked the happy round
That circles Zion's holy ground,
And gladly swelled the choral lays
That hymned my great Redeemer's praise,
What time the hallowed arches rung
Responsive to the solemn song.

4 Ah, why, by passing clouds oppressed,
Should vexing thoughts distract thy breast?
Turn, turn to him in every pain.
Whom suppliants never sought in vain:
Thy strength in joy's ecstatic day,
Thy hope when joy has passed away.

423   *Jehovah the Shepherd.*   L, M.

1 The Lord my pasture shall prepare,
And feed me with a shepherd's care;
His presence shall my wants supply,
And guard me with a watchful eye;
My noonday walks he shall attend,
And all my midnight hours defend.

2 When in the sultry glebe I faint,
Or on the thirsty mountain pant,
To fertile vales, and dewy meads,
My weary, wandering steps he leads,
Where peaceful rivers, soft and slow,
Amid the verdant landscape flow.

3 Though in the paths of death I tread,
With gloomy horrors overspread,
My steadfast heart shall fear no ill,
For thou, O Lord, art with me still;
Thy friendly rod shall give me aid,
And guide me through the dreadful shade.

Admah, Key G.   Petersburgh, Key D.

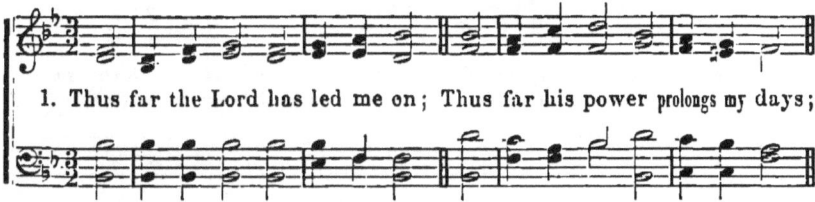

1. Thus far the Lord has led me on; Thus far his power prolongs my days;

And every evening shall make known Some fresh memorial of his grace.

424 *Evening Reflections.* L. M.

1 Thus far the Lord has led me on;
Thus far his power prolongs my days;
And every evening shall make known
Some fresh memorial of his grace.

2 Much of my time has run to waste,
And I, perhaps, am near my home;
But he forgives my follies past,
And gives me strength for days to come.

3 I lay my body down to sleep;
Peace is the pillow for my head;
While well-appointed angels keep
Their watchful stations round my bed.

4 Thus, when the night of death shall come,
My flesh shall rest beneath the ground,
And wait thy voice to break my tomb,
With sweet salvation in the sound.

425 *Prayer for a Minister's Success.* L. M.

1 Father of mercies, bow thine ear,
Attentive to our earnest prayer;
We plead for those who plead for thee:
Successful pleaders may they be.

2 Oh, clothe with energy divine
Their words, and let those words be thine;
To them thy sacred truth reveal,
Suppress their fear, inflame their zeal.

3 Teach them to sow the precious seed;
Teach them thy chosen flock to feed;
Teach them immortal souls to gain,
And thus reward their toil and pain.

4 Let thronging multitudes around
Hear from their lips the joyful sound,
In humble strains thy grace implore,
And feel thy Spirit's living power.

426 *Heaven alone Unfading.* L. M.

1 How vain is all beneath the skies!
How transient every earthly bliss!
How slender all the fondest ties
That bind us to a world like this!

2 The evening cloud, the morning dew,
The withering grass, the fading flower,
Of earthly hopes are emblems true:
The glory of a passing hour.

3 But though earth's fairest blossoms die,
And all beneath the skies is vain,
There is a brighter world on high,
Beyond the reach of care and pain.

4 Then let the hope of joys to come
Dispel our cares, and chase our fears:
If God be ours, we're traveling home,
Though passing through a vale of tears.

Zephyr, Key C.   Brainerd, Key C.   Federal Street, Key A♭.

1. Descend from heaven, immortal Dove; Stoop down and take us on thy wings:
And mount, and bear us far above The reach of these inferior things.

Chorus.

Glo - ry, glory, let us sing, While heaven and earth with glory ring,

Hosan-na! Ho - san-na! Ho-san-na to the Lamb of God!

427   *Longing for Heaven.*   L. M.

2 Beyond, beyond this lower sky,
    Up where eternal ages roll,
Where solid pleasures never die,
    And fruits immortal feast the soul.

3 Oh for a sight, a pleasing sight,
    Of our almighty Father's throne!
There sits our Savior, crowned with light,
    Clothed in a body like our own.

4 Oh, what amazing joys they feel,
    While to their golden harps they sing,
And sit on every heavenly hill,
    And spread the triumphs of their King.

428   *Christ's Kingdom.*   L. M.

1 Jesus shall reign where'er the sun
Does his successive journeys run;
His kingdom stretch from shore to shore,
Till moons shall wax and wane no more.

2 For him shall endless prayer be made,
And endless praises crown his head;
His name, like sweet perfume, shall rise
With every morning sacrifice.

3 People and realms of every tongue
Dwell on his love with sweetest song;
And infant voices shall proclaim
Their early blessings on his name.

4 Let every creature rise and bring
Peculiar honors to our King;
Angels descend with songs again,
And earth repeat the loud Amen!

429   *The Song of Heaven.*   L. M.

1 The countless multitude on high,
    Who tune their songs to Jesus' name,
All merit of their own deny,
    And Jesus' worth alone proclaim.

2 Firm, on the ground of sovereign grace,
    They stand before Jehovah's throne;
The only song in that blest place
    Is, "Thou art worthy, thou alone!"

3 With spotless robes of purest white,
    And branches of triumphal palm,
They shout, with transports of delight,
    The ceaseless, universal psalm.

Uxbridge, Key E♭.   Wells, Key F.   Ward, Key B♭.

1. Anoth-er six days' work is done, Anoth-er Sabbath is be-gun;

Return, my soul, enjoy thy rest, Improve the day that God has blest.

430 *Holy Enjoyment Anticipated.* L. M.

2 Oh that our thoughts and thanks may rise,
As grateful incense, to the skies,
And draw from heaven that sweet repose
Which none but he that feels it knows!

3 A heavenly calm pervades the breast,
The earnest of that glorious rest
Which for the church of God remains,
The end of cares, the end of pains.

4 In holy duties let the day,
In holy pleasures, pass away;
How sweet a Sabbath thus to spend,
In hope of one that ne'er shall end!

431 *The Gracious Promise.* L. M.

1 Where two or three, with sweet accord,
Obedient to their sovereign Lord,
Meet to recount his acts of grace,
And offer solemn prayer and praise,

2 "There," says the Savior, "will I be,
Amid this little company;
To them unvail my smiling face,
And shed my glories round the place."

3 We meet at thy command, dear Lord,
Relying on thy faithful word;
Now send thy Spirit from above,
And fill our hearts with heavenly love.

432 *Dedication Hymn.* L. M.

1 O God the Father, Christ the Son,
And Holy Spirit, Three in One,
Accept this gift our hearts have sought—
Our hands in Christian love have wrought.

2 Here may the light of Gospel truth
Illumine age, enlighten youth:
In many hearts that grace begin,
Which saves from sorrow and from sin.

3 May Jesus here that power display,
Which changes darkness into day,
And open wide those gates of love,
That lead to blessedness above.

4 O Jesus Christ, our sovereign Lord,
By angels and by saints adored,
Accept this tribute of our praise,
And with thy glory fill this place.

433 *Praise.* C. M.

1 With cheerful notes let all the earth
To heaven their voices raise;
Let all, inspired with godly mirth,
Sing solemn hymns of praise.

2 God's tender mercy knows no bound,
His truth shall ne'er decay:
Then let the willing nations round
Their grateful tribute pay.

Luten, Key E♭. Gratitude, Key E♭. Mendon, Key C.
12

UXBRIDGE. L. M.

Dr. LOWELL MASON.

1. The heavens declare thy glory, Lord; In every star thy wisdom shines;

But when our eyes behold thy word, We read thy name in fairer lines.

434   *The Glory of God.*   L. M.

2 The rolling sun, the changing light,
  And nights and days thy power confess;
But that blest volume thou hast writ
  Reveals thy justice and thy grace.

3 Nor shall thy spreading gospel rest
  Till through the world thy truth has run,
Till Christ has all the nations blest
  That see the light or feel the sun.

4 Great Sun of righteousness, arise;
  Oh bless the world with heavenly light;
Thy gospel makes the simple wise;
  Thy laws are pure, thy judgments right.

435   *Song for Morning and Evening.*   L. M.

1 My God, how endless is thy love!
  Thy gifts are every evening new;
And morning mercies from above
  Gently distill like early dew.

2 Thou spread'st the curtains of the night,
  Great Guardian of my sleeping hours;
Thy sovereign word restores the light,
  And quickens all my drowsy powers.

3 I yield my powers to thy command;
  To thee I consecrate my days;
Perpetual blessings from thine hand
  Demand perpetual songs of praise.

Rockingham, Key G.

436   *Glory and Grace in Christ.*   L. M.

1 Now to the Lord a noble song;
  Awake, my soul, awake, my tongue;
Hosanna to the eternal name,
  And all his boundless love proclaim.

2 See where it shines in Jesus' face,
  The brightest image of his grace;
God, in the person of his Son,
  Has all his mightiest works outdone.

3 Grace! 't is a sweet, a charming theme;
  My thoughts rejoice at Jesus' name;
Ye angels, dwell upon the sound;
  Ye heavens, reflect it to the ground.

437   *National Gratitude.*   L. M.

1 Lord, let thy goodness lead our land,
  Still saved by thine almighty hand,
The tribute of its love to bring
  To thee, our Savior and our King.

2 Let every public temple raise
  Triumphant songs of holy praise:
Let every peaceful, private home,
  A temple, Lord, to thee become.

3 Still be it our supreme delight
  To walk as in thy glorious sight;
Still in thy precepts and thy fear,
  Till life's last hour, to persevere.

Missionary Chant, Key A♭.

Dr. LOWELL MASON.

1. The spacious firm-a-ment on high, With all the blue ethere-al sky,

And spangled heavens, a shining frame, Their great Original proclaim.

438 *Divine Perfection.* L. M.

2 The unwearied sun, from day to day,
Doth his Creator's power display,
And publishes to every land
The work of an Almighty Hand.

3 Soon as the evening shades prevail,
The moon takes up the wondrous tale,
And nightly, to the listening earth,
Repeats the story of her birth.

4 While all the stars that round her burn,
And all the planets in their turn,
Confirm the tidings as they roll,
And spread the truth from pole to pole.

439 *The Glory of God in his Works.* L. M.

1 Thine earthly Sabbaths, Lord, we love;
But there's a nobler rest above;
To that our longing souls aspire,
With cheerful hope and strong desire.

2 No more fatigue, no more distress,
Nor sin, nor death, shall reach the place;
No groans shall mingle with the songs
Which dwell upon immortal tongues.

3 No rude alarms of angry foes;
No cares, to break the long repose;
No midnight shade, no clouded sun,
But sacred, high, eternal noon.

440 *Delight in the Sabbath.* L. M.

1 Sweet is the work, my God, my King,
To praise thy name, give thanks, and sing;
To show thy love by morning light,
And talk of all thy truth at night.

2 Sweet is the day of sacred rest;
No mortal care shall fill my breast;
Oh, may my heart in tune be found,
Like David's harp, of solemn sound.

441 *Song of Gratitude and Praise.* L. M.

1 God of my life, through all my days
I'll tune the grateful notes of praise;
The song shall wake with opening light,
And warble to the silent night.

2 When anxious care would break my rest,
And grief would tear my throbbing breast,
The notes of praise, ascending high,
Shall check the murmur and the sigh.

3 When death o'er nature shall prevail,
And all the powers of language fail,
Joy through my swimming eyes shall break,
And mean the thanks I can not speak.

4 But oh, when that last conflict's o'er,
And I am chained to earth no more,
With what glad accents shall I rise,
To join the music of the skies!

Welton, Key B♭. Uxbridge, Key E♭. Brockway, A.

By permission.   B. F. BAKER.

1. He dies! the Friend of sinners dies; Lo! Salem's daughters weep around;

A solemn darkness vails the skies, A sudden trembling shakes the ground.

442 *Death and Resurrection of Christ.* **L. M.**

2 Ye saints, approach!—the anguish view
  Of him who groans beneath your load;
He gives his precious life for you;
  For you he sheds his precious blood.

3 Here's love and grief beyond degree;
  The Lord of glory dies for men;
But, lo! what sudden joys we see!
  Jesus, the dead, revives again.

4 The rising God forsakes the tomb;
  Up to his Father's court he flies;
Cherubic legions guard him home,
  And shout him welcome to the skies.

5 Break off your tears, ye saints, and tell
  How high our great Deliverer reigns;
Sing how he spoiled the hosts of hell,
  And led the tyrant Death in chains.

443   *The Vow Sealed at the Cross.* **L. M.**

1 Lord, I am thine, entirely thine,
  Purchased and saved by blood divine;
With full consent thine I would be,
  And own thy sov'reign right in me.

2 Thine would I live—thine would I die;
  Be thine through all eternity;
The vow is past beyond repeal,
  And now I set the solemn seal.

3 Here, at that cross where flows the blood
  That bought my guilty soul for God,
Thee, my new Master, now I call,
  And consecrate to thee my all.

4 Do thou assist a feeble worm
  The great engagement to perform;
Thy grace can full assistance lend,
  And on that grace I dare depend.

444   *On the Death of a Member.* **L. M.**

1 Another friend we have in heaven:
  New links of love attract us there:
The intervening veil is riven,
  Once more to make our vision clear.

2 He rests from sin, from care, from strife,
  No more the tempter's power he fears,
No shadow now beclouds the life
  He leads within celestial spheres.

3 Transferr'd from toil to heavenly rest,
  From sorrow to unmingled bliss,
Seraphic pleasures fill his breast,
  And faith's fruition now is his.

4 How great his gain, his lot how blest,
  Whom joyous angels welcome home!
Life's work well wrought, how calm his rest,
  Where sin and sorrow ne'er can come.

Dodge, Key A♭.   Rest, Key D.   Federal Street, Key A♭.

1. Awake, my soul, and with the sun Thy dai-ly course of du - ty run;

Shake off dull sloth, and early rise To pay thy morning sac - ri-fice.

445 *Morning Hymn.* L. M.

2 Redeem thy misspent time that's past;
Live this day as if 't were thy last;
To improve thy talents take due care;
'Gainst the great day thyself prepare.

3 Let all thy converse be sincere,
Thy conscience as the noonday clear;
Think how the all-seeing God thy ways
And all thy secret thoughts surveys.

4 Direct, control, suggest this day,
All I design, or do, or say,
That all my powers, with all their might,
In thy sole glory may unite.

446 *Parting with Carnal Joys.* L M.

1 I send the joys of earth away;
Away, ye tempters of the mind;
False as the smooth, deceitful sea,
And empty as the whistling wind.

2 Your streams were floating me along
Down to the gulf of dark despair;
And while I listened to your song,
Your streams had e'en conveyed me there.

3 Lord. I adore thy matchless grace,
That warned me of that dark abyss,
That drew me from those treacherous seas,
And bade me seek superior bliss.

447 *Enjoyment of Christ's Love.* L. M.

1 Jesus, thy boundless love to me
No tho't can reach, no tongue declare;
Unite my thankful heart to thee,
And reign without a rival there.

2 Oh, let thy love my soul inflame,
And to thy service sweetly bind,
Transfuse it thro' my inmost frame,
And mold me wholly to thy mind.

3 Thy love in sufferings be my peace,
Thy love in weakness make me strong;
And when the storms of life shall cease,
Thy love shall be in heaven my song.

448 *Exemplifying the Gospel.* L. M.

1 So let our lips and lives express
The holy Gospel we profess;
So let our works and virtues shine,
To prove the doctrine all divine.

2 Thus shall we best proclaim abroad
The honors of our Savior God,
When his salvation reigns within,
And grace subdues the power of sin.

3 Religion bears our spirits up,
While we expect that blessed hope,
The bright appearance of the Lord,
And faith stands leaning on his word.

Hamburg, Key F.   Brockway, Key A.   Zephyr, Key C.

SPEAK A WORD FOR JESUS.

1. Speak a word for Je - sus, broth - er, 'T will thy heart in - spire;

'T will within thy soul en - kin - dle Love's en - fee-bled fire;

D.S. Show them how in end-less glo - ry They with Christ may reign.

Chorus.

Tell them the old, old sto - ry—Make it ver - y clear and plain.

449   *Speaking for Jesus.*

1 Speak a word for Jesus, brother,
  'T will thy heart inspire;
'T will within thy soul enkindle
  Love's enfeebled fire.

2 Speak a word for Jesus, sister,
  Think what thou may'st do
For the souls that need, around you,
  Christ the Lord to view.

3 Speak a word for Jesus, father,
  Oh, for your delay
Children dear may fail of reaching
  Realms of endless day.

4 Speak a word for Jesus, mother,
  Tell it with the glow
Of the strongest love and pity
  Woman's heart can know.

5 Speak a word for Jesus, Christian;
  Every-where you'll find
Human souls so poor and needy,
  Dark, and drear, and blind.

6 Tell them all the old story,
  Make it clear and plain,
Show them how in endless glory
  They with Christ may reign.

By permission.   WM. B. BRADBURY.

1. Pilgrims we are, to Canaan bound, Our journey lies along this road;
This wil-der-ness we travel round, To reach the ci-ty of our God.
D. C. Our robes are washed in Jesus' blood, And we are trav'ling home to God.

Chorus.

O happy pilgrims, spotless fair, What makes your robes so white appear?

450   *Christian Pilgrimage.*

2 A few more days, or weeks, or years,
   In this dark desert to complain;
A few more sighs, a few more tears,
   And we shall bid adieu to pain.

3 O, blessed land! O, happy land!
   When shall we reach thy golden shore?
And one redeemed, unbroken band
   United be for evermore.

4 We all shall reach that golden shore,
   If here we watch, and fight, and pray;
Straight is the way and straight the door,
   And none but pilgrims find the way.

5 Oh, may we meet at last above,
   Amid the holy blood-washed throng,
And sing forever Jesus' love,
   While saints and angels join the song.

SINNER, COME!

1. Sinner! come, 'mid thy gloom, All thy guilt con-fess-ing,

Trembling now, con-trite bow, Take the proffered bless-ing.

451   *Coming to Jesus.*

2 Sinner! come, while there's room—
   While the feast is waiting;
While the Lord, by his word,
   Kindly is inviting.

3 Sinner! come, ere thy doom
   Shall be sealed forever;
Now return, grieve and mourn,
   Flee to Christ, the Savior.

WELTON. L. M.

DR. MADAN.

1. Once more, in Jesus' holy name, We gather at our Mas - ter's call:

Oh, may his grace our souls inflame, His spirit's influence on us fall.

---

452   *Christ at the Feast.*   L. M.

1 Once more, in Jesus' holy name,
  We gather at our Master's call;
Oh, may his grace our souls inflame,
  His Spirit's influence on us fall.

2 From heart to heart glad greetings fly,
  As, brothers all, again we meet;
A present Savior crowns our joy,
  His welcome makes the joy complete.

3 Immanuel, God with us! He gives
  The promise that ensures such bliss!
Jesus, descending, in us lives;
  He greets us with his holy kiss!

4 Welcome, beloved in the Lord,
  Thrice welcome to this love-spread feast;
With hearts and souls in full accord,
  May each the heavenly manna taste.

5 As God's own guests we gather here;
  His grace the table hath supplied;
Among us, Savior, now appear,
  At thine own table now preside.

6 Thy Spirit give; thy peace impart;
  Fill us with faith, and love, and joy;
Thy welcome speak to every heart,
  Then shall our bliss have no alloy.

453   *Evening Hymn.*   L. M

1 Great God, to thee my evening song,
  With humble gratitude, I raise;
Oh, let thy mercy tune my tongue,
  And fill my heart with lively praise.

2 My days unclouded as they pass,
  And every onward rolling hour,
Are monuments of wondrous grace,
  And witness to thy love and power.

3 And yet this thoughtless, wretched heart,
  Too oft regardless of thy love,
Ungrateful, can from thee depart,
  And from the path of duty rove.

4 Seal my forgiveness in the blood
  Of Christ, my Lord; his name alone
I plead for pardon, gracious God,
  And kind acceptance at thy throne.

454   *Dismission.*   L. M.

1 Dismiss us with thy blessing, Lord,
  Help us to feed upon thy word;
All that has been amiss forgive,
  And let thy truth within us live.

2 Though we are guilty, thou art good;
  Wash all our works in Jesus' blood;
Give every fettered soul release,
  And bid us all depart in peace.

Woodworth, Key Eb.   Rockingham, Key G.   Duryea, Key Bb.

BURDER.

1. Glory to thee, my God, this night, For all the blessings of the light:

Keep me, oh, keep me, King of kings, Beneath the shadow of thy wings.

455 *Trusting God.* L. M.

1 Glory to thee, my God, this night,
For all the blessings of the light:
Keep me, oh, keep me, King of kings,
Beneath the shadow of thy wings.

2 Forgive me, Lord, for thy dear Son,
The ills which I this day have done;
That with the world, myself, and thee,
I, ere I sleep, at peace may be.

3 Be thou my guardian while I sleep;
Thy watchful station near me keep;
My heart with love celestial fill,
And guard me from th' approach of ill.

4 Lord, let my heart forever share
The bliss of thy paternal care:
'T is heaven on earth, 't is heaven above,
To see thy face and sing thy love.

456 *God our Keeper.* L. M.

1 To Zion's hill I lift my eyes,
From thence expecting aid;
From Zion's hill and Zion's God,
Who heaven and earth has made.

2 He will not let my foot be moved,
Thy guardian will not sleep;
Behold, the God who slumbers not
Will favored Israel keep.

3 From common accidents of life
The Lord shall guard thee still;
'T is even he that shall preserve
Thy soul from every ill.

4 At home, abroad, in peace, in war,
Thy God shall thee defend;
Conduct thee through life's pilgrimage,
Safe to thy journey's end.

457 *Rejoicing in Christ.* L. M.

1 He reigns! the Lord, the Savior reigns!
Sing to his name in lofty strains;
Let all the earth in songs rejoice,
And in his praise exalt their voice.

2 Deep are his counsels, and unknown:
But grace and truth support his throne;
Though gloomy clouds his way surround,
Justice is their eternal ground.

3 In robes of judgment, lo! he comes,
Shakes the wide earth and cleaves the tombs:
Before him burns devouring fire:
The mountains melt, the seas retire.

4 His enemies, with sore dismay,
Fly from the sight, and shun the day;
Then lift your heads, ye saints on high,
And sing, for your redemption 's nigh.

Sterling, Key A.   Dayton, Key C.   Mendon, Key C.

By permission.   W. B. BRADBURY.

1. Kindred in Christ, for his dear sake, A hearty welcome here receive,

May we together now partake, The joys which only he can give.

458   *Kindred in Christ.*   L. M.

2 May he, by whose kind care we meet,
    Send his good Spirit from above,
Make our communications sweet,
    And cause our hearts to burn with love.

3 Forgotten be each worldly theme,
    When Christians see each other thus;
We only wish to speak of him
    Who lived, and died, and reigns for us.

4 We'll talk of all he did, and said,
    And suffered for us here below,
The path he marked for us to tread,
    And what he's doing for us now.

·5 Thus, as the moments pass away,
    We'll love, and wonder, and adore,
And long to see the glorious day
    When we shall meet to part no more.

459   *Security of the Believer.*   L. M.

1 How oft have sin and Satan strove
    To rend my soul from thee, my God!
But everlasting is thy love,
    And Jesus seals it with his blood.

2 The oath and promise of the Lord
    Join to confirm his wondrous grace;
Eternal power performs the word,
    And fills all heaven with endless praise.

3 Amidst temptations sharp and long,
    My soul to this dear refuge flies;
Hope is my anchor, firm and strong,
    While tempests blow and billows rise.

4 The gospel bears my spirit up;
    A faithful and unchanging God
Lays the foundation for my hope,
    In oaths, and promises, and blood.

460   *Faithfulness.*   L. M.

1 He lives! he lives! and sits above,
    Forever interceding there:
Who shall divide us from his love?
    Or what should tempt us to despair?

2 Shall persecution, or distress,
    Shall famine, sword, or nakedness?
He who hath loved us bears us through,
    And makes us more than conquerors too.

3 Faith hath an overcoming power;
    It triumphs in the dying hour:
Christ is our life, our joy, our hope,
    Nor can we sink with such a prop.

4 Not all that men on earth can do,
    Nor powers on high, nor powers below,
Shall cause his mercy to remove,
    Or wean our hearts from Christ, our love.

Dodge, Key A♭.   Luton, Key E♭.   Welton, Key B♭.

Rev. W. McDONALD.

1. My heavenly home is bright and fair; Nor pain nor death can enter there;
Its glitt'ring tow'rs the sun outshine; That heavenly mansion shall be mine.

Chorus.

I'm going home, I'm going home, I'm going home to die no more;
To die no more, to die no more, I'm going home to die no more.

461 *The Heavenly Home.* L. M.

2 My Father's house is built on high,
Far, far above the starry sky:
When from this earthy prison free,
That heavenly mansion mine shall be.

3 Let others seek a home below,
Which flames devour, or waves o'erflow;
Be mine a happier lot to own,
A heavenly mansion near the throne.

462 *Haste Thee, Escape.* L. M.

1 Haste, traveler, haste! the night comes on,
And many a shining hour is gone;
The storm is gathering in the west,
And thou far off from home and rest.

2 The rising tempest sweeps the sky;
The rains descend, the winds are high;
The waters swell, and death and fear
Beset thy path, nor refuge near.

3 Oh, yet a shelter you may gain,
A covert from the wind and rain;
A hiding-place, a rest, a home,
A refuge from the wrath to come!

4 Then linger not in all the plain;
Flee for thy life; the mountain gain;
Look not behind; make no delay;
Oh, speed thee, speed thee on thy way!

463 *Resting at the Cross.* L. M.

1 My only Savior! when I feel
O'erwhelmed in spirit, faint, oppressed,
'T is sweet to tell thee, while I kneel
Low at thy feet, thou art my rest.

2 I'm weary of the strife within;
Strong powers against my soul contest;
Oh, let me turn from self and sin
To thy dear cross, for there is rest!

3 Oh! sweet will be the welcome day,
When from her toils and woes released,
My parting soul in death shall say,
"Now, Lord! I come to thee for rest."

464 *Rejoicing in the Sabbath.* L. M.

1 My opening eyes with rapture see
The dawn of thy returning day;
My thoughts, O God, ascend to thee,
While thus my early vows I pay.

2 I yield my heart to thee alone,
Nor would receive another guest:
Eternal King, erect thy throne,
And reign sole monarch in my breast.

3 Then, to thy courts when I repair,
My soul shall rise on joyful wing,
The wonders of thy love declare,
And join the strains which angels sing.

Grammar, Key C.   Retreat, Key C.   Welton, Key B♭.

Arr. by E. Roberts.

1. There are lights by the shore of that country, Where my bark amid perils I

steer, And they ev - er grow brighter and brighter, As that glori - ous

Chorus.

ha - ven I near. Oh! the lights along the shore that never grow dim,

nev - er, nev-er grow dim. Are the souls that are aflame with the

love of Jesus' name, And they guide us, yes, they guide us in - to him.

465

2 There are lights by the shore as we journey,
As we float down the river of time;
All the days of our pilgrimage brighten,
With a radiance truly sublime.

By permission.

W. B. BRADBURY.

1. We are go-ing, we are go-ing To a home beyond the skies,
D. C. We are go-ing, etc.

Where the fields are robed in beauty, And the sunlight never dies.

Where the fount of joy is flowing, In the val-ley green and fair;

We shall dwell in love to-geth-er, There will be no parting there.

466

2 We are going, we are going,
   And the music we have heard,
Like the echo of the woodland,
   Or the carol of a bird;
With the rosy light of morning,
   On the calm and fragrant air,
Still it murmurs, softly murmurs,
   There will be no parting there.

3 We are going, we are going,
   When the day of life is o'er;
To that pure and happy region
   Where our friends have gone before:
They are singing with the angels
   In that land so bright and fair;
We shall dwell with them forever—
   There will be no parting there.

1. Welcome, brothers! voices raising, Thus our glad reun - ion greet,

God, our gracious Fa-ther, praising, Who permits us thus to meet.
D. S. Crave from him a father's blessing, And the sweetest strains prolong.

Let us, then, his grace confessing, Join our hearts in grateful song;

467   *Christian Union.*   8s & 7s.

2 Christian union! joy, O brothers!
  For the soul inspiring words,
Not our own, but each the others',
  Not our own, but each the Lord's.
    One in hoping, one in loving,
    One in faith, and one in prayer;
    By united labors proving
    Toils and burdens too we share.

3 Brothers, sisters, glad we greet you,
  Glad we view your kindling eyes,
May it be our lot to meet you,
  Even thus above the skies.
    There our Father will receive us,
    No more earthly toil or care,
    Strife and parting no more grieve us,
    All is " Christian Union " there.

468   *Missionary Charged.*   8s & 7s.

1 Onward, onward, men of heaven!
  Bear the gospel's banner high!

Rest not till its light is given,
  Star of every Pagan sky.
Send it where the pilgrim stranger
  Faints 'neath Asia's scorching ray;
Bid the red-browed forest ranger
  Hail it, ere he fades away.

2 Where the Arctic ocean thunders,
  Where the tropics fiercely glow,
Broadly spread its page of wonders,
  Brightly bid its radiance flow.
India marks its luster stealing,
  Shiv'ring Greenland loves its rays,
Afric 'mid her deserts kneeling
  Lifts the untaught strain of praise.

3 Rude in speech or grim in feature,
  Dark in spirit tho' they be,
Show that light to every creature—
  Prince or vassal—bond or free.
Lo! they haste to every nation.
  Host on host the ranks supply;
Onward! Christ is your salvation,
  And your death is victory.

Song of Welcome, Key G.   Autumn, Key G.

468   *Hymn of Welcome.*   8s & 7s.

1 Grateful hearts and cheerful voices
   Swell our sacred song to-night,
Sending up to God thanksgiving
   For the scenes which greet our sight.
Thanks we give for that sweet spirit
   Which hath hither drawn, from far,
Such a goodly band of pilgrims,
   Guided by love's gentle star.

2 Christian friends, we bid you welcome!
   Welcome to this sacred place,
For we joy, with untold gladness,
   Here to meet you, face to face.
Welcome to our homes; we bid you
   Welcome to our social cheer,
Hearts and hands we give you freely,
   For you all are brethren here.

3 Like the gentle dews on Hermon,
   So refreshing, sweet, and still,
Giving life, and strength, and beauty,
   Unto Zion's holy hill,
So may now the Holy Spirit
   Gently on each heart descend,
And in one sweet bond of union
   All our waiting spirits blend.

4 Thus shall all our hearts be strengthened,
   Filled with love, and holy fear,
Wisdom crown our acts and counsels,
   In these days of converse here.
Thus the Savior shall be honored,
   In this feast of Christian love,
And these gatherings be the foretaste
   Of reunion sweet above.

470   *Work for All.*   8s & 7s.

1 Hark! the voice of Jesus, crying,
   Who will go and work to-day?
Fields are white, and harvests waiting,
   Who will bear the sheaves away?
Loud and long the Master calleth,
   Rich reward he offers free;
Who will answer, gladly saying,
   "Here am I, send me, send me?"

2 If you can not cross the ocean,
   And the heathen lands explore,
You can find the heathen nearer,
   You can help them at your door.

If you can not give your thousands,
   You can give the widow's mite;
And the least you give for Jesus
   Will be precious in his sight.

3 If you can not speak like angels,
   If you can not preach like Paul,
You can tell the love of Jesus,
   You can say he died for all;
If you can not rouse the wicked
   With the judgment's dread alarms,
You can lead the little children
   To the Savior's waiting arms.

4 While the souls of men are dying,
   And the Master calls for you,
Let none hear you idly saying,
   "There is nothing I can do!"
Take the task he gives you gladly,
   Let his work your pleasure be;
Answer quickly, when he calleth,
   "Here am I, send me, send me!"

471   *Christian Soldiers, Welcome.*   8s & 7s.

1 Soldiers in the ranks of Jesus,
   Workers in the field of grace,
Preachers of our blessed Gospel,
   Welcome to this chosen place.
What an hour of holy transport—
   God is in our midst to-day!
Praise the Lord this happy union,
   How it cheers us on our way.

2 Tell us, brethren, are you planting
   Goodly seed on fertile ground?
Is the glorious work progressing?
   Does the fruit of joy abound?
Though you sometimes feel discouraged,
   And your labor seems in vain,
Look to God, and seek his blessing—
   He will bring the promised reign.

3 Sow thy seed, be never weary,
   Let not fears thy mind employ;
Be the prospect ne'er so dreary,
   Thou may'st reap the fruits of joy.
Lo! the scene of verdure brightening,
   See the rising grain appear!
Look again! the fields are whitening:
   Sure the harvest time is near.

Harwell, Key G.   Ripley, Key E♭.

1. Welcome, brothers, from the woodlands, From the cities by the sea,

From the heaven kiss-ing mountains, Here we meet in u-ni - ty.

Chorus.

Let us join the an - gel cho-rus, Let us shout a - gain, a - gain,

Glo - ry be to God the high-est, Peace on earth, good will to men.

472

2 Welcome, brothers, bonds fraternal,
  Make our hearts responsive beat,
Giving strength to aid the erring,
  Rendering communion sweet.

Chorus.

Join we then the angel chorus,
  Shouting loud. again, again,
Glory be to God the highest,
  Peace on earth, good will to men.

3 Welcome, brothers, strong in council,
  May we prove in virtue brave,
Brave to aid the broken-hearted,
  Strong to comfort and to save.

Chorus.

Swelling still the angel chorus,
  Shouting still again. again,
Glory be to God the highest,
  Peace on earth, good will to men.

Stockwell, Key B♭.   Harwell, Key G.

From "Bright Jewels," by per.

1. When these weary days are over, When our griefs have passed away,

S.　　　　　　　　　　　　　　**End.**

Like the clouds that melt and vanish In the sun's effulgent ray;
Far away from sin or sadness, Brothers, we shall meet and rest.

D. S. S.

Then with light, and joy, and gladness, Making sunshine in the breast,

Chorus.

Brothers, we shall meet and rest, Meet and rest, yes, meet and rest.

Brothers, we shall meet and rest,

Safe at home, and safe forever, Brothers, we shall meet and rest.

ever, safe forever,

473

2 Soon the earthly chain will sever;
　Soon to higher joys we 'll rise;
Soon we 'll meet the blessed Savior
　In the realms of paradise.
Then our hearts will cease to languish,
　By their load of guilt oppressed;
There, beyond this toil and anguish,
　Brothers, we shall meet and rest !

3 Oh, the blissful, joyous meeting!
　Bliss and joy beyond compare !
When the saints, in rapture greeting,
　Their Redeemer's love declare !
Storms and doubts shall vex us never,
　In those mansions of the blest;
Safe at home, and safe forever,
　Brothers, we shall meet and rest!

13

1. Brothers, clasp hands, the brief moments are flying; Here up-on
earth but as pil-grims we dwell; Glad-ly we met, yet we
Chorus. In his dear name, the All
part without sighing, Look-ing be-yond the fra-ter-nal farewell.
Loving, All Seeing, Hand clasped in hand for him, brothers farewell.

474 *Hymn of Parting.* C. M.

2 Rich in our faith, in our love, in
our union,
Foretastes of heaven together we 've known,
Ours is the bliss of a saintly communion,
Granted to lovers of Jesus alone.

3 Now to our work again, stronger
for meeting,
Pledged to our Master as never before,
Warm are the hearts that are loyally
beating,
Longing to serve and to honor him more.

4 Jesus we own as the Lord of our
being;
Let our last song rich in gratitude
swell;
In his dear name, the All Loving, All
Seeing.
Hand clasped in hand, for him.
brothers, farewell.

475 *Farewell Hymn.*

1 Brothers, farewell; the sad word
must be spoken;
Jesus. our Master, hath work to be done:
The spell that hath charmed us now
must be broken,
Labor and conflict be once more begun.

2 Linger no longer, but up and be doing,
Faithful and earnest go forth to
the fight;
Satan is fleeing, our Leader pursuing,
Donning our armor, let's dare to
do right.

3 Parting is painful. but 'tis not eternal;
Farewells. to Christians, are simply good-byes;
When we have vanquished the legions
infernal,
Jesus will bind us in still stronger
ties.

1. Meet we a-gain for one more friendly greeting, Grasp we each oth - er once more by the hand; Quickly, too quickly, the moments are fleeting, Broken and scattered must soon be our band.

---

476   *For Closing Conventions.*

2 Friends have we found here, whose
    friendship shall never
Cease till the current of life flow
    no more ;
Seas may divide us, but ne'er shall
    they sever
Hearts filled with fond recollec-
    tions of yore.

3 Fondly we think on the place we
    are leaving,
Boldly we seek what the future may give,
Knowledge and strength we have
    here been receiving.
God grant us all that we know how to live.

4 Onward we'll march, then, with
    shoulder to shoulder,
Ready to meet all that life has in store,
Blood leaping quicker, and hearts
    beating bolder,
Hoping to meet where we'll part
    nevermore.

477   *At Close of Meeting.*

1 Spirit divine, as these blest scenes
    are closing,
Lend us thy presence and grant us
    thy grace;
May we, on Jesus' dear bosom reposing,
Commune with our Savior and see
    his loved face.

2 Strong in the food on which, here,
    thou hast fed us,
Renewed in our souls, hence home-
    ward we go;
Trusting in Jesus, who thus far hath led us,
Nothing shall daunt us: we fear
    naught below.

3 Clad with the armor that ne'er can
    be broken,
Lead us, dear Savior, the victory
    to gain;
Sure of the conquest thy cross hath
    bespoken,
Soldiers of Zion shall never be slain.

1. Come in our midst, O gracious Lord, Unveil thy smiling face;

Dis-till in ev - ery wait-ing heart, The dew of heavenly grace;
D. S. We worship in thy ho - ly name, Oh bless this hour of prayer.

From earthly scenes we turn aside, On thee we cast our care.

478 *Holy Spirit Invoked.*

2 Come in our midst, oh gracious Lord,
　Thy promise we believe,
That bids us seek and we shall find,
　Ask, and we shall receive.
We gather at thy mercy-seat,
　Our only hope is there,
We plead the merits of thy blood,
　Oh, bless this hour of prayer!

3 Come in our midst, oh gracious Lord,
　Eternal King of kings,
And fold the children of the law
　Beneath thy mighty wings.
Support the weak, the mourner cheer,
　Help all their cross to bear;
Thou Spring of Joy, thou Source of Life,
　Oh bless this hour of prayer!

Thane, Key B♭.

479 *Prayer.*

1 Prayer is the soul's sincere desire,
　Uttered or unexpressed:
The motion of a hidden fire
　That trembles in the breast.
Prayer is the burden of a sigh,
　The falling of a tear,
The upward glancing of an eye,
　When none but God is near.

2 Prayer is the Christian's vital breath
　The Christian's native air,
His watch-word at the gates of death,
　He enters heaven with prayer.
Prayer is the contrite sinner's voice,
　Returning from his ways;
While angels in their songs rejoice,
　And cry, "Behold, he prays!"

Lucius, Key C.

1. How sweet the name of Je - sus sounds In a be - liev - er's ear;

Cuo. I do be - lieve, I now be - lieve, That Jesus died for me;

It soothes his sorrows, heals his wounds, And drives away his fear.

And through his blood, his precious blood, I shall from sin be free.

480   *Believe.*   C. M.

2 It makes the wounded spirit whole,
   And calms the troubled breast;
'T is manna to the hungry soul,
   And to the weary rest.

3 Weak is the effort of my heart,
   And cold my warmest thought;
But when I see thee as thou art,
   I 'll praise thee as I ought.

4 Till then I would thy love proclaim
   With every fleeting breath;
And may the music of thy name
   Refresh my soul in death.

481   *Jesus precious to the Believer.*   C. M.

1 Jesus, I love thy charming name;
   'T is music to my ear;
Fain would I sound it out so loud
   That earth and heaven might hear.

2 Yes, thou art precious to my soul,
   My transport and my trust;
Jewels to thee are gaudy toys,
   And gold is sordid dust.

3 All my capacious powers can wish
   In thee doth richly meet;
Nor to my eyes is light so dear,
   Nor friendship half so sweet.

4 Thy grace shall dwell upon my heart,
   And shed its fragrance there:
The noblest balm of all its wounds,
   The cordial of its care.

5 I 'll speak the honors of thy name
   With my last, laboring breath,
And, dying, clasp thee in my arms,
   The antidote of death.

482   *Lord, I Believe.*   C. M.

1 Lord, I believe; thy power I own;
   Thy word I would obey;
I wander comfortless and lone,
   When from thy truth I stray.

2 Lord, I believe; but gloomy fears
   Sometimes bedim my sight;
I look to thee with prayers and tears,
   And cry for strength and light.

3 Lord, I believe; but oft, I know,
   My faith is cold and weak;
Strengthen my weakness, and bestow
   The confidence I seek.

4 Yes, I believe; and only thou
   Canst give my soul relief;
Lord, to thy truth my spirit bow;
   Help thou my unbelief.

Arlington, Key G.   Ortonville, Key B♭.   Claxton, Key E♭.

TUCKER.

1. Oh, for a thousand tongues to sing My great Re-deemer's praise;

The glo-ries of my God and King, The triumphs of his grace.

483   *Praise to the Savior.*   C. M.

2 My gracious Master, and my God,
    Assist me to proclaim,
To spread thro' all the earth abroad,
    The honors of thy name.

3 Jesus! the name that charms our fears,
    That bids our sorrows cease;
'T is music in the sinner's ears;
    'T is life, and health, and peace,

4 He breaks the power of reigning sin,
    He sets the prisoner free;
His blood can make the foulest clean;
    His blood availed for me.

484   *The Church Triumphant.*   C. M.

1 A host of spirits round the throne
    In humble posture stand,
On every head a starry crown,
    A palm in every hand.

2 From different regions of the globe,
    These happy spirits came;
In Jesus' blood they washed their robes,
    And triumphed in his name.

3 One glorious body now they make,
    More glorious far their Head;
Their souls to rapturous joys awake;
    Their sorrows all are fled.

485   *The Gospel Trumpet.*   C. M.

1 Let every mortal ear attend,
    And every heart rejoice;
The trumpet of the gospel sounds
    With an inviting voice.

2 Ho! ye that pant for living streams,
    And pine away, and die..
Here you may quench your raging thirst
    With springs that never dry.

3 The happy gates of gospel grace
    Stand open night and day;
Lord, we are come to seek supplies,
    And drive our wants away.

486   *Zion's Enlargement Desired.*   C. M.

1 Shine, mighty God, on Zion shine,
    With beams of heavenly grace;
Reveal thy power thro' every land,
    And show thy smiling face.

2 When shall thy name from shore to shore,
    Sound through the earth abroad.
And distant nations know and love
    Their Savior and their God?

3 Sing to the Lord, ye distant lands;
    Sing loud, with joyful voice;
Let every tongue exalt his praise,
    And every heart rejoice.

Brown, Key C.   Burnell, Key F.   Peterboro, Key G.

1. Once more, my soul, the ris-ing day Sa-lutes thy wak-ing eyes;

Once more, my voice, thy tribute pay To him who rules the skies.

487 *Divine Forbearance.* C. M.

2 'Tis he supports my mortal frame;
  My tongue shall speak his praise;
My sins would rouse his wrath to flame,
  And yet his wrath delays.

3 Great God, let all my hours be thine,
  While I enjoy the light;
Then shall my sun in smiles decline,
  And bring a peaceful night.

488 *Prayer for Strong Faith.* C. M.

1 Oh for a faith that will not shrink,
  Though pressed by every foe.
That will not tremble on the brink
  Of any earthly woe!

2 That will not murmur nor complain
  Beneath the chastening rod.
But, in the hour of grief or pain,
  Will lean upon its God.

3 A faith that keeps the narrow way
  Till life's last hour is fled,
And with a pure and heavenly ray
  Lights up a dying bed.

4 Lord, give us such a faith as this,
  And then, whate'er may come,
We'll taste, e'en here, the hallowed bliss
  Of an eternal home.

489 *Gospel a Savor of Life or Death.* C. M.

1 Christ and his cross are all our theme;
  The mysteries that we speak
Are scandal in the Jews' esteem,
  And folly to the Greek.

2 But souls enlightened from above
  With joy receive the word;
They see what wisdom, power, and love
  Shine in their dying Lord.

3 The vital savor of his name
  Restores their fainting breath;
But unbelief perverts the same
  To guilt, despair, and death.

4 Till God diffuse his graces down,
  Like showers of heavenly rain,
In vain Apollo sows the ground,
  And Paul may plant in vain.

490 *Joy over Converts.* C. M.

1 Dear Savior, we rejoice to hear
  Poor sinners sweetly tell,
How thou art pleased to save from sin,
  From sorrow, death, and hell.

2 Lord, we unite to praise thy name
  For grace so freely given;
Still may we keep in Zion's road,
  And dwell at last in heaven.

Arlington, Key G. Marlow, Key F. Christmas, Key D.

SCOTCH.

1. As o'er the past my mem'ry strays, Why heaves the secret sigh?

'T is that I mourn de-part-ed days, Still un-pre-pared to die.

491   *Painful Recollections.*   C. M.

2 The world and worldly things beloved,
   My anxious thoughts employed;
And time unhallowed, unimproved,
   Presents a fearful void.

3 Yet, holy Father, wild despair
   Chase from my laboring breast,
Thy grace it is which prompts the prayer,
   That grace can do the rest.

4 My life's brief remnant all be thine!
   And when thy sure decree
Bids me this fleeting breath resign,
   Oh speed my soul to thee.

492   *A Parting Blessing Invoked.*   C. M.

1 One more petition, O our God,
   We lay before thy throne;
That thou wouldst bless us as we part,
   And our weak efforts own.

2 Oh ever may the love of God
   Within our bosoms glow;
And love to man in all our acts,
   The humble Christian show.

3 That when thou makest up thy gems
   In yonder world of bliss,
It may be known that not in vain
   Our mission was in this.

493   *Brevity of Life.*   C. M.

1 Life is a span—a fleeting hour:
   How soon the vapor flies!   •
Man is a tender, transient flower,
   That e'en in blooming dies.

2 The once-loved form, now cold and dead,
   Each mournful thought employs;
And Nature weeps her comforts fled,
   And withered all her joys.

3 Hope looks beyond the bounds of time
   When what we now deplore
Shall rise in full, immortal prime,
   And bloom to fade no more.

4 Cease, then, fond Nature, cease thy tears;
   Thy Savior dwells on high;
There everlasting spring appears;
   There joys shall never die.

494   *Praise to Christ.*   C. M.

1 To him who loved the souls of men,
   And washed us in his blood,
To royal honors raised our head,
   And made us priests to God,—

2 To him let every tongue be praise,
   And every heart be love,
All grateful honors paid on earth,
   And nobler songs above.

Downs, Key E♭.   Farwell, Key E♭.   Naomi, Key D.

1. Lord, lead the way the Sav-ior went, By lane and cell obscure,

And let our treasures still be spent Like his up-on the poor.

495 *Invitation to Christ's Kingdom.* C. M.

2 Like him through scenes of deep distress
  Who bore the world's sad weight,
We, in their gloomy loneliness,
  Would seek the desolate.

3 For thou hast placed us side by side
  In this wide world of ill,
And that thy followers may be tried—
  The poor are with us still.

4 Small are the offerings we can make,
  Yet thou hast taught us, Lord,
If given for the Savior's sake,
  They lose not their reward.

496 *The True Guide.* C. M.

1 Thy word is to my feet a lamp,
  The way of truth to show;
A watch-light, to point out the path
  In which I ought to go.

2 Let still my sacrifice of praise
  With thee acceptance find;
And in thy righteous judgments, Lord,
  Instruct my willing mind.

3 Thy testimonies I have made
  My heritage and choice;
For they, when other comforts fail,
  My drooping heart rejoice.

497 *The Way, the Truth, the Life.* C. M.

1 Thou art the Way, to thee alone
  From sin and death we flee;
And he who would the Father seek,
  Must seek him, Lord, by thee.

2 Thou art the Truth, thy word alone
  True wisdom can impart;
Thou only canst inform the mind
  And purify the heart.

3 Thou art the Life, the rending tomb
  Proclaims thy conquering arm,
And those who put their trust in thee
  Nor death nor hell shall harm.

4 Thou art the Way, the Truth, the Life;
  Grant us that way to know,
That truth to keep, that life to win,
  Whose joys eternal flow.

498 *Treasure in Heaven.* C. M.

1 Yes, there are joys that can not die,
  With God laid up in store—
Treasures, beyond the changing sky,
  More bright than golden ore.

2 To that bright world my soul aspires,
  With rapturous delight:
Oh for the Spirit's quickening powers,
  To speed me in my flight!

Marlow, Key G.   Avon, Key A.   Siloam, Key D.

1. Be-hold! be-hold! the Lamb of God, On the cross, on the cross; ⎫
For you he shed his precious blood, On the cross, on the cross; ⎬
D. C. Draw near and see your Savior die, On the cross, on the cross.

Slower. *D. C.*

Now hear his all im-por-tant cry, "E - loi la - ma sa-bach-tha-ni."

499 *Behold the Lamb.*

2 Come, sinners, see him lifted up,
On the cross, on the cross;
He drinks for you the bitter cup,
On the cross, on the cross;
The rocks do rend, the mountains quake,
While Jesus doth atonement make,
While Jesus suffers for our sake,
On the cross, on the cross.

3 And now the mighty deed is done,
On the cross, on the cross;
The battle's fought, the vict'ry's won,
On the cross, on the cross;

To heaven he turns his languid eyes:
"'Tis finished now," the conq'ror cries,
Then bows his sacred head and dies,
On the cross, on the cross.

4 Let every mourner rise and cling
To the cross, to the cross;
Let every Christian come and sing
Round the cross, round the cross;
There let the preacher take his stand,
And, with the Bible in his hand,
Go preach the doctrine through the land
Of the cross, of the cross.

500 OH, HOW I LOVE JESUS.

1. Oh, how I love Je - sus, Oh, how I love Je - sus,
2. How can I for - get thee? How can I for - get thee?

Oh, how I love Je - sus. Be - cause he first loved me.
How can I for - get thee? Dear Lord, remem - ber me.

1. A - las! and did my Sa-vior bleed? And did my Sovereign die?

Would he de-vote that sa - cred head, For such a worm as I?

501 *Godly Sorrow at the Cross.* C. M.

2 Was it for crimes that I had done
He groaned upon the tree?
Amazing pity! grace unknown!
And love beyond degree!

3 Well might the sun in darkness hide,
And shut his glories in,
When Christ, the mighty Maker, died
For man—the creature's sin.

4 Thus might I hide my blushing face
While his dear cross appears,
Dissolve my heart in thankfulness,
And melt mine eyes to tears.

5 But drops of grief can ne'er repay
The debt of love I owe:
Here, Lord, I give myself away;
'T is all that I can do.

502 *The Gospel Feast.* C. M.

1 How sweet and awful is the place,
With Christ within the doors,
While everlasting love displays
The choicest of her stores!

2 While all our hearts, and every song,
Join to admire the feast,
Each of us cries, with thankful tongue,
"Lord, why was I a guest?

3 "Why was I made to hear thy voice,
And enter while there's room,
When thousands make a wretched choice,
And rather starve than come?"

4 'T was the same love that spread the feast
That sweetly forced us in;
Else we had still refused to taste,
And perished in our sin.

5 We long to see thy churches full,
That all the chosen race
May, with one voice, and heart, and soul,
Sing thy redeeming grace.

503 *Divine Help.* C. M.

1 Forever blessed be the Lord,
My Savior and my shield;
He sends his Spirit with his word,
To arm me for the field.

2 When sin and hell their force unite,
He makes my soul his care,
Instructs me to the heavenly fight,
And guards me through the war.

3 A Friend and Helper so divine
Doth my weak courage raise;
He makes the glorious victory mine,
And his shall be the praise.

China, Key C.   Claxton, Key B♭.   Balerma, B♭.

By permission.   Dr. LOWELL MASON.

Andante. Soprano.

1. Watchman! tell us of the night, What its signs of promise are.

Tenor.

Traveler! o'er yon mountain's height, See that glory beaming star!

Soprano.

Watchman! does its beauteous ray Aught of hope or joy foretell?

Tenor.

Traveler! yes! it brings the day, Promised day of Is - ra - el.

Chorus to 1st and 2d stanzas.   **Chorus to 3d stanza.**

Traveler! yes! it brings the day, Promised day of Isra - el! Traveler!
Traveler! ages are its own, See, it bursts o'er all the earth.

lo! the Prince of Peace! Lo! the Son of God is come! Lo! the Son of God is come!

504   *Watchman! Tell us of the Night.*

2 Watchman! tell us of the night,
  Higher yet the star ascends:
Traveler! blessedness and light,
  Peace and truth its course portends!
Watchman! will its beams alone
  Gild the spot that gave them birth?
Traveler! ages are its own,
  See, it bursts o'er all the earth.

3 Watchman! tell us of the night,
  For the morning seems to dawn;
Traveler! darkness takes its flight,
  Doubt and terror are withdrawn.
Watchman! let thy wand'rings cease;
  Hie thee to thy quiet home;
Traveler! lo! the Prince of Peace,
  Lo! the Son of God is come.

1. O-ver the ocean wave, far, far a-way, There the poor heathen live,
Chor. Pity them, pity them, Christians at home, Haste with the bread of life,

End.　　　　　　　　　　　　*D. C. Chorus.*

wait-ing for day; { Groping in ig - norance, dark as the night, }
hasten and come. { No blessed Bi - ble to give them the light. }

505　　　　　　　*Missionary.*

2 Here in this happy land we have the light
Shining from God's own word, free,
　　pure, and bright;
Shall we not send to them Bibles to read,
Teachers, and preachers, and all that
　　they need?

3 Then, while the mission ships glad
　　tidings bring,
List! as that heathen band joyfully sing,
"Over the ocean wave, oh, see them come,
Bringing the bread of life, guiding
　　us home."

WAITING BY THE RIVER.

Arr. by W. H. D.

Duet. Repeat in full Chorus.

1. Tho' the mist hang o'er the river,　And its billows loudly roar,
2. And the bright celes-tial city,　We have caught such radiant gleams.

Cho. We are wait-ing by the river,　We are watching on the shore,

Yet we hear the song of angels,　Wafted from the oth - er shore.
Of its towers, like dazzling sunlight, With its sweet and peaceful streams.

On - ly waiting for the angels,　Soon they'll come to bear us o'er.

506　　　　　　*Waiting by the River.*

3 He has called for many a loved one,
　We have seen them leave our side;
With our Savior we shall meet them
When we too have crossed the tide.

4 When we've passed that vale of shadows,
　With its dark and chilling tide;
In that bright and glorious city
We shall evermore abide.

HENRY. C. M.

S. B. POND.

1. Joy to the world! the Lord is come! Let earth re-ceive her King;

Let ev-ery heart prepare him room, And heaven and na-ture sing.

507 *Joy to the World.* C. M.

2 Joy to the earth! the Savior reigns!
Let men their songs employ;
While fields, and floods, rocks, hills, and plains
Repeat the sounding joy.

3 No more let sins and sorrows grow,
Nor thorns infest the ground;
He comes to make his blessings flow
Far as the curse is found.

4 He rules the world with truth and grace,
And makes the nations prove
The glories of his righteousness,
And wonders of his love.

508 *Holy Spirit Desired.* C. M.

1 Enthroned on high, Almighty Lord!
The Holy Ghost send down;
Fulfill in us thy faithful word,
And all thy mercies crown.

2 Though on our heads no tongues of fire
Their wondrous powers impart,
Grant, Savior, what we more desire,
Thy Spirit in our heart.

3 Spirit of life, and light, and love,
Thy heavenly influence give;
Quicken our souls, our guilt remove,
That we in Christ may live.

509 *Joy in Christ's Love.* C. M.

1 Sweet was the time when first I felt
The Savior's pardoning blood
Applied to cleanse my soul from guilt,
And bring me home to God.

2 Soon as the morn the light revealed,
His praises tuned my tongue;
And when the evening shades prevailed,
His love was all my song.

3 In prayer my soul drew near the Lord,
And saw his glory shine;
And when I read his holy word,
I called each promise mine.

510 *Spring.* C. M.

1 When verdure clothes the fertile vale,
And blossoms deck the spray,
And fragrance breathes in every gale,
How sweet the vernal day!

2 Hark! how the feathered warblers sing!
'Tis nature's cheerful voice;
Soft music hails the lovely spring,
And woods and fields rejoice.

3 Oh God of nature and of grace,
Thy heavenly gifts impart;
Then shall my meditation trace
Spring, blooming in my heart.

Peterboro, Key G.   Marlow, Key G.   Christmas, Key D.

Dr. L. MASON.

1. For-ev - er with thyself, dear Lord, What thought can comprehend

The glo - ries of that bless - ed place, Where thou dost ev-er dwell.

511 *Love of Christ.* C. M.

2 That love that brought thee down to earth
From Glory's bright abode,
To seek the guilty and the lost
And bring them back to God.

3 Thy life thou gavest on the cross
Thy blood has cleansed from sin,
Thy power has reached the vilest ones,
And songs of praise they sing.

4 We sing thy love that met our need
When ruined in our sins,
That took us all and made us clean,
And fixed our hearts on thee.

512 *Preciousness of the Bible.* C. M.

1 How precious is the book divine,
By inspiration given!
Bright as a lamp its doctrines shine,
To guide our souls to heaven.

2 It sweetly cheers our drooping hearts
In this dark vale of tears;
Life, light, and joy, it still imparts,
And quells our rising fears.

3 This lamp, through all the tedious night
Of life, shall guide our way.
Till we behold the clearer light
Of an eternal day.

513 *Importance of the Bible.* C. M.

1 How shall the young secure their hearts
And guard their lives from sin ?
Thy word the choicest rules imparts,
To keep the conscience clean.

2 'T is like the sun, a heavenly light,
That guides us all the day,
And, through the dangers of the night,
A lamp to lead our way.

3 Thy precepts make us truly wise :
We hate the sinner's road ;
We hate our own vain thoughts that rise
But love thy law, O God.

4 Thy word is everlasting truth ;
How pure is every page !
That holy book shall guide our youth,
And well support our age.

514 *Looking for Direction.* C. M.

1 Lord, in the morning thou shalt hear
My voice ascending high ;
To thee will I direct my prayer,
To thee lift up mine eye ;—

2 Oh, may thy Spirit guide my feet
In ways of righteousness,
Make every path of duty straight
And plain before my face.

Brown, Key E. Lanesboro, Key C. Burnell, Key F.

WOODLAND. C. M.

N. D. GOULD.

1. There is an hour of peaceful rest To mourning wand'rers given; There is a joy for

souls distressed, A balm for every wounded breast, 'T is found above in heaven.

515 *The Land of Rest.* C. M.

1 There is an hour of peaceful rest
  To mourning wand'rers given;
There is a joy for souls distressed,
A balm for every wounded breast,—
  'T is found above in heaven.

2 There is a home for weary souls
  By sin and sorrow driven,
When tossed on life's tempestuous shoals,
Where storms arise and ocean rolls,
  And all is drear but heaven.

3 There faith lifts up the tearless eye
  To brighter prospects given;
And views the tempest passing by,
The evening shadows quickly fly,
  And all serene in heaven.

516 *On Earth Peace.* C. M.

1 Calm on the listening ear of night
  Come heaven's melodious strains,
Where wild Judea stretches far
  Her silver-mantled plains.

2 Celestial choirs, from courts above,
  Shed sacred glories there,
And angels, with their sparkling lyres,
  Make music on the air.

3 The joyous hills of Palestine
  Send back the glad reply,

And greet, from all their holy heights,
  The dayspring from on high.

4 O'er the blue depths of Galilee
  There comes a holier calm,
And Sharon waves, in solemn praise,
  Her silent groves of palm.

5 "Glory to God!" the sounding skies
  Aloud with anthems ring;
"Peace to the earth, good-will to men,
  From heaven's eternal King!"

517 *Remembering Christ.* C. M.

1 If human kindness meets return,
  And owns the grateful tie;
If tender thoughts within us burn,
  To feel a friend is nigh,—

2 Oh! shall not warmer accents tell
  The gratitude we owe
To him who died our fears to quell—
  Our more than orphan's woe?

3 While yet his anguished soul surveyed,
  Those pangs he would not flee,
What love his latest words displayed:
  "Meet, and remember me!"

4 Remember thee—thy death, thy shame,
  Our sinful hearts to share!—
Oh, mem'ry! leave no other name
  But his recorded there.

Dundee, Key F.   Chimes, Key C.   Avon, Key A.

1. Where Je-sus is there is no night, All darkness flees a-way;

His presence sheds a ho-ly light, And brings eter-nal day.

518 *Longings Heavenward.* C. M.

2 In the glad sunshine of his smile
My soul is all aglow,
And spreads itself in praises, while
Imprisoned here below.

3 I pant to reach the heavenly rest,
The victor's crown to win;
To lay my head on Jesus' breast,
Forever freed from sin.

4 That rest belongs to weary souls,
That freedom must be won:
The welcoming Savior's arm enfolds
His faithful ones alone.

5 Then let me work, that rest to gain,
My freedom let me win;
And, faithful, patiently remain
Till Christ says, "Enter in!"

519 *Load of Sin.* C. M.

1 Beneath my load of sin borne down,
A wasted life I mourn;
How dare I hope to wear the crown
By saints in glory worn?

2 My bankrupt soul all helpless lies,
No earthly succor near;
In faith to heaven I turn my eyes,
And see my surety there.

3 Yes, Jesus died my soul to save,
The cross for me endured;
To pay my debt his life he gave,
His blood the debt secured.

4 He asks from me but small return,
An humble, trustful heart,
That shall in him all grace discern,
And from him ne'er depart.

5 My soul redeemed, to him belongs;
It shall to him be given;
And when life ends I'll sing the songs
The angels sing in heaven.

520 *Expostulation with Sinners.* C. M.

1 Sinner, the voice of God regard;
His mercy speaks to-day;
He calls you, by his sovereign word,
From sin's destructive way.

2 Like the rough sea, that can not rest,
You live devoid of peace;
A thousand stings within your breast
Deprive your soul of ease.

3 But he who turns to God shall live,
Through his abounding grace;
His mercy will the guilt forgive
Of those who seek his face.

Balerma, Key B♭. Burnell, Key F. Melody, Key A♭.

14

1. A-las! what hourly dangers rise! What snares beset my way!

To heaven, oh let me lift mine eyes, And hourly watch and pray.

521   *Divine and Implored.*   C. M.

2 How oft my mournful thoughts complain,
And melt in flowing tears!
My weak resistance, ah, how vain!
How strong my foes and fears!

3 Oh gracious God, in whom I live,
My feeble efforts aid;
Help me to watch, and pray, and strive,
Though trembling and afraid.

4 Whene'er temptations lure my heart,
Or draw my feet aside,
My God, thy powerful aid impart,
My Guardian and my Guide.

522   *Winter.*   C. M.

1 Stern Winter throws his icy chains,
Encircling nature round;
How bleak, how comfortless, the plains,
Late with gay verdure crowned!

2 The sun withholds his vital beams,
And light and warmth depart;
And drooping, lifeless nature seems
An emblem of my heart.

3 Return, oh blissful sun, and bring
Thy soul-reviving ray:
This mental winter shall be spring
This darkness cheerful day.

523   *Reflections at the End of the Year.* C. M.

1 And now, my soul, another year
Of thy short life is past;
I can not long continue here,
And this may be my last.

2 Much of my hasty life is gone,
Nor will return again;
And swift my passing moments run—
The few that yet remain.

3 Awake, my soul; with utmost care
Thy true condition learn:
What are thy hopes? how sure? how fair?
What is thy great concern?

4 Behold, another year begins;
Set out afresh for heaven;
Seek pardon for thy former sins,
In Christ so freely given.

524   *A Blessing Sought.*   C. M.

1 Great Shepherd of thy people, hear;
Thy presence now display;
We kneel within thy house of prayer;
Oh, give us hearts to pray.

2 Help us, with holy fear and joy,
To kneel before thy face;
Oh, make us creatures of thy power,
The children of thy grace.

Downs, Key E♭.   Siloam, Key D.   Claxton, Key B♭.

525 *Thanksgiving for Deliverance.* C. M.

1 Our little bark, on boisterous seas,
  By cruel tempests tossed,
Without one cheerful beam of hope,
  Expecting to be lost,—

2 We to the Lord, in humble prayer,
  Breathed out our sad distress;
Though feeble, yet with contrite hearts,
  We begged return of peace.

3 Then ceased the stormy winds to blow;
  The surges ceased to roll;
And soon again a placid sea
  Spoke comfort to the soul.

4 Oh, may our grateful, trembling hearts
  Their hallelujahs sing
To him who hath our lives preserved,
  Our Savior and our King.

526 *Habitual Devotion.* C. M.

1 While thee I seek, protecting Power,
  Be my vain wishes stilled;
And may this consecrated hour
  With better hopes be filled.

2 Thy love the power of thought bestowed;
  To thee my thoughts would soar;
Thy mercy o'er my life has flowed,
  That mercy I adore.

3 In each event of life, how clear
  Thy ruling hand I see!
Each blessing to my soul more dear
  Because conferred by thee.

4 In every joy that crowns my days,
  In every pain I bear,
My heart shall find delight in praise,
  Or seek relief in prayer.

5 When gladness wings my favored hour,
  Thy love my thoughts shall fill;
Resigned, when storms of sorrow lower,
  My soul shall meet thy will.

6 My lifted eye, without a tear,
  The gathering storm shall see;
My steadfast heart shall know no fear;
  That heart shall rest on thee.

527 *Secret Communion with God.* C. M.

1 Sweet is the prayer whose holy stream,
  In earnest pleading flows;
Devotion dwells upon the theme,
  And warm and warmer glows.

2 Faith grasps the blessing she desires;
  Hope points the upward gaze;
And love, celestial love, inspires
  The eloquence of praise.

3 But sweeter far the still small voice,
  Unheard by human ear,
When God has made the heart rejoice,
  And dried the bitter tear.

4 No accents flow, no words ascend;
  All utt'rance faileth there;
But God himself doth comprehend,
  And answer, silent prayer.

528 *Secret Prayer at Twilight.* C. M.

1 I love to steal awhile away
  From every cumbering care,
And spend the hours of setting day
  In humble, grateful prayer.

2 I love in solitude to shed
  The penitential tear,
And all his promises to plead
  Where none but God can hear.

3 I love to think on mercies past,
  And future good implore,
And all my cares and sorrows cast
  On him whom I adore.

529 *Hinder me Not.* C. M.

1 In all my Lord's appointed ways
  My journey I'll pursue;
"Hinder me not," ye much-loved saints,
  For I must go with you.

2 Through duties, and through trials too,
  I'll go at his command;
"Hinder me not," for I am bound
  To my Immanuel's land.

3 And when my Savior calls me home,
  Still this my cry shall be—
"Hinder me not!" come, welcome, death,
  I'll gladly go with thee.

Brattle Street, Key E♭.   Naomi, Key D.

Arr. by Dr. L. Mason.

1. Oh, it is hard to work for God, To rise and take his part,

Up - on this bat - tle - field of earth, And not some-times lose heart.

530   *The Right Must Win.*   C. M.

2 He hides himself so wondrously,
    As though there was no God;
He is least seen when all the powers
    Of ill are most abroad.

3 Or he deserts us in the hour,
    The fight is all but lost,
And seems to leave us to ourselves
    Just when we need him most.

4 Workman of God, oh lose not heart,
    But learn what God is like,
And in the darkest battle-field
    Thou shalt know where to strike.

5 For right is right, since God is God,
    And right the day must win;
To doubt would be disloyalty,
    To falter would be sin.

531   *Praise to God from all Nations.*   C. M.

1 Oh, all ye nations, praise the Lord;
    His glorious acts proclaim;
The fullness of his grace record,
    And magnify his name.

2 His love is great, his mercy sure,
    And faithful is his word;
His truth forever shall endure;
    Forever praise the Lord.

532   *Overcoming Evil.*   C. M.

1 A youthful band, we tune our praise
    To him whose name we bear,
And to our Elder Brother raise
    In unison our prayer.

2 May he, who once was crucified,
    To us new life impart;
And may his gracious word abide
    Forever in our heart.

533   *The Invitation.*   C. M.

1 The King of heaven his table spreads,
    And blessings crown the board;
Not Paradise, with all its joys,
    Could such delight afford.

2 Pardon and peace to dying men,
    And endless life are given,
Through the rich blood that Jesus shed,
    To raise our souls to heaven.

3 Millions of souls, in glory now,
    Were fed and feasted here;
And millions more, still on the way,
    Around the board appear.

4 All things are ready, come away.
    Nor weak excuses frame;
Crowd to your places at the feast,
    And bless the Founder's name.

Peterboro', Key G.   Jacobs, Key A♭.   Chimes, Key C.

534 *Light in Darkness.* C. M.

1 Dark shadows on our pathway lie;
Thick clouds obscure the light;
Hope trembles, and our graces die,
If thou be not in sight.

2 Oh! give us Faith's all-piercing eye,
Beyond the gloom to see;
On Hope's swift pinions may we fly,
Till we find rest in thee.

3 Revive our fainting, flickering love,
Cast out our faithless fear;
Send down thy Spirit from above,
Thy voice, oh, make us hear!

4 Dispel the blindness from our eyes;
A Savior's charms reveal;
Oh, Sun of Righteousness, arise!
Thy beams alone can heal!

5 Thou great Physician, make us whole;
All lasting grace supply;
Speak peace to every storm-tossed soul,
Say, "Fear not: it is I!"

535 *The Prodigal's Return.* C. M.

1 The long-lost son, with streaming eyes,
From folly just awake,
Reviews his wanderings with surprise,
His heart begins to break.

2 I starve, he cries, nor can I bear
The famine in this land,
While servants of my Father share
The bounty of his hand.

3 With deep repentance I'll return,
And seek my Father's face,
Unworthy to be called a son,
I'll ask a servant's place.

4 Far off the Father saw him move—
In pensive silence mourn—
And quickly ran, with arms of love,
To welcome his return.

5 Thro' all the courts the tidings flew,
And spread the joy around;
The angels tuned their harps anew—
The long-lost son is found!

536 *Warning.* C. M.

1 There is a way that seemeth right;
The steps go on with ease;
And conscience slumbers while the soul
Forsakes the path of peace.

2 There is a way that leads to death,
God hath the warning given;
And multitudes pursue that way,
Still dreaming on of heaven.

3 Then let me tremble at the word
That shows this danger nigh;
And wake, and pray, and keep the path
That leads to joys on high.

4 For God will teach the contrite mind
The way of death to shun;
He ne'er will leave a praying soul
By sin to be undone.

537 *Gratitude.* C. M.

1 When all thy mercies, oh my God,
My rising soul surveys,
Transported with the view, I'm lost
In wonder, love, and praise.

2 Unnumbered comforts on my soul
Thy tender care bestowed,
Before my infant heart conceived
From whom those comforts flowed.

3 When in the slippery paths of youth
With heedless steps I ran,
Thine arm, unseen, conveyed me safe,
And led me up to man.

4 Ten thousand thousand precious gifts
My daily thanks employ;
Nor is the least a cheerful heart,
That tastes those gifts with joy.

5 Through every period of my life,
Thy goodness I'll pursue;
And after death, in distant worlds,
The glorious theme renew.

538 *Doxology.* C. M.

To Father, Son, and Holy Ghost,
One God, whom we adore,
Be glory as it was, is now,
And shall be evermore!

Ortonville, Key Bb.   Jacobs, Key Ab.   Burnell, Key F.

1. How pleasant thus to dwell below In fellowship of love!
And, tho' we part, 't is bliss to know The good shall meet above. } The

D. S. To

good shall meet above, The good shall meet above; And tho' we part, 't is
meet to part no more, On Canaan's happy shore, And sing the ever-

End. Chorus.

bliss to know The good shall meet above. Oh, that will be joyful, joyful,
lasting song With those who 've gone before.

D. S. S.

joy - ful! Oh, that will be joy-ful, To meet to part no more.

539　　　*Fellowship of Love.*　　　C. M.

2 Yes, happy tho't! when we are free
　From earthly grief and pain,
In heaven we shall each other see,
　And never part again.
　　Oh, that will be joyful, etc.

3 Then let us each, in strength divine,
　Still walk in wisdom's ways,
That we with those we love may join
　In never-ending praise.
　　Oh, that will be joyful, etc.

Ortonville, Key Bb.　　Brown, Key C.

540 *The Society of Heaven.* C. M.

1 Jerusalem, my happy home,
Name ever dear to me!
When shall my labors have an end,
In joy, and peace, and thee?

2 When shall these eyes thy heaven-built walls
And pearly gates behold?
Thy bulwarks, with salvation strong,
And streets of shining gold?

3 Oh when, thou city of my God,
Shall I thy courts ascend,
Where congregations ne'er break up,
And sabbaths have no end?

4 There happier bowers than Eden's bloom,
Nor sin, nor sorrow, know ;
Blest seats! through rude and stormy scenes
I onward press to you.

541 *The Heavenly Canaan.* C. M.

1 There is a land of pure delight,
Where saints immortal reign;
Eternal day excludes the night,
And pleasures banish pain.

2 There everlasting spring abides,
And never-fading flowers ;
Death, like a narrow sea, divides
That heavenly land from ours.

3 Sweet fields, beyond the swelling flood,
Stand dressed in living green ;
So to the Jews fair Canaan stood,
While Jordan rolled between.

4 Could we but climb where Moses stood,
And view the landscape o'er,
Not Jordan's stream, nor death's cold flood,
Should fright us from the shore.

542 *Heaven in Prospect.* C. M.

1 On Jordan's stormy banks I stand,
And cast a wishful eye
To Canaan's fair and happy land,
Where my possessions lie.

2 Oh, the transporting, rapturous scene,
That rises to my sight!
Sweet fields, arrayed in living green,
And rivers of delight.

3 O'er all those wide-extended plains
Shines one eternal day;
There God the Son forever reigns,
And scatters night away.

4 No chilling winds, nor poisonous breath,
Can reach that healthful shore;
Sickness and sorrow, pain and death,
Are felt and feared no more.

543 *The Hope of Heaven.* C. M.

1 When I can read my title clear
To mansions in the skies,
I bid farewell to every fear,
And wipe my weeping eyes.

2 Should earth against my soul engage,
And fiery darts be hurled,
Then I can smile at Satan's rage,
And face a frowning world.

3 Let cares, like a wild deluge, come,
And storms of sorrow fall,
May I but safely reach my home,
My God, my heaven, my all.

4 There shall I bathe my weary soul
In seas of heavenly rest,
And not a wave of trouble roll
Across my peaceful breast.

544 *Winter.* C. M.

1 The hoary frost, the fleecy snow,
Descend, and clothe the ground;
The liquid streams forbear to flow,
In icy fetters bound.

2 When, from his dreadful stores on high,
God pours the sounding hail,
The man that does his power defy
Shall find his courage fail.

3 God sends his word, and melts the snow;
The fields no longer mourn;
He calls the warmer gales to blow,
And bids the spring return.

4 The changing wind, the flying cloud,
Obey his mighty word;
With songs and honors sounding loud,
Praise ye the sovereign Lord.

Arlington, Key G.   Heber, Key C.   Thane, Key B♭.

W. B. B.

1. I love to think of the heavenly land, Where white-robed angels are;
Where many a friend is gathered safe From fear, and toil, and care.

Refrain.

There 'll be no part - ing, There 'll be no part - ing,

There 'll be no part-ing, There 'll be no part-ing there.

545   *The Heavenly Land.*   C. M.

2 I love to think of the heavenly land,
  Where my Redeemer reigns,
Where rapturous songs of triumph rise
  In endless, joyous strains.

3 I love to think of the heavenly land,
  The saints' eternal home,
Where palms, and robes, and crowns ne'er fade,
  And all our joys are one.

4 I love to think of the heavenly land,
  The greetings there we'll meet,
The harps—the songs forever ours—
  The walks—the golden streets.

5 I love to think of the heavenly land,
  That promised land so fair,
Oh, how my raptured spirit longs
  To be forever there !

REMEMBER ME. C. M.

End.

1. Je - sus, thou art the sinner's friend, As such I look to thee ;
Now in the full-ness of thy love, O Lord, re-mem - ber me.

Cho. Re - member me, re-mem-ber me, Dear Lord ! remem-ber me.

546   *The Sinner's Friend.*   C. M.

2 Remember thy pure word of grace,
  Remember Calvary;
Remember all thy dying groans,
  And then remember me.

3 Lord ! I am guilty—I am vile,
  But thy salvation's free;
Then, in thine all-abounding grace,
  Dear Lord ! remember me.

Slow.

1. I gave my life for thee, My precious blood I shed, That thou might'st ransom'd be,

And quickened from the dead; I gave my life for thee; What hast thou done for me?

Chorus.

This I did for thee, What hast thou done for me?

This I did for thee, What hast thou done for me? Yes,

This I did for thee, What hast thou done for me?

this I did for thee.

547   *This I Did for Thee.*   C. M.

2 I spent long years for thee
  In weariness and woe,
That one eternity
  Of joy thou mightest know;
I spent long years for thee;
Hast thou spent one for me?

3 My Father's house of light,
  My rainbow-circled throne,
I left for earthly night,
  For wand'rings sad and lone;
I left it all for thee;
Hast thou left aught for me?

4 I suffered much for thee,—
  More than thy tongue can tell,
Of bitterest agony,
  To rescue thee from hell;
I suffered much for thee;
What dost thou bear for me?

5 And I have brought to thee,
  Down from my house above,
Salvation full and free,
  My pardon and my love;
Great gifts I brought to thee;
What hast thou brought to me?

6 Oh, let thy life be given,
  Thy years for me be spent,
World fetters all be riven,
  And joy with suffering blent;
Give thou thyself to me,
And I will welcome thee!

By permission.   HASTINGS.

1. Now be - gin the heavenly theme, Sing a - loud in Jesus' name; }
Ye, who his sal - va-tion prove, Triumph in re - deeming love. }

Ye, who see the Father's grace Beaming in the Savior's face,

As to Ca-naan on ye move, Praise, and bless redeeming love.

548   *The Heavenly Theme.*   7s.

1 Now begin the heavenly theme,
Sing aloud in Jesus' name;
Ye who his salvation prove,
Triumph in redeeming love.
Ye who see the Father's grace
Beaming in the Savior's face,
As to Canaan on ye move,
Praise and bless redeeming love.

2 Mourning souls, dry up your tears!
Banish all your sinful fears;
See your guilt and curse removed,—
Canceled by redeeming love.
When his Spirit leads us home,
When we to his glory come,
We shall all the fullness prove
Of the Lord's redeeming love.

549   *Seamen.*   7s.

1 They that toil upon the deep,
And in vessels light and frail

O'er the mighty waters sweep,
   With the billow and the gale,
Mark what wonders God performs,
   When he speaks, and, unconfined,
Rush to battle all his storms,
   In the chariots of the wind.

2 Up to heaven their bark is whirled
   On the mountain of the wave;
Downward suddenly 't is hurled,
   To th' abysses of the grave;
'Mid the tempest now they roll,
   As intoxicate with wine;
Terrors paralyze their soul,
   Helm they quit, and hope resign.

3 Then unto the Lord they cry;
   He inclines his gracious ear,
Sends deliverance from on high,
   Rescues them from all their fear.
Oh that men would praise the Lord
   For his goodness to their race;
For the wonders of his word,
   And the riches of his grace

Martin, Key F.   Aletta, Key F.

1. Jesus, merciful and mild, Lead me as a helpless child: . . .
On no other arm but thine, Would my weary . . . soul recline.
D.C. Guide the wanderer, day by day, In the straight and . . . narrow way.

Thou art read - y to for-give, Thou canst bid the sin-ner live;

550 *Leaning on Jesus.* 7s.

1 Jesus, merciful and mild,
Lead me as a helpless child;
On no other arm but thine
Would my weary soul recline.
Thou art ready to forgive;
Thou canst bid the sinner live;
Guide the wanderer, day by day,
In the straight and narrow way.

2 Thou canst fit me by thy grace
For the heavenly dwelling-place;
All thy promises are sure,
Ever shall thy love endure.
Then what more could I desire,
How to greater bliss aspire?
All I need in thee I see,
Thou art all in all to me.

3 Jesus, Savior all divine,
Hast thou made me truly thine?
Hast thou bought me by thy blood?
Reconciled my heart to God?
Hearken to my tender prayer,
Let me thine own image bear;
Let me love thee more and more,
Till I reach heaven's blissful shore.

Simmons, Key Eb.

551 *Longing for Rest.* 7s.

1 Does the gospel word proclaim
Rest for those that weary be?
Then, my soul, advance thy claim—
Sure that promise speaks to thee!
Marks of grace I can not show,
All polluted is my best;
But I weary am, I know,
And the weary long for rest.

2 Burdened with a load of sin,
Harassed with tormenting doubt,
Hourly conflicts from within,
Hourly crosses from without,
All my little strength is gone,
Sink I must without supply;
Sure upon the earth is none
Can more weary be than I.

3 In the ark the weary dove
Found a welcome resting-place;
Thus my spirit longs to prove
Rest in Christ, the Ark of Grace.
Tempest-tossed I long have been,
And the flood increases fast;
Open, Lord, and take me in,
Till the storm be overpast.

Watchman, Key Eb.

AMBOY. 7s.

Dr. Lowell Mason.

1. Hark! the song of ju-bi-lee, Loud as mighty thunders roar, }
   Or the fullness of the sea, When it breaks upon the shore. }

D.C. Now the kingdoms of this world, Are the kingdoms of his Son.

See Je-hovah's banner furled, Sheathed his sword—he speaks, 't is done!

552　　*Jubilee Song.*　　7s.

2 He shall reign from pole to pole
　With supreme, unbounded sway;
He shall reign, when, like a scroll,
　Yonder heavens have passed away.
Hallelujah! for the Lord
　God omnipotent shall reign:
Hallelujah!—let the word
　Echo round the earth and main.

553　　*Hymn of Dedication.*　　7s.

1 Lord of hosts to thee we raise
Here a house of prayer and praise;
Thou thy people's hearts prepare
Here to meet for praise and prayer.
Let the living here be fed
With thy word, the heavenly bread;
Here in hope of glory blest,
May the dead be laid to rest.

2 Here to thee a temple stand,
While the sea shall gird the land;
Here reveal thy mercy sure,
While the sun and moon endure.
Hallelujah! earth and sky
To the joyful sound reply;
Hallelujah! hence ascend
Prayer and praise till time shall end.

554　　*The Call of Heaven.*　　7s.

1 Sleep not, soldier of the cross!
　Foes are lurking all around;
Look not here to find repose:
　This is but thy battle ground.
Up! and take thy shield and sword;
　Up! it is the call of Heaven:
Shrink not faithless from thy Lord;
　Nobly strive as he hath striven.

2 Break through all the force of ill;
　Tread the might of passion down,
Struggling onward, onward still,
　To the conqu'ring Savior's crown!
Through the midst of toil and pain,
　Let this thought ne'er leave thy breast,
Every triumph thou dost gain
　Makes more sweet thy coming rest.

555　　*The Friend Near.*　　7s.

Brethren! while we sojourn here,
Fight we must, but should not fear;
Foes we have, but we've a Friend,
One that loves us to the end:
Forward, then, with courage go:
Long we shall not dwell below;
Soon the joyful news will come,
" Child, your Father calls—*come home.*"

Wannamaker, Key B♭.　　Simmons, Key D.

1. Pilgrim, burdened with thy sin, Come this way to Zion's gate;
There, till mercy speaks within, Knock and weep and . . . watch and wait.
D.C. Watch, for saving grace is nigh, Wait, till heavenly . . grace appears.

Knock—he knows the sinner's cry, Weep—he loves the mourner's tears;

556 *Burdened Pilgrim.* 7s.

2 Hark, it is the Savior's voice!
"Welcome, pilgrim, to thy rest!"
Now within the gate rejoice,
Safe, and owned, and bought and blest,
Safe, from all the lures of vice;
Owned, by joys the contrite know;
Bought by love, and life the price;
Blest, the mighty debt we owe.

3 Holy pilgrim! what for thee
In a world like this remains?
From thy guarded breast shall flee
Fear, and shame, and doubts, and pains;
Fear—the hope of heaven shall fly,
Shame, from glory's view retire;
Doubt, in full belief shall die,
Pain, in endless bliss expire.

557 *Deep Contrition.* 7s.

1 Jesus save my dying soul;
Make the broken spirit whole:
Humble in the dust I lie:
Savior, leave me not to die.
Jesus, full of every grace,
Now reveal thy smiling face;
Grant the joys of sin forgiven,
Foretaste of the bliss of heaven.

2 All my guilt to thee is known,
Thou art righteous, thou alone;
All my help is from thy cross,
All beside I count but loss.
Lord, in thee I now believe;
Wilt thou, wilt thou not forgive?
Helpless at thy feet I lie;
Savior, leave me not to die.

558 *I Know Thee Not.* 7s.

1 Seek, my soul, the narrow gate,
Enter ere it be too late;
Many ask to enter there
When too late to offer prayer.
God from mercy's seat shall rise,
And forever bar the skies:
Then, though sinners cry without,
He will say, "I know you not."

2 Mournfully will they exclaim:
"Lord, we have profess'd thy Name;
We have ate with thee, and heard
Heavenly teaching in thy word."
Vain, alas, will be their plea,
Workers of iniquity;
Sad their everlasting lot;
Christ will say, "I know you not."

Martin, Key F.   Aletta, Key F.

1. Safe in the arms of Je - sus, Safe on his gen-tle breast;

D. C. Safe in the arms of Je - sus, Safe on his gen-tle breast;

Rit.   *End.*

There by his love o'er - shad - ed, Sweetly my soul shall rest.

There by his love o'er - shad - ed, Sweetly my soul shall rest.

Hark! 'tis the voice of an - gels, Borne in a song to me,

D. C. Chorus.

O - ver the fields of glo - ry, O - ver the Jas-per sea.

559

2 Safe in the arms of Jesus,
Safe from corroding care;
Safe from the world's temptations,
Sin can not harm me there.
Free from the blight of sorrow,
Free from my doubts and fears;
Only a few more trials,
Only a few more tears.
Safe in the arms, etc.

3 Jesus, my heart's dear refuge.
Jesus has died for me;
Firm on the Rock of Ages,
Ever my trust shall be.
Here let me wait with patience,
Wait till the night is o'er;
Wait till I see the morning
Break on the golden shore.
Safe in the arms, etc.

WHITE ROBES.

By permission. W. B. BRADBURY.

1. Who are these in bright array, This exulting, happy throng,
Round the altar night and day, Singing one - - - - triumphant song?

Chorus.

They have clean robes, white robes, White robes are waiting for me!

Yes, clean robes, white robes, Washed in the blood of the Lamb.

560 *White Robes.*

2 These thro' fiery trials trod,
These from great afflictions came;
Now before the throne of God,
Sealed with his almighty name.

3 Joy and gladness banish sighs;
Perfect love dispels all fears;
And forever from their eyes
God shall wipe away their tears.

JESUS LOVES ME.

Rev. R. LOWRY.

1. Let the shadows round me gather, And the day Pass away—Jesus loves me.

Chorus. Jesus loves me, always loves me; You may have All the world—Jesus loves me.

561 *Jesus Loves Me.*

2 Tho' the tide of sorrow 'whelm me,
In the flow
This I know—
Jesus loves me.

3 Neither sin nor death can fright me,
Jesus died,
He'll provide—
Jesus loves me.

J. PLEYEL.

1. Haste, O sin-ner! now be wise; Stay not for the morrow's sun;

Wis-dom if you still de-spise, Hard-er is it to be won.

562   *Danger of Delay.*   7s.

2 Haste, and mercy now implore;
  Stay not for the morrow's sun,
Lest thy season should be o'er
  Ere this evening's stage be run.

3 Haste, O sinner; now return;
  Stay not for the morrow's sun,
Lest thy lamp should cease to burn
  Ere salvation's work is done.

4 Haste, O sinner; now be blest;
  Stay not for the morrow's sun,
Lest perdition thee arrest
  Ere the morrow is begun.

563   *Song of Praise.*   7s.

1 Songs of praise the angels sang,
Heaven with hallelujahs rang,
When Jehovah's work begun,
When he spake, and it was done.

2 Songs of praise awoke the morn,
When the Prince of Peace was born;
Songs of praise arose, when he
Captive led captivity.

3 Heaven and earth must pass away—
Songs of praise shall crown that day;
God will make new heavens and earth—
Songs of praise shall hail their birth.

564   *The Body and Blood of Christ.*   7s.

1 Bread of heaven, on thee we feed,
For thy flesh is meat indeed;
Ever let our souls be fed
With this true and living bread.

2 Vine of heaven, thy blood supplies
This blest cup of sacrifice;
Lord, thy wounds our healing give;
To thy cross we look and live.

3 Day by day with strength supplied,
Through the life of him who died,
Lord of life, oh, let us be
Rooted, grafted, built on thee.

565   *Trials.*   7s.

1 'T is my happiness below
  Not to live without the cross;
But the Savior's power to know,
  Sanctifying every loss.

2 Trials must and will befall;
  But with humble faith to see
Love inscribed upon them all—
  This is happiness to me.

3 Trials make the promise sweet;
  Trials give new life to prayer;
Bring me to my Savior's feet,
  Lay me low and keep me there.

Dallas, Key E♭.   Nuremberg, Key G.

566 *New Year's Day.* 7s.

1 While, with ceaseless course, the sun
Hasted through the former year,
Many souls their race have run,
Never more to meet us here.

2 Fixed in an eternal state,
They have done with all below;
We a little longer wait,
But how little none can know.

3 As the winged arrow flies,
Speedily the mark to find;
As the lightning from the skies
Darts, and leaves no trace behind;

4 Swiftly thus our fleeting days
Bear us down life's rapid stream.
Upward, Lord, our spirits raise;
All below is but a dream.

5 Thanks for mercies past receive;
Pardon of our sins renew;
Teach us, henceforth, how to live,
With eternity in view.

6 Bless thy word to old and young;
Fill us with a Savior's love;
When our life's short race is run,
May we dwell with thee above.

567 *Resurrection of Christ.* 7s.

1 Christ, the Lord, is risen to-day,
Sons of men and angels say;
Raise your songs of triumph high;
Sing, ye heavens, and, earth, reply.

2 Love's redeeming work is done,
Fought the fight, the battle won;
Lo! our Sun's eclipse is o'er;
Lo! he sets in blood no more.

3 Vain the stone, the watch, the seal;
Christ hath burst the gates of hell;
Death in vain forbids his rise;
Christ hath opened Paradise.

4 Lives again our glorious King;
Where, O Death, is now thy sting?
Once he died our souls to save;
Where thy victory, boasting Grave?

568 *Joined to God's People.* 7s.

1 People of the living God,
I have sought the world around,
Paths of sin and sorrow trod,
Peace and comfort nowhere found.

2 Now to you my spirit turns—
Turns, a fugitive unblest;
Brethren, where your altar burns,
Oh, receive me into rest!

3 Lonely I no longer roam,
Like the cloud, the wind, the wave;
Where you dwell shall be my home,
Where you die shall be by grave;

4 Mine the God whom you adore,
Your Redeemer shall be mine;
Earth can fill my soul no more,
Every idol I resign.

569 *Invitation to the intemperate.* 7s.

1 Brother, hast thou wandered far
From thy Father's happy home,
With thyself and God at war?
Turn thee, brother; homeward come,

2 Hast thou wasted all the powers
God for noble uses gave?
Squandered life's most golden hours?
Turn thee, brother; God can save.

3 He can heal thy bitterest wound,
He thy faintest prayer can hear:
Seek him, for he may be found;
Call upon him; he is near.

570 *Waiting upon God.* 7s.

1 Wait, my soul upon the Lord,
To his gracious promise flee,
Laying hold upon his word,
"As thy days thy strength shall be."

2 If the sorrows of thy case
Seem peculiar still to thee,
God has promised needful grace.
"As thy days thy strength shall be."

3 Days of trial, days of grief,
In succession thou may'st see;
This is still thy sweet relief,
"As thy days thy strength shall be."

DALLAS. 7s.

Dolce.   CHERUBINI.

1. Lord! I can not let thee go,   Till a blessing thou bestow;

Do not turn a-way thy face,   Mine's an urgent, pressing case.

571   *Persistent Prayer.*   7s.

2 Once a sinner, near despair,
Sought thy mercy-seat by prayer;
Mercy heard and set him free—
Lord! that mercy came to me.

3 Thou hast helped in every need—
This emboldens me to plead;
After so much mercy past,
Canst thou let me sink at last?

4 No—I must maintain my hold;
'T is thy goodness makes me bold;
I can no denial take,
Since I plead for Jesus' sake.

572   *Hear my Cry.*   7s.

1 Jesus! Master! hear my cry,
  Save me, heal me, with a word;
Fainting at thy feet I lie,
  Thou my whispered plaint hast heard,

2 Jesus! Master! mercy show;
  Thou art passing near my soul;
Thou my inward grief dost know,
  Thou alone canst make me whole.

3 Jesus! Master! as of yore
  Thou didst make the blind man see,
Light upon my soul restore;
  Jesus! Master! heal thou me.

573   *Prayer for Healing.*

1 Gently, gently, lay the rod
On my sinful head, O God!
Stay the wrath, in mercy stay,
Lest I sink beneath its sway.

2 Heal me, for my flesh is weak;
Heal me, for thy grace I seek;
This my only plea I make,—
Heal me for thy mercy's sake.

3 Lo! he comes—he heeds my plea;
Lo! he comes—the shadows flee;
Glory round me dawns once more;
Rise, my spirit! and adore.

574   *Resignation of Will.*   7s.

1 Prince of Peace, control my will;
Bid this struggling heart be still;
Bid my fears and doubtings cease;
Hush my spirit into peace.

2 Thou hast bought me with thy blood,
Opened wide the gate of God:
Peace I ask—but peace must be,
Lord, in being one with thee.

3 May thy will, not mine, be done;
May thy will and mine be one;
Chase those doubtings from my heart,
Now thy perfect peace impart.

Martyn. Key F.   Nuremberg, Key G.   Pleyel's Hymn, Key G.

575 *Sabbath Evening.* 7s.

1 Softly fades the twilight ray
Of the holy Sabbath day;
Gently as life's setting sun,
When the Christian's course is run.

2 Night her solemn mantle spreads
O'er the earth, as daylight fades;
All things tell of calm repose
At the holy Sabbath's close.

3 Peace is on the world abroad;
'T is the holy peace of God—
Symbol of the peace within
When the spirit rests from sin.

4 Still the Spirit lingers near,
Where the evening worshiper
Seeks communion with the skies,
Pressing onward to the prize.

576 *Parting of Christians.* 7s.

1 For a season called to part,
Let us now ourselves commend
To the gracious eye and heart
Of our ever-present Friend.

2 Jesus, hear our humble prayer;
Tender Shepherd of thy sheep,
Let thy mercy and thy care
All our souls in safety keep.

3 In thy strength may we be strong;
Sweeten every cross and pain;
And our wasting lives prolong,
Till we meet on earth again.

577 *Desiring more love to God.* 7s.

1 Lord, my God, I long to know,
Oft it causes anxious thought;
Do I love thee, Lord, or no?
Am I thine, or am I not?

2 Could my heart so hard remain,
Prayer a task and burden prove,
Any duty give me pain,
If I knew a Savior's love?

3 Savior, let me love thee more,
If I love at all, I pray;
If I have not loved before,
Help me to begin to-day.

578 *Thanksgiving.* 7s.

1 Swell the anthem, raise the song;
Praises to our God belong;
Saints and angels, join to sing
Praises to the heavenly King.

2 Blessings from his liberal hand
Flow around this happy land:
Kept by him, no foes annoy;
Peace and freedom we enjoy.

3 Here, beneath a virtuous sway,
May we cheerfully obey,—
Never feel oppression's rod,—
Ever own and worship God.

4 Hark! the voice of nature sing
Praises to the King of kings;
Let us join the choral song,
And the grateful notes prolong.

579 *New Year.* 7s.

1 Bless, O Lord, the opening year
To each soul assembled here;
Clothe thy word with power divine,
Make us willing to be thine.

2 Where thou hast thy work begun,
Give new strength the race to run;
Scatter darkness, doubts, and fears;
Wipe away the mourner's tears.

3 Bless us all, both old and young;
Call forth praise from every tongue;
Let the whole assembly prove
All thy power, and all thy love.

580 *Book Divine.* 7s.

1 Holy Bible, book divine,
Precious treasure, thou art mine!
Mine, to tell me whence I came;
Mine, to teach me what I am.

2 Mine, to chide me when I rove;
Mine, to show a Savior's love,
Mine art thou, to guide my feet;
Mine, to judge, condemn, acquit.

3 Mine to comfort in distress,
If the Holy Spirit bless;
Mine, to show, by living faith,
How to triumph over death.

Horton, Key B♭.   Aletta, Key F.

End.

1. O Lamb of God, still keep me Near to thy wounded side; }
   'T is on - ly there in safe-ty And peace I can a - bide. }

D.C. The grace that sought and found me, Alone can keep me clean.

D. C.

What foes and snares surround me! What doubts and fears within!

581   *Safety in Christ.*   7s & 6s.

2 'T is only in thee hiding,
   I feel my life secure;
Only in thee abiding,
   The conflict can endure.
Thine arm the victory gaineth
   O'er every hateful foe;
Thy love my heart sustaineth
   In all its care and woe.

3 Soon shall my eyes behold thee,
   With rapture, face to face;
One-half hath not been told me
   Of all thy power and grace:
Thy beauty, Lord, and glory,
   The wonders of thy love,
Shall be the endless story
   Of all thy saints above.

582   *Sovereign Mercy.*   7s & 6s.

1 'T is not that I did choose thee,
   For, Lord, that could not be—
This heart would still refuse thee;
   But thou hast chosen me:
Hast, from the sin that stained me,
   Washed me and set me free,
And to this end ordained me,
   That I should live to thee.

2 'T was sovereign mercy called me,
   And taught my opening mind;
The world had else enthralled me
   To heavenly glories blind.
My heart owns none above thee,
   For thy rich grace I thirst;
This knowing—if I love thee,
   Thou must have loved me first.

583   *Repentance.*   7s & 6s.

1 We stand in deep repentance,
   Before thy throne of love;
O God of grace, forgive us;
   The stain of guilt remove;
Behold us while with weeping
   We lift our eyes to thee;
And all our sins subduing,
   Our Father, set us free!

2 Our souls—on thee we cast them,
   Our only refuge thou!
Thy cheering words revive us,
   When pressed with grief we bow:
Thou bear'st the trusting spirit
   Upon thy loving breast,
And givest all thy ransomed
   A sweet, unending rest.

Mendebras, Key F.   Webb, Key B♭.

By permission.

1. In heavenly love a - biding, No change my heart shall fear,
And safe is such con-fid-ing, ... For

D. S. But God is round about me, ... And

End. *D. S.*

nothing changes here. The storm may roar without me, My heart may low be laid,
can I be dismayed?

584   *Heavenly Love Abiding.*   7s & 6s.

1 In heavenly love abiding,
  No change my heart shall fear,
And safe is such confiding,
  For nothing changes here:
The storm may roar without me,
  My heart may low be laid,
But God is round about me,
  And can I be dismayed?

2 Wherever he may guide me,
  No want shall turn me back;
My Shepherd is beside me,
  And nothing can I lack:
His wisdom ever waketh,
  His sight is never dim;
He knows the way he taketh,
  And I will walk with him.

585   *Early Piety.*   7s & 6s.

1 Go thou in life's fair morning,
  Go in thy bloom of youth,
And seek, for thine adorning,
  The precious pearl of truth.
Secure the heavenly treasure,
  And bind it on thy heart;
And let no earthly pleasure
  E'er cause it to depart.

2 Go, ere the cloud of sorrow
  Steals o'er thy bloom of youth;
Defer not till to-morrow—
  Go now and buy the truth.
Go, seek thy great Creator;
  Learn early to be wise;
Go, place upon the altar
  A morning sacrifice.

586   *When shall I Pray?*   7s & 6s.

1 Pray when the dawn is beaming
  Upon the sunny hills,
When half the world is dreaming
  On scenes which fancy fills
Pray at the silent hour,
  As, pensively, you stray
By mead or fragrant bower,
  To while the time away.

2 Pray when the evening closes—
  All nature sinks to rest:
Beast in the lair reposes,
  Bird in the downy nest.
Pray at the midnight season,
  Enveloped in its gloom;
Oh, then, indeed, there's reason—
  'Tis kindred to the tomb.

Immanuel's Land, Key G.   Farmer, Key C.

WORTHING. 8s & 7s.

GERMAN.

1. Hail, thou long-ex-pect-ed Je-sus, Born to set thy peo-ple free!

From our sins and fears release us; Let us find our rest in thee.

587 *Christ Welcomed as a Savior.* 8s & 7s.

1 Hail, thou long-expected Jesus,
Born to set thy people free!
From our sins and fears release us;
Let us find our rest in thee.

2 Israel's strength and consolation,
Hope of all the saints, thou art;
Long desired of every nation,
Joy of every waiting heart.

3 Born thy people to deliver,
Born a child, yet God our King,
Born to reign in us forever,
Now thy gracious kingdom bring.

4 By thine own eternal Spirit,
Rule in all our hearts alone;
By thine all-sufficient merit,
Raise us to thy glorious throne.

588 *Jesus Exalted to the Throne.* 8s & 7s.

1 Jesus, hail! enthroned in glory,
There forever to abide;
All the heavenly hosts adore thee,
Seated at Thy Father's side.

2 There for sinners thou art pleading,
There thou dost our place prepare,
Ever for us interceding,
Till in glory we appear.

3 Worship, honor, power, and blessing,
When unworthy to receive;
Loudest praises without ceasing,
Meet it is for us to give.

4 Help, ye bright, angelic spirits;
Bring your sweetest, noblest lays;
Help to sing our Savior's merit;
Help to chant Immanuel's praise.

589 *Confidence in God's Protection.* 8s & 7s.

1 Savior, breathe an evening blessing
Ere repose our spirits seal;
Sin and want we come confessing;
Thou canst save and thou canst heal.

2 Though destruction walk around us,
Though the arrows past us fly,
Angel guards from thee surround us;
We are safe, if thou art nigh.

3 Though the night be dark and dreary,
Darkness can not hide from thee;
Thou art he who, never weary,
Watchest where thy people be.

4 Should swift death this night o'ertake us,
And command us to the tomb,
May the morn in heaven awake us,
Clad in bright, eternal bloom.

Harwell, Key G.   Ripley, Key E.   Autumn, Key A.

590 *Praise the Lord.* 8s & 7s.

1 Praise the Lord; ye heavens, adore him;
Praise him, angels, in the height;
Sun and moon, rejoice before him;
Praise him, all ye stars of light.

2 Praise the Lord, for he hath spoken;
Worlds his mighty voice obeyed;
Laws, which never can be broken,
For their guidance he hath made.

3 Praise the Lord, for he is glorious;
Never shall his promise fail;
God hath made his saints victorious,
Sin and death shall not prevail.

4 Praise the God of our salvation;
Hosts on high, his power proclaim;
Heaven and earth, and all creation,
Praise and magnify his name.

591 *Mercy Implored.* 8s & 7s.

1 Savior, source of every blessing,
Tune my heart to grateful lays;
Streams of mercy, never ceasing,
Call for ceaseless songs of praise.

2 Teach me some melodious measure,
Sung by raptured saints above;
Fill my soul with sacred pleasure,
While I sing redeeming love.

3 Thou didst seek me when a stranger,
Wandering from the fold of God;
Thou, to save my soul from danger,
Didst redeem me with thy blood.

4 By thy hand restored, defended,
Safe through life, thus far, I 'm come;
Safe, O Lord, when life is ended,
Bring me to my heavenly home.

592 *Onward, Christian.* 8s & 7s.

1 Onward, Christian, though the region
Where thou art be drear and lone;
God has set a guardian legion
Very near thee; press thou on.

2 Listen, Christian, their hosanna
Rolleth o'er thee: "God is love,"
Write upon thy red-cross banner,
"Upward ever; heaven's above."

3 By the thorn-road, and none other,
Is the mount of vision won;
Tread it without shrinking, brother,
Jesus trod it; press thou on.

4 Be this world the wiser, stronger,
For thy life of pain and peace,
While it needs thee; oh! no longer
Pray thou for thy quick release.

5 Pray thou, Christian, daily rather,
That thou be a faithful son;
By the prayer of Jesus, "Father,
Not my will, but thine, be done."

593 *Prayer for Light.* 8s & 7s.

1 Light of those whose dreary dwelling
Borders on the shades of death,
Come and, by thyself revealing,
Dissipate the clouds beneath.

2 Still we wait for thy appearing;
Life and joy thy beams impart,
Chasing all our fears, and cheering
Every poor, benighted heart.

3 Come, extend thy wonted favor,
To our ruined, guilty race;
Come, thou blest, exalted Savior,
Come, apply thy saving grace.

4 By thine all-atoning merit
Every burdened soul release;
By the teachings of thy Spirit
Guide us into perfect peace.

594 *Temperance.* 8s & 7s.

1 O'er the dark abodes of sorrow,
Cheered by no reviving ray,
Brightly temperance arising,
Brings a bright and glorious day.

2 Thousands long in bondage groaning,
Hail the bright and glorious light,
See, from eastern coast to western,
Quickly fly the shades of night.

3 May the heart-reviving story
Win and conquer—never cease;
May the ranks of temperance ever
Multiply and still increase.

Sicily, Key E. Greenville, Key F. Stockwell, B♭.

1. Glorious things of thee are spoken, Zion, cit - y of our God!

:S:

End.

He, whose word can not be broken, Formed thee for his own abode.
D. S. With salvation's walls surrounded, Thou mayst smile at all thy foes.

D. S.

On the Rock of Ages founded, What can shake thy sure repose?

595 *Glory of the Church.* 8s & 7s.

2 See, the streams of living waters,
  Springing from eternal love,
Well supply thy sons and daughters,
  And all fear of want remove:
Who can faint, while such a river
  Ever flows their thirst t' assuage?
Grace, which, like the Lord, the giver,
  Never fails from age to age.

3 Round each habitation hovering,
  See the cloud and fire appear!
For a glory and a covering,
  Showing that the Lord is near;
He who gives them daily manna,
  He who listens when they cry,—
Let him hear the loud hosanna,
  Rising to his throne on high.

596 *Glorying in the Cross.* 8s & 7s.

1 In the cross of Christ I glory,
  Towering o'er the wrecks of time;
All the light of sacred story
  Gathers round its head sublime.
When the woes of life o'ertake me,
  Hopes deceive and fears annoy,
Never shall the cross forsake me;
  Lo! it glows with peace and joy.

2 When the sun of bliss is beaming
  Light and love upon my way,
From the cross the radiance streaming
  Adds new luster to the day.
Bane and blessing, pain and pleasure,
  By the cross are sanctified;
Peace is there that knows no measure,
  Joys that through all time abide.

Worthing, Key F.   Ripley, Key E.

End.

1. Je - sus, I my cross have taken, All to leave and follow thee;
Naked, poor, despised, forsak-en, Thou, from hence, my all shalt be.

D. C. Yet how rich is my con-di-tion, God and heaven are still my own.

D. C.

Perish every fond ambition, All I've sought, or hoped, or known;

Perish ev' - - ry fond am-bition, All I 've sought, or hoped, or known;

---

597 *" Jesus, I my Cross."* 8s & 7s.

2 Let the world despise and leave me,
  They have left my Savior, too;
Human hearts and looks deceive me;
  Thou art not, like them, untrue:
And while thou shalt smile upon me,
  God of wisdom, love, and might,
Foes may hate, and friends may scorn me;
  Show thy face, and all is bright.

3 Man may trouble and distress me,
  'T will but drive me to thy breast;
Life with trials hard may press me,
  Heaven will bring me sweeter rest.
Oh! 't is not in grief to harm me,
  While thy love is left to me ;
Oh! 't were not in joy to charm me,
  Were that joy unmixed with thee.

598 *Christian workers.* 8s & 7s.

1 Brother, you may work for Jesus;
  God has given you a place
In some portion of his vineyard,
  And will give sustaining grace.
He has bidden you " go labor,"
  And has promised a reward,
Even joy and life eternal,
  In the kingdom of your Lord.

2 Brother, you may pray to Jesus,
  In your closet and at home,
In the village, in the city,
  Or wherever you may roam ;
Pray that God may send the Spirit
  Into some dear sinner's heart,
And that in his soul's salvation
  You may bear an humble part.

599 *Christ the Lamb enthroned.* 8s & 7s.

1 Hark! ten thousand harps and voices
  Sound the note of praise above ;
Jesus reigns, and heaven rejoices ;
  Jesus reigns, the God of love ;
See, he sits on yonder throne;
Jesus rules the world alone.

2 Jesus, hail! whose glory brightens
  All above, and gives it worth;
Lord of life, thy smile enlightens,
  Cheers, and charms, thy saints on earth ;
When we think of love like thine,
Lord, we own it love divine.

3 King of glory, reign forever;
  Thine an everlasting crown ;
Nothing from thy love shall sever
  Those whom thou hast made thine own:
Happy objects of thy grace,
Destined to behold thy face.

Nettleton, Key E♭.   Cheer thee, Brother, Key C.

1. Lord, dismiss us with thy blessing, Fill our hearts with joy and peace;

Let us each, thy love possessing, Triumph in redeeming grace. }
Oh, refresh us, oh, refresh us, Trav'ling through this wilderness. }

600   *Dismission.*   8s & 7s.

2 Thanks we give, and adoration,
   For thy gospel's joyful sound;
May the fruits of thy salvation
   In our hearts and lives abound;
     May thy presence, may thy presence,
   With us evermore be found.

3 Then, when'er the signal's given
   Us from earth to call away,
Borne on angel's wings to heaven,
   Glad the summons to obey,
     May we ever, may we ever,
   Reign with Christ in endless day!

601   *Trusting in the Lord.*   8s & 7s.

1 Gently, Lord! oh gently lead us,
   Through this lonely vale of tears;
Through the changes thou'st decreed us,
   Till our last great change appears:

2 When temptation's darts assail us,
   When in devious paths we stray,
Let thy goodness never fail us,
   Lead us in thy perfect way.

3 In the hour of pain and anguish,
   In the hour when death draws near,
Suffer not our hearts to languish,
   Suffer not our souls to fear;

4 And when mortal life is ended,
   Bid us on thy bosom rest,
Till, by angel bands attended,
   We awake among the blest.

602   *The Apostolic Benediction.*   8s & 7s.

1 May the grace of Christ our Savior,
   And the Father's boundless love,
With the Holy Spirit's favor,
   Rest upon us from above.

2 Thus may we abide in union
   With each other and the Lord;
And possess, in sweet communion,
   Joys which earth can not afford.

603   *Prayer for Humility.*   8s & 7s.

1 Let thy grace, Lord, make me lowly,
   Humble all my swelling pride:
Fallen, guilty, and unholy,
   Greatness from my eyes I'll hide.

2 I'll forbid my vain aspiring,
   Nor at earthly honors aim,
No ambitious heights desiring,
   Far above my humble claim.

3 Weaned from earth's delusive pleasures,
   In thy love I'll seek for mine;
Placed in heaven my nobler treasures,
   Earth I quietly resign.

4 Thus the transient world despising,
   On the Lord my hopes rely;
Thus my joys from him arising,
   Like himself, shall never die,

Greenville, Key F.   Autumn, Key A.

From a GREGORIAN CHANT.

End.

1. Always with us, always with us, Words of cheer and words of love; }
Thus the ris - en Savior whispers, From his dwelling-place above. }
D. C. Telling us that in the fu - ture, Gold-en harvests shall be won.

With us when we toil in sadness, Sowing much and reaping none;

D. C.

604 *Christ Ever Present.* 8s & 7s.

1 Always with us, always with us—
    Words of cheer and words of love;
Thus the risen Savior whispers,
    From his dwelling-place above.
With us when we toil in sadness,
    Sowing much and reaping none
Telling us that in the future
    Golden harvests shall be won.

2 With us when the storm is sweeping
    O'er our pathway dark and drear;
Waking hope within our bosoms,
    Stilling every anxious fear.
With us in the lonely valley,
    When we cross the chilling stream;
Lighting up the steps to glory
    With salvation's radiant beam.

605 *Opening of School.* 8s & 7s.

1 We have met in peace together
    In this house of God again;
Constant friends have led us hither,
    Here to chant the solemn strain;
Here to breathe our adoration,
    Here the Savior's praise to sing;
May the Spirit of salvation
    Come with healing in his wing.

2 We have met, and Time is flying;
    We shall part, and still his wing,
Sweeping o'er the dead and dying,
    Will the changeful seasons bring:
Let us, while our hearts are lightest,
    In our fresh and early years,
Turn to him whose smile is brightest,
    And whose grace will calm our fears.

606 *Birth of Christ.* 8s & 7s.

1 Hark! what mean those holy voices,
    Sweetly sounding thro' the skies?
Lo! th' angelic host rejoices;
    Heavenly hallelujahs rise.
Hear them tell the wondrous story,
    Hear them chant in hymns of joy:
"Glory in the highest, glory!
    Glory be to God Most High!

2 "Peace on earth, good will from heaven,
    Reaching far as man is found;
Souls redeemed, and sins forgiven!
    Loud our golden harps shall sound.
Christ is born, the great Anointed;
    Heaven and earth his praises sing!
Oh, receive whom God appointed
    For your Prophet, Priest, and King!"

Harwell, Key G.   Stockwell, Key B♭.

236 MEEK AND LOWLY. 8s & 7s.

GLOVER.

1. Meek and lowly, pure and ho-ly, Chief among the blessed three;
Cho. Meek and lowly, pure and ho-ly, Chief among the blessed three;

End.

Turn-ing sadness in - to gladness, Heaven-born art thou, charity.
Turn-ing sadness in - to gladness, Heaven-born art thou, charity.

Pit - y dwelleth in thy bosom, Kindness reigneth o'er thy heart;

D. C. Chorus.

Gentle thoughts alone can sway thee, Judgment hath in thee no part.

607 *Charity.* 8s & 7s.

1 Meek and lowly, pure and holy,
  Chief among the blessed three,
Turning sadness into gladness,
  Heaven-born art thou, charity!
Pity dwelleth in thy bosom,
  Kindness reigneth o'er thy heart;
Gentle thoughts alone can sway thee—
  Judgment hath in thee no part.

2 Hoping ever, failing never,
  Though deceived, believing still;
Long abiding, all confiding
  To thy heavenly Father's will;
Never weary of well-doing,
  Never fearful of the end;
Claiming all mankind as brothers,
  Thou dost all alike befriend.

608 *Seamen.* 8s & 7s.

1 Tossed upon life's raging billow,
  Sweet it is, O Lord, to know
Thou didst press a sailor's pillow,
  And canst feel a sailor's woe;
Never slumbering, never sleeping,
  Though the night be dark and drear,
Thou the faithful watch art keeping;
  "All, all's well," thy constant cheer.

2 Thus my heart the hope will cherish,
  While to thee I lift mine eye,
Thou wilt save me ere I perish,
  Thou wilt hear the sailor's cry:
And though mast and sail be riven,
  Soon life's voyage will be o'er;
Safely moored in heaven's wide haven,
  Storm and tempest vex no more.

Slow and soft.   From "CARMINA SACRA."

1. Sis - ter, thou wast mild and lovely, Gentle as the summer breeze,

Pleasant as the air of eve-ning When it floats a-mong the trees.

---

609   *Death of a Schoolmate.*   8s & 7s.

1 Sister, thou wast mild and lovely,
  Gentle as the summer breeze,
Pleasant as the air of evening
  When it floats among the trees.

2 Peaceful be thy silent slumber,
  Peaceful in the grave so low;
Thou no more wilt join our number,
  Thou no more our songs shall know.

3 Dearest Sister, thou hast left
  Here thy loss we deeply feel,
But 't is God that hath bereft us,
  He can all our sorrows heal.

4 Yet again we hope to meet thee,
  When the day of life is fled,
Then, in heaven, with joy to greet thee,
  Where no farewell tear is shed.

610   *Bereavement and Resignation.* 8s & 7s.

1 Jesus, while our hearts are bleeding
  O'er the spoils that death has won,
We would, at this solemn meeting,
  Calmly say—thy will be done.

2 Though cast down, we're not forsaken;
  Though afflicted, not alone:
Thou didst give, and thou hast taken:
  Blessed Lord—thy will be done.

3 Though to-day we're fill'd with mourning,
  Mercy still is on the throne;
With thy smiles of love returning,
  We can sing,—thy will be done.

4 By thy hands the boon was given;
  Thou hast taken but thine own;
Lord of earth, and God of heaven,
  Evermore,—thy will be done.

611   *Death of the Christian.*   8s & 7s.

1 Cease, ye mourners, cease to languish
  O'er the grave of those you love;
Pain and death, and night and anguish
  Enter not the world above.

2 While our silent steps are straying,
  Lonely, through night's deepening shade,
Glory's brightest beams are playing
  Round the happy Christian's head.

3 Light and peace at once deriving
  From the hand of God most high,
In his glorious presence living,
  They shall never, never die.

4 Endless pleasure, pain excluding,
  Sickness, there, no more can come:
There, no fear of woe, intruding,
  Sheds o'er heaven a moment's gloom.

1. Ye Christian sons from distant parts, Met 'neath the cross to-day,

We give to you our hands, our hearts, And join in joyful lays.

Chorus.

Dear Christian friends, in ho-ly joy, A wel-come we ex-tend;

May Je - sus grant that all our hearts, In mu - tual love may blend.

612 *Christian Welcome.*

2 Come, Christian hearts, speak forth
the joy
That beams in every eye;
In sacred song each voice employ,
To raise the welcome high.

3 In Christian love swell forth the
song,
That thrills in every breast,
This happy greeting loud prolong,
A welcome to each guest.

613 *Beneath the Cross.* C. M.

1 Opprest with noon-day's scorching heat,
To yonder cross I flee;
Beneath its shelter take my seat:
No shade like this for me!

2 Beneath that cross clear waters burst—
A fountain sparkling free;
And there I quench my desert thirst:
No spring like this for me!

3 A stranger here, I pitch my tent
Beneath this spreading tree;
Here shall my pilgrim life be spent:
No home like this for me!

4 For burdened ones a resting-place,
Beside that cross I see;
I here cast off my weariness:
No rest like this for me!

Slow and gentle.

1. Hast thou, my Master, aught for me to do To hon-or thee to-day?

Hast thou a word of love to some poor soul, That mine may say?
D.S. Thousands are lonely, thousands sigh and weep, But few are glad.

For see, this world that thou hast made so fair, Within its heart is sad.

614   *Where shall I Work To-day?*

2 To which of them shall I stretch
forth my hand?
With sympathetic grasp,
Whose fainting form, shall I for thy
dear sake,
Fondly enclasp?
Straight from my heart, each day, a
blessing goes
Warmly, through thee, to theirs;
They are enfolded in my inmost soul,
And in my prayers.

3 But which, among them all, is mine
to-day?
O guide my willing feet
To some poor soul that fainting on
the way,
Needs counsel sweet.

Or into some sick-room, where I may
speak
With tenderness of thee;
And showing who and what thou art,
O Christ,
Bid sorrow flee.

4 Or unto one whose straits call not
for words;
To one in want, in need;
Who wills not counsel, but would
take from me
A loving deed.
Sure thou hast some work for me to
do!
Oh, open thou mine eyes,
To see how thou wouldst have it done,
And where it lies!

1. There's a beautiful home for thee, Christian, A holy, happy place,

And no sin is there, nor a grief to bear, And never a tearful face.

Chorus.

A beau-ti-ful, peaceful home, O Christian, for thee doth wait,

And the angels stand, with beck'ning hands, Inside of the shining gate.

615   *The Christians Beautiful Home.*

1 There's a beautiful home for thee, Christian,
A holy, happy place,
And no sin is there, nor a grief to bear,
And never a tearful face.

Chorus.

A beautiful, peaceful home,
O Christian, for thee doth wait,
And the angels stand, with beck'ning hands,
Inside of the shining gate.

2 In that beautiful, changeless home, Christian,
There'll be no cross to bear;
All your prayers will end in praises grand,
For Jesus, your Lord, is there.

3 Then go patiently on and on, Christian,
And short the way will seem;
You are nearly there, its mansions fair,
Just over the river gleam.

A FRIEND THAT'S EVER NEAR.

241

By permission.   W. B. BRADBURY.

616

2 All thy prospects will seem brighter
　When the shadow leaves the heart,
And the steps of time beat lighter,
　When the gloomy clouds depart.
Many days have dawned serenely,
　While the birds sang with delight;
But the skies were dark and gloomy
　Ere the sun had reached its height.
　　There's a friend, etc.

3 Soon will dawn a brighter morning,
　On a blessed tranquil shore;
Sighs will then give place to singing,
　Tears to bliss for evermore.
Thou shalt see a world of glory,
　And eternal joy and bliss;
Let not, then, thy soul be moaning
　O'er the woes and cares of this.
　　There's a friend, etc.

16

617 *" Never be Afraid."*

Key F.

1 Never be afraid to speak for Jesus,
  Think how much a word can do;
Never be afraid to own your Savior,
  He who loves and cares for you.

Chorus.

  Never be afraid, never be afraid,
  Never, never, never;
  Jesus is your loving Savior,
  Therefore never be afraid.

2 Never be afraid to work for Jesus,
  In his vineyard, day by day;
Labor with a kind and willing spirit,
  He will all your toil repay.

3 Never be afraid to bear for Jesus
  Keen reproaches when they fall;
Patiently endure your every trial,
  Jesus meekly bore them all.

4 Never be afraid to live for Jesus;
  If you on his care depend,
Safely shall you pass thro' every trial,
  He will bring you to the end.

618 *Dare to do Right.*

Key E.

1 Dare to do right! dare to be true!
You have a work that no other can do;
Do it so bravely, so kindly, so well,
Angels will hasten the story to tell.

Chorus.

  Dare, dare, dare to do right!
  Dare, dare, dare to be true!
  Dare to be true! dare to be true!

2 Dare to do right! dare to be true!
Other men's failures can never save you;
Stand by your conscience, your honor, your faith,
Stand like a hero, and battle till death.

3 Dare to do right! dare to be true!
Keep the great judgment-seat always in view;
Look at your work as you'll look at it then,
Scanned by Jehovah, and angels, and men.

4 Dare to do right! dare to be true!
Jesus, your Savior, will carry you through;
City, and mansion, and throne all in sight,
Can you not dare to be true and do right?

619 *I want to be like Jesus.*

Tune, Watcher, Key D.

1 I want to be like Jesus,
  All gentle, pure, and mild;
His seal upon my forehead,
  And owned as his dear child.
My heart, so weak and sinful,
  All changed by grace divine,
And all my life to serve him,
  And ever call him mine.

2 I want to do like Jesus,
  To mark each passing day
With deeds of love and mercy,
  Or cheer some lonely way;
Speak gentle words of counsel,
  Avoid each secret sin,
And to my precious Savior
  The lost ones seek to win.

3 I want to live like Jesus,
  Whose words with love were fraught;
I want to find his favor,
  By him be truly taught.
Oh, then I'm sure that ever
  His hand will guide me on,
Until the heavenly portals
  And glory shall be won.

620 *Oh, do not be Discouraged.*

Key G.

1 Oh, do not be discouraged,
  For Jesus is your Friend!
Oh, do not be discouraged,
  For Jesus is your Friend!
He will give you grace to conquer,
He will give you grace to conquer,
  And keep you to the end.

Chorus.

I am glad I'm in this army,
Yes, I'm glad I'm in this army,
Yes, I'm glad I'm in this army,
  And I'll battle for the Lord.

2 Fight on, ye Christian soldiers,
  The battle you shall win;
Fight on, ye Christian soldiers,
  The battle you shall win;
For the Savior is your Captain,
For the Savior is your Captain,
  And he has vanquished sin.

621 *The Land of Beulah.*

Key C.

1 My latest sun is sinking fast,
My race is nearly run;
My strongest trials now are past,
My triumph is begun.

Chorus.

Oh come, angel band,
Come and around me stand,
Oh bear me away on your snowy wings,
To my immortal home.

2 I know I'm nearing the holy ranks,
Of friends and kindred dear,
For I brush the dews on Jordan's banks—
The crossing must be near.

3 I've almost gained my heavenly home,
My spirit loudly sings;
The holy ones, behold, they come—
I hear the noise of wings.

4 Oh, bear my longing heart to him
Who bled and died for me;
Whose blood now cleanses from all sin,
And gives me victory.

622 *That Beautiful Land.*

Key B♭.

1 A beautiful land by faith I see,
A land of rest, from sorrow free;
The home of the ransomed, bright and fair,
And beautiful angels too are there.

Chorus.

Will you go? will you go, go to that
beautiful land with me?
Will you go? will you go, go to that
beautiful land?

2 That land is called the city of Light;
It ne'er has known the shades of night;
The glory of God, the light of day,
Hath driven the darkness far away.

3 In vision I see its streets of gold,
Its gates of pearl, too, I behold;
The river of life, the crystal sea,
The ambrosial fruit of life's fair tree.

4 The ransomed throng, arrayed in white,
In rapture range the plains of light;
In one harmonious choir they praise
Their glorious Savior's matchless grace.

623 *Your Mission.*

Key F.

1 If you can not on the ocean
Sail among the swiftest fleet,
Rocking on the highest billow,
Laughing at the storms you meet,

2 You can stand among the sailors,
Anchored yet within the bay,
You can lend a hand to help them,
As they launch their boats away.

3 If you are too weak to journey
Up the mountain, steep and high,
You can stand within the valley,
Where the multitudes go by.

4 You can chant in happy measure,
As they slowly pass along,
Though they may forget the singer,
They will not forget the song.

5 If you have not gold and silver
Ever ready to command;
If you can not t'wards the needy
Reach an ever open hand;

6 You can visit the afflicted,
O'er the erring you can weep,
You can be a true disciple,
Sitting at the Savior's feet.

7 If you can not in the conflict
Prove yourself a soldier true,
If, where fire and smoke are thickest,
There's no work for you to do,

8 When the battle-field is silent,
You can go with careful tread,
You can bear away the wounded,
You can cover up the dead.

9 Do not, then, stand idly waiting
For some greater work to do;
Fortune is a lazy goddess,
She will never come to you.

10 Go and toil in any vineyard,
Do not fear to do or dare,
If you want a field of labor,
You can find it anywhere.

624 *The Prodigal Child.*

1 Come home! come home!
You are weary at heart,
For the way has been dark
And so lonely and wild.
O Prodigal Child!
Come home, oh, come home!

2 Come home! come home!
For we watch and we wait,
And we stand at the gate,
While the shadows are piled.
O Prodigal Child!
Come home, oh, come home!

3 Come home! come home!
From the sorrow and blame,
From the sin and the shame,
And the tempter that smiled.
O Prodigal Child!
Come home, oh, come home!

4 Come home! come home!
There is bread and to spare,
And a warm welcome there,
Then, to friends reconciled,
O Prodigal Child!
Come home, oh, come home!

Very gentle and tender.

1. Wea-ry of wan-der-ing long, My sore heart saith,
D. C. Wea-ry of wan-der-ing, etc.

"Show me thy way, O Lord! Teach me thy path!"

I thought these wea-ry feet Straightway would find

All rough and rug-ged paths Left far be-hind.

625   *Weary of Wandering Long.*

2 But, as I onward passed,
   The way grew steep;
And black clouds gathered fast,
   And skies did weep,
And darkness seemed to hide
   The toilsome road;
Amazed, again I cried,
   "Thy way, O God!"

3 "A lamp unto my feet"
   God's word did prove;
A "still, small voice," and sweet,
   Spoke thus in love:—

"Whoso, through night and day,
   God's way pursues,
'Him shall he teach the way
   That he shall choose.'"

4 Then, since he chose for me
   This rugged path,
My hand in his shall be
   With steadfast faith:
Each step, this darksome night,
   Is bringing me
Still nearer to the bright
   Eternity.

WILL YOU GO? 8s & 3s.

End.

1. We are trav'ling home to heaven above, Will you go? Will you go?
To sing the Sav-ior's dy-ing love; Will you go? Will you go?
D. C. And millions more are on the road; Will you go? Will you go?

D. C.

Millions have reached that blest abode, Anointed kings and priests to God;

626

2 We're going to walk the plains of light,
Will you go?
Far, far from curse and death and night;
Will you go?
The crown of life we then shall wear,
The conqueror's palm we then shall bear,
And all the joys of heaven we'll share;
Will you go?

3 The way to heaven is straight and plain;
Will you go?
Repent, believe, be born again;
Will you go?
The Savior cries aloud to thee,
"Take up your cross and follow me,
And thou shalt my salvation see."
Will you go?

THE SWEETEST NAME.

By permission. WM. B. BRADBURY.

| 1st. | 2d. End.

1. There is no name so sweet on earth, No name so sweet in heaven,
The name before his wondrous birth To Christ, the Savior, . . . giv-en.
D.C. For there's no word ear ever heard, So dear, so sweet as . . . Je-sus.

Refrain *D. C.*

We love to sing around our King, And hail him blessed Je - sus;

627

2 And when he hung upon the tree,
They wrote his name above him,
That all might see the reason we
For evermore must love him.

3 So now upon his Father's throne,
Almighty to release us
From sin and pains, he gladly reigns,
The Prince and Savior, Jesus.

1. Broken in spirit, And laden with care, Sweet is thy refuge, Find it in prayer.

Chorus.

Tell it to Jesus! Tell it to Jesus! Tell it to Jesus! He will give peace.

628

2 Art thou neglected
  And sighing to know
Joys that in friendship
  Tenderly flow?

3 Art thou recalling
  The years that have fled?

Weeping in sorrow,
  Mourning the dead?

4 Bear thy affliction,
  Whatever it be,
Jesus, thy Savior,
  Bore it for thee.

OH, THERE WILL BE MOURNING.

1. Oh, there will be mourning, Mourning, mourn-ing, mourn-ing,

Oh, there will be mourning At the judgment-seat of Christ;

Parents and children there will part, Parents and children there will part,

Parents and children there will part, Will part to meet no more.

629

2 Wives and husbands there will part.
3 Brothers and sisters there will part.
4 Friends and neighbors there will part.
5 Pastors and people there will part.

6 Teachers and children there will part.

7 Oh, there will be shouting,
  Saints and angels there will meet,
  Will meet to part no more.

REVIVE US AGAIN.

By per.

1. We praise thee, O God! for the Son of thy love, For Jesus who died, and is now gone a-bove.

Chorus.

{ Hallelujah! Thine the glory, Hallelujah! A-men. }
{ Hallelujah! Thine the glory, ... } Revive us a-gain.

630

2 We praise thee, O God! for thy
Spirit of light,
Who has shown us our Savior, and
scattered our night.

3 All glory and praise to the Lamb
that was slain,
Who has borne all our sins, and has
cleansed every stain.

4 All glory and praise to the God of
all grace,
Who has bought us, and sought us,
and guided our ways.

5 Revive us again; fill each heart
with thy love;
May each soul be rekindled with fire
from above.

"STAR OF PEACE."   From a MS. by G. E. P.

1. Star of Peace, to wand'rers weary. Bright the beams that smile on me;

Cheer the pi - lot's vis - ion dreary, Far, far at sea.

631   *Seamen's Song.*

1 Star of Peace, to wand'rers weary,
Bright the beams that smile on me;
Cheer the pilot's vision dreary,
Far, far at sea.

2 Star of Hope, gleam on the billow,
Bless the soul that sighs for thee;
Bless the sailor's lonely pillow,
Far, far at sea.

3 Star of Faith, when winds are mocking
All his toil, he flies to thee;
Save him, on the billows rocking,
Far, far at sea.

4 Star Divine! oh, safely guide him—
Bring the wanderer home to thee;
Sore temptations long have tried him,
Far, far at sea.

1. My Je - sus, I love thee, I know thou art mine; For thee all the pleasures of sin I resign; My gracious Redeemer, my Sa - vior art thou; If ev - er I loved thee, If ev - er I loved thee, If ev - er I loved thee, My Jesus, 't is now.

632
Love to Jesus.

1 My Jesus I love thee, I know thou art mine,
For thee all the pleasures of sin I resign;
My gracious Redeemer, my Savior art thou.
"If ever I loved thee, my Jesus, 't is now."

2 I love thee, because thou hast first loved me,
And purchased my pardon on Calvary's tree;
I love thee for wearing the thorns on thy brow.
"If ever I loved thee, my Jesus, 't is now."

3 I'll love thee in life, and I'll love thee in death,
And praise thee as long as thou lendest me breath;
And say, when the death-dew lies cold on my brow,
"If ever I loved thee, my Jesus, 't is now."

4 In mansions of glory and endless delight,
I'll ever adore thee in yon heaven of light,
I'll sing with the glittering crown on my brow,
"If ever I loved thee, my Jesus, 't is now."

250 **HE IS COMING OUT TO MEET US.**

From "BRIGHT JEWELS," by per.   CHESTER G. ALLEN.

1. When we turn to God and leave the path of sin, When the heart repenting feels the need of him; Then our gentle loving Father full of pardoning grace, Comes to meet us with a kind embrace. Coming out to meet us on the way, Coming out to meet us, coming out to meet us, Oh, the joyful welcome, see the Fa-ther now, Coming out to meet us on the way.

633   *Coming Out to Meet Us.*

2 He will guide our feet where quiet
    waters flow,
He will lead us onward thro' the vale
    below;
With his presence and his blessing
    cheer us day by day,
He will come to meet us on the way.

3 At the cold, dark stream of Jordan
    when we stand,
He will bear us safely to the promised
    land:
With his loving arm around us we
    shall hear him say,
I have come to meet you on the way.

W. H. DOANE.

1. There's a gen-tle voice within calls a-way, (calls a-way,) 'Tis a
But my heart is melted now, I o-bey, (I o-bey,) From my

warning I have heard o'er and o'er, (o'er and o'er;) Yes, I will go,
Savior I will wander no . . . . . . more.

yes, I will go; To Je-sus I will go and be saved;

Yes, I will go, yes, I will go; To Jesus I will go and be saved.

634   *The Gentle Voice.*

2 He has promised all my sins to forgive,
 If I ask in simple faith for his love;
In his holy word I learn how to live,
 And to labor for his kingdom above.

3 I will try to bear the cross in my youth,
 And be faithful to its cause till I die;

If with cheerful step I walk in the truth,
 I shall wear a starry crown by and by.

4 Still the gentle voice within calls away,
 And its warning I have heard o'er and o'er;
But my heart is melted now, I obey;
 From my Savior I will wander no more.

May be sung as a duet first time.

Slow and gliding.

1. { Je - sus, my Savior, Cleanse me from sin; Make me thy temple—
   { Gen-tle and ho-ly, Lov-ing and mild, Make me to wor-ship

Chorus.

Dwell thou therein; } Je - sus, thou on - ly Canst comfort me when
Thee, as   a   child. }

lonely;   O   Je - sus, my Sa-vior, Draw near un-to   me.

635

Prayer to Jesus.

1 Jesus, my Savior,
   Cleanse me from sin :
Make me thy temple—
   Dwell thou therein;
Gentle and holy,
   Loving and mild;
Make me to worship
   Thee, as a child.

2 May I with ardor
   Serve thee each day;
Learning to praise thee,
   Learning to pray.
Filled with thy Spirit,
   Lord, I would be,
Humble and holy,
   Like unto thee.

3 Longing for something
   Earth can not give;
Hoping and striving,
   Daily I live.
But in thy presence
   Conflict must cease;
Savior, dear Savior,
   Grant me thy peace.

4 Cleanse me, oh cleanse me
   From every stain;
Near me, oh near me
   Ever remain.
Jesus, my Savior,
   Never depart,
Make thy pure temple
   Here in my heart.

By permission.   W. B. BRADBURY.

1. Traveler, whither art thou go-ing, Heedless of the clouds that form?
Naught to me the wind's rough blowing, Mine 's a land without a storm.

Chorus.

And I 'm go-ing, yes, I 'm going To that land that has no storms.

And I 'm go-ing, yes, I 'm go-ing To the land that has no storms.

636   *A Land without a Storm.*

2 Traveler, not a moment linger,
  Soon the darkness will be o'er.
No! I see a beckoning finger,
  Guiding to a far-off shore.

3 Traveler, yonder narrow portal
  Opens to receive thy form.
Yes! but I shall be immortal
  In that land without a storm.

637   CHRISTIAN MISSION.

Tune.—Your Mission. Key F.

1 Brother, art thou faint and weary
With life's battle just begun;
Falter not till thou hast conquered,
Rest not till thy work is done.
Earth-stained toil thy hands may harden,
Sorrow's furnace try thy soul;
And 'mid hours of deepest anguish
Sin may seek to gain control.

2 Labor, then, with zeal untiring,
Life's great mission to fulfill;
Enter now the Master's vineyard,
Seeking there some spot to till.
'Neath the frowning storm-cloud's shadow,
'Mid the glare of noon-day sun,
Through night's starless depths of darkness,
Labor till thy work is done.

3 If upon the towering mountain
Thou can'st find no place to toil,
Seek it in the lowly valley
Where the dews enrich the soil.
If thou can'st not with the reapers
Gather in the bearded sheaves,
Go and glean where they have trodden
Golden grain among the leaves.

4 On the shores of sounding ocean,
By the river's rolling tide;
On the banks of flowing streamlet,
Scatter truth on every side.
Where earth's noxious weeds are growing,
Thou can'st plant some seed of love,
Whose eternal bloom shall greet thee,
In the far-off realms above.

MY HOME IS THERE.

WM. B. BRADBURY.

1. Above the waves of earthly strife, Above the ills and cares of life,
2. Where living fountains sweetly flow, Where buds and flowers immortal grow,

Where all is peaceful, bright, and fair; My home is there, my home is there.
Where trees their fruits celestial bear; My home is there, my home is there.

Chorus.

My beauti-ful home, My beau-ti-ful home,

My beau-ti-ful home, My beau-ti-ful home,

In the land where the glorified ever shall roam, Where an-gels

In the land where the glo-ri-fied ev-er shall roam, Where an-gels,

bright wear crowns of light, My home is there, my home is there.

angels bright, wear crowns, wear crowns of light, My home is there, My home is there.

638

3 Away from sorrow, doubt and pain,
Away from worldly loss and gain,
From all temptation, tears and care;
My home is there, my home is there.

4 Beyond the bright and pearly gates,
Where Jesus, loving Savior, waits,
Where all is peaceful, bright, and fair;
My home is there, my home is there.

1. Sa-vior, keep me near thy side, Hum-ble, meek, and low-ly,

In thy love may I a-bide, Ear-nest, pure, and ho-ly.

Chorus.

At thy side, At thy side, Pu-ri-fied, forgiv-en,

At thy side, At thy side,

Let me ev-er dwell, dear Lord, With the saints in heav-en.

639

2 With mine eyes still fixed on thee,
Oh divinest treasure,
I would sit and be content
With thy love's full measure.

3 I would cast my sins on thee
While I seek thy favor,
Trusting in thy precious blood
All sufficient Savior.

4 Savior, keep me near the cross,
Clinging, fondly clinging,
Till I hear death's welcome call
And the angels singing.

5 Till I pass on pinions soft,
Through the golden portal,
And my raptured soul shall know
Joys that are immortal.

By permission.　　　　　　　　　　　　　　W. B. BRADBURY.

Moderato, with expression.

1. Oh, I see the shining angels Gath'ring round my dying bed; . . . .
With their harps and crowns of glory. Thus a faith - - - - - ful mother said,

While celestial songs were ringing Thro' the heavenly courts above, Seraphs

came from glory bringing Blessed words of peace and love. When I near death's stormy

Chorus.
Expressive and distinct.

billow, And earth's scenes no more can see; When I press my dying

cres.

dim. *ritard.* *p*

pillow, Will the angels come to me? Will they come?　　　　　Will they

Will they come?

640

2 Earthly joys, I know, are fleeting;
  Earthly pleasures quickly go;
But the joys that last forever,
  From the heavenly fountain flow!
When released from life's short duty,
  My glad spirit would be free;—
From that land of peace and beauty,
  Will the angels come to me.

3 Oh, how sweet to feel their presence,
  In the hushed and silent room;
With their bright and shining faces,
  Gilding all the dreaded gloom!
When from loved friends I've parted,
  And their tears are flowing free;
When from Jordan's banks I've started,
  Will the angels come to me?

WE'LL HELP THE CAUSE ALONG.

641 *Temperance.*

2 In defense of truth and justice,
Like a bulwark we must stand,
And the soul that's full of courage
Will give courage to the hand.

3 We must work and not be weary,
Though we conquer not to-day;

For the rescue of our brothers,
We must work as well as pray.

4 Hark! the crystal streams and fountains,
Swell the chorus of our song;
And they seem to be rejoicing
As they help the cause along.

17

1. Rescue the perishing, Care for the dying, Snatch them in pity from
Weep o'er the erring one, Lift up the fallen, Tell them of Je-sus, the

1st.   *2d.*   *Chorus.*

sin and the grave;
(*Omit.*) . . . . . mighty to save. } Res-cue the per-ish-ing,

Care for the dy-ing; Je-sus is mer-ci-ful, Je-sus will save.

642   *Rescue the Perishing.*

2 Though they are slighting him,
   Still he is waiting,
Waiting the penitent child to receive.
   Plead with them earnestly,
   Plead with them gently,
He will forgive if they only believe.

3 Down in the human heart,
   Crushed by the tempter,
Feelings lie buried, that grace can restore.
   Touched by a loving heart,
   Wakened by kindness,
Chords that were broken, will vibrate once more.

4 Rescue the perishing,
   Duty demands it;
Strength for thy labor the Lord will provide.
   Back to the narrow way
   Patiently win them;
Tell the poor wand'rer, a Savior has died.

643   *The Wandering Sheep.*

Tune, Lebanon, Key F.

1 I was a wandering sheep,
   I did not love the fold:
I did not love my Shepherd's voice,
   I would not be controlled;

2 I was a wayward child,
   I did not love my home,
I did not love my Father's voice,
   I loved afar to roam.

3 The Shepherd sought his sheep,
   The Father sought his child;
He followed me o'er vale and hill,
   O'er deserts waste and wild;

4 He found me nigh to death,
   Famished, and faint, and lone;
He bound me with the bands of love,
   He saved the wandering one.

1. Reach me thy hand, my child, Help-less and lone-ly;
2. Reach me thy hand, my child, Home-less and friendless,

Thro' the drear and des-ert wild, 'Tis I and I
Un-to me now re-con-ciled, Thy bliss shall be

on-ly, Can safe-ly conduct thee, Can safe-ly conduct thee.
end-less In mansions e-ter-nal, In mansions e-ter-nal.

644

Reach me Thy Hand.

3 Reach me thy hand, my child,
I am thy Savior;
Perfect and undefiled,
Thy sinful behavior,
I will not remember.

4 Reach me thy hand, my child,
What can betide thee,
If the Savior, meek and mild,
Is walking beside thee,
And loving thee always?

CHANT—"OUR FATHER."

GREGORIAN.

645

The Lord's Prayer.

1 Our Father, who art in heaven, | hallowed | be thy | name; ||
Thy kingdom come, thy will be done on | earth, . . as it | is in | heaven;
2 Give us this | day our | daily | bread;
And forgive us our trespasses, as we forgive | them that | tres- . .pass a- | gainst us.
3 And lead us not into temptation, but deliver | us from | evil;
For thine is the kingdom, and the power, and the glory, for- | ever. | A- | men

1. On the sweet E-den shore so peaceful and bright, The spirits made perfect are dwelling in light.

Their white wings are wafting them gently along, Thro' beautiful regions of glory and song.

Chorus

On the sweet E-den shore so peace-ful and bright, On the

On the sweet E-den shore

sweet E-den shore, The home of the blest, with friends gone before, We'll

On the sweet E-den shore

tar-ry and rest, tar-ry and rest, Tar-ry and rest on the shore.

646 *Sweet Eden Shore.*

2 Oh, blessed to rise when life's pangs are o'er,
To mount up to heaven and dwell evermore,
To never grow weary and never know care,
In those beautiful regions so blooming and fair.

3 On the sweet Eden shore, the home of the blest,
With friends gone before soon we'll tarry and rest,
Content there with Jesus our Savior to stay,
We'll delight in the pleasures that never decay.

1. When angry storms are beating, When, weak and tempest-tost, You cry with bitter

weeping, "Help, Lord, or I am lost!" Still, on some word of Jesus, Your

:S:

End.

soul may all be stayed, Let not your heart be troubled, Nor let it be afraid.
D. S. Since he will never leave us, Nor let us be afraid.

Chorus.

D. S. :S:

Oh, bless - ed words of Je - sus! Why should we be a - fraid,

647   *"Let not your Heart be Troubled."*

2 Should dearest hopes be floating,
  Like drift-wood on the sea,
Each treasure worth the keeping,
  Shall yet come back to thee;
Thy God is watching o'er thee,
  Go forward undismayed;
Let not your heart be troubled,
  Nor let it be afraid.

3 When care and grief oppress you,
  When sore temptations try,
And when no star of promise
  Breaks through the clouded sky:

Remembering how the Savior
  For all his children prayed,
Let not your heart be troubled,
  Nor let it be afraid.

4 When from the great hereafter,
  A voice doth call and call,
And from your failing fingers
  The pilgrim staff shall fall:
Still leaning on some promise
  Your risen Lord has made,
Let not your heart be troubled,
  Nor let it be afraid.

1. When shall we meet again—Meet ne'er to sever?
When will peace wreathe her chain . . . . . . Round us for-ev-er?

Our hearts will ne'er repose
Safe from each blast that blows In this dark vale of woes, Never, no, never!

648 *When shall we meet?*

2 When shall love freely flow,
   Pure as life's river;
When shall sweet friendship glow,
   Changeless forever?
Where joys celestial thrill,
Where bliss each heart shall fill,
And fears of parting chill,
   Never, no, never!

3 Up to that world of light
   Take us, dear Savior;
May we all there unite,
   Happy forever!
Where kindred spirits dwell,
There may our music swell
And time our joys dispel,
   Never, no, never.

JESUS, GUIDE. Chant.

1. The way is dark; | I can not see at all. | My Jesus, guide, | my Jesus, guide!

Oh, let me feel | the clasping of thy hand | Close by my side, | Close by my side,

649 *Jesus, Guide.*

2 The way is rough; my | feet are very sore.
   My Jesus, aid, | My Jesus, aid!
Oh, let me lean | while yet thou leadest on,
   Nor me upbraid, | nor me upbraid!

3 The way is long; I | fear I yet may fall.
   My Jesus, keep, | my Jesus, keep!

Oh, let my faith | outlast the weary road,
   No more to weep, | no more to weep!

4 The way—it ends; | the radiant gate appears!
   All trials past, | all trials past!
My spirit hastes | and bounds with joy, to be
   At home at last, | at home at last!

650 *Sinners Entreated.* 7s.
Martyn, Key F.

1 Sinners, turn; why will ye die?
God, your Maker, asks you why;
God, who did your being give,
Made you with himself to live.

2 Sinners, turn; why will ye die?
God, your Savior, asks you why;
He who did your souls retrieve,
He who died, that ye might live.

3 Sinners, turn; why will ye die?
God, the Spirit, asks you why;
He who all your lives hath strove,
Wooed you to embrace his love.

4 Will ye not his grace receive?
Will ye still refuse to live?
Oh! ye dying sinners, why
Will ye grieve your God, and die?

651 *The Joyful Sound.* C. M.
Marlow, Key G.

1 Salvation! oh, the joyful sound!
What pleasure to our ears!
A sov'reign balm for every wound,
A cordial for our fears.

2 Salvation! let the echo fly
The spacious earth around,
While all the armies of the sky
Conspire to raise the sound.

3 Salvation! oh, thou bleeding Lamb!
To thee the praise belongs;
Salvation shall inspire our hearts,
And dwell upon our tongues.

652 *The Wanderer Returning.* S. M.
Balerma, Key Bb.

1 How oft this wretched heart
Has wandered from the Lord;
How oft my roving thoughts depart,
Forgetful of his word.

2 Yet mercy calls—Return;
Savior, to thee I come;
My vile ingratitude I mourn,
Oh, take the wanderer home!

3 Thy love, so free, so sweet,
Blest Savior, I adore;
Oh, keep me at thy sacred feet,
And let me rove no more!

653 *Nearer my Home.* S. M.
Olmutz, Key Bb.

1 One sweetly solemn thought
Comes to me o'er and o'er:
I'm nearer to my home to-day
Than e'er I've been before.

2 Nearer my Father's house,
Where many mansions be;
I'm nearer to the great white throne,
Nearer the jasper sea.

654 *Glorying only in the Cross.* L. M.
Hamburg, Key F.

1 When I survey the wondrous cross
On which the Prince of glory died,
My richest gain I count but loss,
And pour contempt on all my pride.

2 Forbid it, Lord, that I should boast,
Save in the death of Christ, my God;
All the vain things that charm me most,
I sacrifice them to his blood.

3 See, from his head, his hands, his feet,
Sorrow and love flow mingled down;
Did e'er such love and sorrow meet,
Or thorns compose so rich a crown?

4 Were the whole realm of nature mine,
That were a present far too small;
Love so amazing, so divine,
Demands my soul, my life, my all.

655 *Earnest of Eternal Rest.* 7s.
Pleyel's Hymn, Key Ab.

1 Gracious Spirit, Love divine!
Let thy light within me shine;
All my guilty fears remove,
Fill me with thy heavenly love.

2 Speak thy pardoning grace to me,
Set the burdened sinner free;
Lead me to the Lamb of God,
Wash me in his precious blood.

3 Life and peace to me impart,
Seal salvation on my heart;
Breathe thyself into my breast—
Earnest of immortal rest.

4 Let me never from thee stray,
Keep me in the narrow way;
Fill my soul with joy divine,
Keep me, Lord, forever thine!

INDEX OF FIRST LINES.

The Figures refer to the Number of the Hymn.

(261)

INDEX OF TUNES.

The Figures refer to the Page.

(275)

METRICAL INDEX.

The Figures refer to the Page.

(277)

INDEX OF TUNES.

CLASSIFICATION OF HYMNS.

THE FIGURES INDICATE THE HYMNS.

PRAISE.—1, 2, 3, 23, 40, 41, 42, 118, 124, 126, 150, 151, 180, 183, 186, 187, 168, 189, 192, 267, 279, 288, 289, 306, 307, 308, 322, 328, 342, 350, 375, 376, 406, 428, 433, 440, 441, 480, 483, 494, 531, 538, 588, 590, 591, 606, 630.

WORSHIP—42, 90, 111, 131, 166, 186, 255, 278, 304, 305, 306, 307, 308, 346, 352, 361, 375, 376, 407, 430, 439, 524.

GOD—3, 5, 13, 16, 21, 34, 57, 67, 83, 91, 92, 97, 113, 128, 181, 182, 186, 198, 202, 225, 234, 235, 252, 255, 273, 288, 299, 362, 398, 423, 433, 438, 456, 537, 558, 583, 597, 633.

CHRIST—6, 17, 20, 26, 33, 35, 36, 37, 39, 40, 53, 64, 74, 75, 93, 102, 122, 124, 132, 137, 147, 153, 157, 169, 175, 188, 202, 207, 210, 212, 214, 229, 234, 259, 261, 262, 297, 300, 316, 320, 323, 351, 385, 410, 419, 422, 424, 428, 450, 457, 460, 473, 481, 483, 484, 497, 504, 507, 509, 511, 520, 526, 534, 550, 552, 557, 587, 593, 599, 601, 604, 606, 620, 630, 647, 648, 651, 653.

CHURCH.

I. COMMUNION OF SAINTS—15, 82, 84, 96, 148, 169, 193, 230, 292, 315, 458, 467, 471, 472, 539, 602, 641.

II. PROGRESS—123, 182, 265, 272, 276, 280, 293, 298, 339, 416, 428, 434, 484, 486, 502, 504, 552, 595.

III. REVIVAL—7, 100, 182, 265, 630.

IV. MISSIONS—104, 105, 106, 107, 182, 265, 271, 276, 280, 339, 468, 505.

HOLY SPIRIT—30, 33, 48, 170, 218, 227, 235, 319, 390, 399, 508, 514, 654.

REDEMPTION.

I. SIN—11, 25, 29, 32, 51, 52, 79, 117, 134, 139, 217, 357, 359, 384, 385, 400, 446, 491, 519, 536, 546, 551, 557, 624, 651.

II. WARNING—63, 168, 171, 199, 213, 217, 218, 219, 247, 259, 327, 378, 462, 520, 536, 558, 562, 634.

III. INVITATION—25, 52, 59, 61, 68, 112, 134, 138, 169, 170, 201, 203, 226, 236, 303, 310, 321, 343, 353, 357, 360, 378, 451, 485, 533, 556.

IV. REPENTANCE—22, 29, 54, 62, 68, 78, 117, 138, 172, 209, 262, 296, 324, 357, 359, 535, 536, 557, 569, 583, 633.

V. DELIVERANCE—22, 43, 46, 128, 138, 151, 152, 157, 188, 189, 199, 224, 229, 236, 259, 297, 549, 591, 593, 643, 650.

VI. DIVINE LOVE—17, 20, 33, 222, 351, 362, 442, 447, 449, 459, 480, 494, 502, 509, 511, 526, 548, 550, 561, 565, 581, 584, 591, 599, 630, 639, 651, 653.

CHRISTIAN LIFE.

I. FAITH—12, 15, 28, 29, 34, 36, 74, 75, 98, 143, 147, 156, 157, 163, 169, 172, 198, 250, 258, 268, 273, 316, 318, 323, 488, 520, 526, 534, 550, 559, 564, 583, 601, 625, 634, 639.

II. COMMUNION WITH CHRIST—24, 111, 140, 166, 208, 233, 251, 284, 295, 326, 431, 452, 502, 508, 517, 581, 584, 604, 616, 635, 639, 642.

III. HOLINESS—17, 37, 58, 109, 128, 144, 177, 223, 235, 249, 251, 286, 290, 295, 443, 448, 491, 550, 619, 635, 639, 654.

IV. ACTIVITY—159, 161, 163, 164, 170, 174, 175, 233, 239, 266, 270, 337, 341, 368, 396, 405, 409, 411, 412, 415, 417, 420, 470, 471, 495, 518, 598, 604, 614, 616, 617, 618, 619, 623, 637, 641.

V. CONFLICTS—12, 38, 50, 132, 137, 162, 173, 185, 211, 212, 263, 372, 373, 414, 416, 503, 543, 551, 554, 555, 581, 618, 620, 635, 637, 641.

VI. TRIALS—28, 49, 50, 67, 153, 176, 202, 215, 239, 262, 313, 377, 421, 515, 543, 551, 565, 570, 584, 592, 596, 597, 604, 617.

VII. ENCOURAGEMENTS—34, 47, 50, 132, 133, 135, 137, 143, 150, 158, 160, 162, 163, 184, 185, 202, 211, 212, 239, 281, 365, 366, 373, 414, 421, 503, 530, 554, 555, 584, 592, 618, 620, 623, 637.

VIII. GRACES—4, 12, 19, 29, 82, 84, 85, 132, 133, 135, 158, 159, 161, 164, 167, 178, 193, 202, 230, 239, 256, 287, 292, 315, 323, 338, 359, 364, 389, 419, 420, 421, 526, 539, 554, 557, 559, 565, 574, 592, 603, 607, 610, 635, 637.

IX. PRIVILEGES—88, 120, 221, 323, 347, 356, 360, 364, 390, 459, 556, 595, 581, 654.

X. PRAYER—7, 12, 13, 29, 70, 113, 114, 134, 163, 169, 197, 257, 258, 295, 317, 338, 348, 389, 393, 479, 527, 571, 598, 628, 645.

THE FUTURE STATE.

I. DEATH—9, 10, 86, 87, 242, 243, 244, 245, 247, 329, 330, 331, 332, 333, 335, 336, 387, 401, 444, 493, 506, 541, 609, 610, 611.

II. JUDGMENT—149, 220, 457, 558, 618, 629.

III. HEAVEN—73, 86, 87, 88, 89, 133, 158, 173, 178, 193, 196, 214, 215, 221, 280, 281, 312, 313, 377, 382, 383, 394, 426, 427, 429, 439, 461, 466, 515, 518, 540, 541, 542, 543, 545, 554, 559, 561, 581, 615, 616, 621, 622, 626, 636, 638, 646, 648, 652.

IV. ETERNAL LIFE AND DEATH—8, 558.

SPECIAL OCCASIONS.

I. NATIONAL—32, 186, 371, 374, 486, 578.

II. NEW YEAR—179, 523, 566, 579.

III. DEDICATION OF CHURCHES—301, 302, 395, 482, 553.

IV. ASSOCIATIONS AND ASSEMBLIES—264, 269, 270, 345, 346, 458, 467, 712.

PARTING HYMNS—82, 121, 314, 492, 576.

DOXOLOGIES—2, 23, 41, 118, 279, 322, 328, 406, 538.

INDEX OF SUBJECTS.

The Figures refer to the Number of the Hymn.

www.ingramcontent.com/pod-product-compliance
Lightning Source LLC
Chambersburg PA
CBHW020511270326
41926CB00008B/825